THE elea WAY

Social entrepreneurship and impact investing contribute to a more inclusive capitalism and bring innovative solutions to global challenges, such as fighting poverty and protecting planet earth. This book offers practical advice on how to best integrate entrepreneurship and capital for impact and innovation by using elea's philanthropic investing approach to fight absolute poverty with entrepreneurial means as an example.

Written by two leading experts, the book summarizes insights from elea's 15-year pioneering journey, from creating an investment organization, choosing purposeful themes, and sourcing opportunities, to partnering with entrepreneurs for impact creation. This includes suggestions on how to lead impact enterprises in such areas as developing strategies, plans, and models; building effective teams and organizations; managing resources; and handling crises. Using real-life examples, this is valuable reading for entrepreneurs, investors, executives, philanthropists, policymakers, and anyone curious about entrepreneurship and inclusive capitalism.

Vanina Farber, PhD, is an economist and political scientist with 20 years of teaching, researching, and consultancy experience. She holds the elea Chair for Social Innovation at IMD. Previously, Vanina was Dean of the Graduate School of Business and Associate Professor at Universidad del Pacífico in Peru.

Peter Wuffli, PhD, is a senior leader and entrepreneurial philanthropist. He is the Founder and Chairman of elea Foundation for Ethics in Globalization and the Honorary Chairman of IMD. Previously, Peter was a partner at McKinsey & Company, the CEO of UBS Group and the Chairman of Partners Group, respectively IMD. In 2015, he published the book *Inclusive Leadership*.

THE elea WAY

A Learning Journey Toward Sustainable Impact

Vanina Farber and Peter Wuffli

LONDON AND NEW YORK

First published 2021
by Routledge
2 Park Square, Milton Park, Abingdon, Oxon OX14 4RN

and by Routledge
52 Vanderbilt Avenue, New York, NY 10017

Routledge is an imprint of the Taylor & Francis Group, an informa business.

British Library Cataloguing-in-Publication Data
A catalogue record for this book is available from the British Library.

Library of Congress Cataloguing-in-Publication Data
Names: Farber, Vanina, author. | Wuffli, Peter A., 1957- author.
Title: The elea way : a learning journey toward sustainable impact /
Vanina Farber and Peter Wuffli.
Description: Abingdon, Oxon ; New York, NY : Routledge, 2021. | Includes
bibliographical references and index. |
Identifiers: LCCN 2020026556 (print) | LCCN 2020026557 (ebook) | ISBN
9780367549213 (hardback) | ISBN 9781003094807 (ebook)
Subjects: LCSH: elea Foundation for Ethics in Globalization. | Social
entrepreneurship. | Venture capital—Social aspects. |
Investments—Social aspects. | Social responsibility of business.
Classification: LCC HD60 .F367 2021 (print) | LCC HD60 (ebook) | DDC
362.5/8—dc23
LC record available at https://lccn.loc.gov/2020026556
LC ebook record available at https://lccn.loc.gov/2020026557

ISBN: 978-0-367-54921-3 (hbk)
ISBN: 978-1-003-09480-7 (ebk)

Typeset in Scala Sans Pro and Bembo Std
by KnowledgeWorks Global Ltd.

Printed and bound by CPI Group (UK) Ltd, Croydon, CR0 4YY

CONTENTS

FIGURES

BOXES

PREFACE BY BILL DRAYTON

The new entrepreneurship

The rate of change is accelerating exponentially. So is the extent and degree of interconnection. Indeed, each feeds the other.

These are *facts*. Facts that define everyone's new strategic reality.

To play in an everything–is–changing world, you must be a change-maker. This requires complex, learned abilities that are radically opposite to those needed in the old efficiency-in-repetition order (think assembly lines and law firms).

Much of humanity has made this leap and is doing very well. Their economies are accelerating, and, organized in fluid, open, integrated teams, they help one another become even more skilled. That's how teams work.

The other half does not have the new abilities and, therefore, can't contribute, which means that they fall further and further behind. Their economies are dying faster and faster. They are being crushed. They are depressed. They are losing years of life (four years in the United States). They have the psychological need to blame someone else for the fact that they are failing. Hence, the rapid spread of "us versus them" politics across the world in the last half dozen years.

This is the "new inequality". It is especially dangerous because it is deepening at an exponential rate. It is creating divisions that make solving other problems – be they financial or climate-related – much, much harder. And it is deeply unethical.

How do we solve this "new inequality"? First, we have to see and acknowledge it. Then, we have to ensure that *everyone* has the abilities to be a giver, to be powerful for the good; that is, to be a changemaker.

This is the central goal of Ashoka: *Everyone* a changemaker.

How does one achieve this – or any of society's other major goals?

This critical catalytic force is almost always a big pattern change idea – but only if it is in the hands of a great entrepreneur committed to the good of all. That's why the roughly 4,000 Ashoka Fellows (working everywhere and in all areas of need) are very leading social entrepreneurs. Three-quarters have changed the patterns in the field at the national and/or international level within five years of launch, and over half have changed national policy also within five years. We are even more powerful working together.

The most powerful form of change is that of new forms of human organization. This book opens with the example of the creation of the limited liability trading collaboration in Venice and how that helped to open global trade.

This book is about how to bring together these greatest of forces – entrepreneurship for the good and new forms of organizing.

However, it is Peter Wuffli, whom I have long known and admired, and his elea team who are pressing forward the frontier of organizing in new and more effective ways.

How can one keep the business entrepreneurial engine, complete with Schumpeterian creative destruction, going while expanding its purpose from the owners' interests to the good of all? How can one marry the worlds of entrepreneurs for the good with those of philanthropy, business finance, and modern management? (Both Peter and I were previously McKinsey management consultants.)

This is what elea's experiments and learnings are about. The results, captured and made beautifully accessible in this book, are an insightful contribution both to these profound issues of how to redesign human society and how all these key actors can work together well. There is both real vision and a lot of practical wisdom here.

Bill Drayton,
Founder of Ashoka: *Everyone* a Changemaker.
May 2020

FOREWORD BY DR. ANDREW KUPER

Capitalism at a crossroads

Over the past two centuries, capitalism – twinned with scientific revolution – has enabled unprecedented growth in wealth and well-being, globally. Billions of people have lifted themselves out of poverty. Middle-income people in many countries now enjoy lives that are longer, healthier, and richer in choice than kings and queens in the 18th century. Yet this breathtaking achievement is incomplete and inadequate. For all the progress, capitalism has left billions of people behind, vulnerable, and excluded from modern economies. In fact, four billion people – half of humanity – are accessing none or few of the many products, services, and support that would enable them to change their own lives. This uneven and unequal progress is a threat to the sustainability of social order and economic growth – and to human flourishing for us all.

We are in urgent need of an improved kind of capitalism that helps to solve the most pressing global challenges of today and tomorrow.

Growing up in apartheid South Africa, the structural origins of inequality and exclusion were apparent to me daily. It was only later, while studying politics and philosophy in the UK and the U.S. and then helping to finance social enterprises around the world, that I came to understand the extent to which other societies contain their own discriminatory structural barriers. This is not about cosmic unfairness; rather, we have made economic choices, and reform is within our collective grasp.

State resources and political will are inherently limited. So markets and business have a powerful role to play in leveling the playing field and empowering vulnerable people as agents of their own destiny.

In 2007, I founded LeapFrog Investments to invest in and grow businesses that serve lower-income people with essential services. My dream was to demonstrate our credo and methodology of "Profit with Purpose": there can be strong synergies between outsized social impact and financial returns. Later that year, the term "impact investing" was coined.

As of today, LeapFrog companies reach over 200 million people with financial tools or healthcare. Over 80% of those people are low-income, living on an income of under USD 10 per day, as defined by the World Bank. Over 100 million of the individuals empowered via access to these products and services are women and girls. At the same time, LeapFrog has been able to raise over USD 1.5 billion from private equity investors utilizing this investment strategy, and has often doubled or tripled institutions' money after repeatedly growing and selling successful social businesses.

As is evident from these numbers, we place a high value on rigorously measuring and consistently managing impact – applying the same level of discipline as in financial measurement and management. In the comparatively new, unfamiliar, and diffuse domain of "impact," it is crucial to understand what metrics best capture the social success of one's mission – and how those metrics link to commercial sustainability. Otherwise, impact too easily becomes a sideshow to the old mode of capitalism. We do this for every one of the dozens of companies we own stakes in, grow, and govern. Truly symbiotic profit and purpose require intentionality and the tracking of impact to be at the core of every major investment and operating decision.

This symbiosis also requires integrity and accountability. As many institutions followed us into the impact investment industry, we supported the development of industry-wide Operating Principles for Impact Management under the International Finance Corporation (IFC), which is part of the World Bank Group. LeapFrog announced the world's first impact audit based on those agreed principles. Many others have also recorded decisive successes in impact investing.

In short, the critics who claimed that a new form of capitalism is vague, uncommercial, nonscalable, and a pipe dream have been proven wrong – again and again – not simply in theory but in practice. That said, there is a long journey ahead to turn "Profit with Purpose" into a norm for the capital markets.

When I met Peter Wuffli on the journey, I found a kindred spirit. I was delighted to learn about elea and its distinctive approach as a philanthropic impact investor with a focus on early stage impact enterprises. The elea model allows for the mobilization of philanthropic capital in order to fund the critical "pioneer gap" of enterprise development, when risks are still high and much support is needed. Within the impact investing ecosystem, elea plays a crucial role in systematically identifying and nurturing new and promising impact ventures, which can then become an exciting focus for commercial impact investors.

While elea and LeapFrog complement each other in their focus, as well as the size and stage of companies they invest in, we share a common vision of capitalism as a solution to some of the world's most pressing challenges. We share the same values regarding freedom and responsibility, and we believe that a close integration of capital and entrepreneurship is critically important to achieving impact and innovation. Ultimately, we are both committed to being held accountable for our impact, based on transparent measurement and an independent audit.

Such a substantial and enduring commitment to philanthropy twinned with entrepreneurship, as demonstrated by elea, is rare. Even rarer is a thorough reflection on insights and lessons learned, as documented in this book. Peter Wuffli and his academic partner Professor Vanina Farber of the elea Center for Social Innovation at IMD have developed a treasure trove of practical resources for impact entrepreneurs, impact investment professionals, and entrepreneurial philanthropists. This book should expand the imaginations and tool kits of everyone committed to reinventing capitalism.

Dr. Andrew Kuper,
Founder and CEO of LeapFrog Investments
April 2020

INTRODUCTION

REINVENTING CAPITALISM[1]

How can capitalism become more inclusive, and what can a philan-thropic impact investment organization like elea Foundation for Ethics in Globalization (elea) contribute to this quest? To answer these questions, let us first take a look at the origins of capitalism.

Around the 10th century, merchants in Venice and Genoa introduced a contract called "Commenda" (or "Collegantia") to finance maritime commercial ventures. Their challenge was to link traveling merchants and sedentary merchants. Traveling merchants had adventurous, entre-preneurial ambitions to conquer new markets along the Silk Road to Asia, but they lacked capital. Sedentary merchants, on the other hand, had substantial wealth but lacked the vision and energy for undertak-ing such ventures themselves. Under such contracts, sedentary merchants invested capital or goods, while the traveling merchants invested time and energy – and took significant personal risk – to transport and sell the goods overseas. The upfront contributions of the sedentary merchants were typically two-thirds to three-quarters of total capital invested. The contract stipulated this total value (the "joint stock") and its components, provided an itinerary of ports to be visited, and stated how profits would be split. It also confirmed that the responsibility of the sedentary mer-chants for losses incurred would not exceed their capital contribution, so their liability would be limited.

Economic historians agree that this – highly successful – construct was at the origin of the wealth created by Venetian and Genoese merchants over several hundred years. It was also one of the mechanisms that pioneered modern capitalism, whereby entrepreneurship and capital were integrated to achieve shared objectives, which were – of course – often much broader than to just accumulate financial wealth (Reinert & Fredona, 2017). The rise of capitalism was reinforced by two waves of globalization over the last two centuries. The first, which largely happened within the confines of the British Empire, reached its peak before World War I. In an analysis of the economic consequences of World War I that was published in 1920, the great economist John Maynard Keynes observed that before the war "the inhabitant of London could order by telephone, sipping his morning tea in bed, the various products of the whole earth, in such quantity as he might see fit ... and he regarded this state of affairs as normal, certain and permanent, except in the direction of further improvement" (Keynes, 1920).

According to historians Tony Judt and Timothy Snyder, it took over 50 years; i.e., two World Wars, one Cold War, several regional conflicts, and some extremely disruptive communist revolutions, until, – in the mid-1970s, – the world's core economies were back at the levels of global economic integration that had prevailed before World War I (Judt & Snyder, 2012). Since then, we have witnessed a further acceleration of the second wave of globalization, which has only met with some serious roadblocks in recent years, following the Great Financial Crisis of 2007/2008.

The Commenda contract focused on the creation and distribution of financial wealth (in this example, through financing trade), as do many successive forms of limited liability companies across the world. Yet, important trends and developments in recent decades have provoked ever louder calls for a "new, more inclusive capitalism" that serves humanity in a more convincing, visible way rather than concentrating primarily on financial wealth creation and distribution. In the wake of severe financial, economic, and, most recently, health crises, economists have increasingly substituted the picture of an abstract, profit-maximizing "economic man" with a more realistic view of mankind as beings with both self-serving and altruistic characteristics. Moreover, globalization has created a basis for awareness and growing alignment around the essential challenges facing humanity as they have crystallized; e.g., in the 17 United Nations

(UN) Sustainable Development Goals (SDGs). A reinvented form of capitalism is thereby often seen as an important solution that can contribute to tackling such challenges.

elea's journey

In 2021, elea will celebrate its 15th anniversary. Created in 2006, its purpose is to fight absolute poverty[2] (i.e., a daily income below USD 3.00) with entrepreneurial means. Poverty is the number one global social challenge that humanity faces. For this reason, the first of the 17 SDGs is to "end poverty in all its forms". In 2015, over 1.9 billion people lived on less than USD 3.20 per day. Of those, 734 million people – or 10% of the world population – lived in extreme poverty; i.e., below USD 1.90 per day (The World Bank, 2018). Due to the Global Covid-19 Crisis, the World Bank expects poverty rates to increase and estimates that an additional 40–60 million people will fall into extreme poverty in 2020 (The World Bank, 2020).

As a philanthropic impact investment organization, elea addresses themes such as agricultural value chains, informal retail and last-mile distribution, employable skills building, and digital solutions. It searches for innovative social impact enterprises and helps them to grow. Because it invests in such companies at an early stage – when risks are high and therefore the probabilities for success are limited – and because much support is needed beyond financial capital, elea is partly funded by philanthropic capital in addition to funds originating from the repayment of debt and the divestment of equity participations.

elea's journey to date has resulted in many lessons and insights that may help to inspire impact investors, social entrepreneurs, and philanthropists on their own respective journeys. One insight is that such an evolutionary path is not linear and calls for continuous reflection on the successes and failures, experiences made along the way, and adjustments needed going forward. However, we have never compromised on ethics and have always strictly adhered to our virtues and guiding principles. Integrity, partnership, professionalism, and additionality are among the signposts that have led us to where we are now and will show us the way forward. Another key lesson is how much value can be gained from close and sustained personal collaboration between investors and entrepreneurs in a spirit of partnership. This is particularly true when such collaboration is underpinned by professionalism, relevant skills, and the deep expertise gained from sharing experiences.

Yet, the most important insight that elea has gained from over a decade of building and running its organization is that capitalism needs a new formula that goes beyond the wealth-oriented Commenda contract of old Venice and Genoa. According to this new formula, entrepreneurship and capital must be closely integrated in an effective way to achieve positive financial returns and impact. It is this formula that we will explore in this book:

> **Entrepreneurship times Capital equals Profit and Impact**

With this formula, we establish that there is a multiplier relationship between entrepreneurship and capital on the basis of a strong integration of the two. Why is profit an essential part of this formula as well, and what is its relationship with impact? As we will discuss throughout this book, profitability is a necessary condition for sustainable impact and innovation. This is not about extracting profit for "greedy" investors and owners. Rather, it is about achieving profit as the lifeblood of an impact enterprise to ensure survival and allow for investments in growth, thereby sustaining impact and innovation. There is an ongoing debate about whether a trade-off exists between profit and impact, and if so, what type. In our view, whether profit and impact reinforce each other or whether part of the impact will have to be achieved by sacrificing a certain portion of the profit, depends on the chosen business model.

Bringing this formula to life and effectively integrating entrepreneurship and capital toward measurable impact is challenging. Many social entrepreneurs find it hard to attract and make good use of capital, and many impact investors are not set up to collaborate with entrepreneurs in a way that will help them to achieve both social impact and financial returns. This is why we feel it is valuable to share what we have learned on how such linkages between entrepreneurship and capital can be built and how impact and innovation can be sustained. Based on both our practical experience and academic research, we will address and debate relevant issues around this formula, and we will provide practical guidance and suggestions that may be helpful to others. This book targets entrepreneurs, investors, corporate executives, philanthropists, policymakers, academic teachers, and students, as well as anyone who is curious to learn about entrepreneurship and capital or seeks inspiration on how to further evolve capitalism toward delivering higher and more equitable benefits to society.

Our perspective on impact is guided by elea's purpose; namely, to fight absolute poverty with entrepreneurial means. Although we recognize that there are other important impact areas (e.g., climate change and other environmental issues) in different locations than the ones we mention, these cannot be covered. Also, while most examples of impact enterprises are located in African, South-Asian, and Latin-American geographies, and while we try very hard to familiarize ourselves with local characteristics, we must acknowledge that there is a clear Western bias in many of our perspectives.

Underlying convictions

The specific approach to building elea was strongly influenced by several philosophical ethical convictions.[3] Chief among them was liberalism as a framework, with individual liberty at the core but underpinned by the ethics of responsibility. Individual liberty was a concept invented in Europe two millennia ago as a fortunate combination of Greek philosophy and Christian faith.[4] Along the journey of freedom, responsibility was developed as its ethical counterpart. The great liberal thinker Friedrich August von Hayek emphasized that liberty and responsibility are inseparable: "Liberty not only means that the individual has both the opportunity and the burden of choice; it also means that he must bear the consequences of his actions ..." (Hayek, 2006 [first published in 1960], p. 63).

Evolutionary pragmatism is a related conviction that is based on a Darwinian worldview that is true to Charles Darwin's original empirical insights and looks at the development of mankind as a continuous process of gradual development, whereby comprehension follows competence.[5] This view is in stark contrast to a dogmatic stance according to which ideologies (secular or transcendental) guide the world's development. Alongside these two fundamental convictions is a belief in the overall benefits of capitalism in a "Schumpeterian-sense" (according to the great Austrian economist Joseph Schumpeter); namely, as a continuous process of creative destruction driven by entrepreneurial initiative and competitive forces. Accordingly, market solutions in a competitive context are often superior to central planning approaches in solving social problems.

Structure

In the first chapter of this book, we explore the first component of our formula; namely, entrepreneurship. We search for entrepreneurial qualities by placing some of our elea enterprises and their entrepreneurs in the limelight and by reviewing the findings of academic research on the topic of social entrepreneurship. Such insights help us to understand, inform, and develop entrepreneurship in a systematic fashion.

In the subsequent chapter, we describe the second component of our formula; namely, capital by referring to the strong momentum of the impact investing trend over the past decade. We identify the driving forces of this trend, discuss controversial issues with respect to its scope, and argue in favor of the principle of additionality (i.e., a positive difference achieved that would not have happened without this investment) as a distinctive feature of this way of investing. Moreover, we strongly encourage industry leaders to go deeper in defining impact and in articulating its ethical roots.

elea's foundation and operating model are the themes of the third chapter. We look at how elea was created, exploring its founders' motivation and intentions, as well as underlying ethics, virtues, and guiding principles. Then, we describe the different components of its operating model; namely, investment management, the investors' circle, and professional development. We also explain how elea sources and evaluates new investment opportunities and then actively supports the respective companies during the period of its active engagement.

In the fourth chapter, we dive deeper into elea's investment focus. Its concentration on earlystage impact enterprises explains its positioning as a philanthropic impact investment organization. Its chosen four investment themes, which reflect the important challenges posed by absolute poverty and point to impactful market solutions, are all about access: access to skills, essential and affordable goods and services, income opportunities, finance and digital solutions. We also discuss how elea is always striving to find effective ways to grow the companies in its portfolio, so that these enterprises can achieve their full impact potential.

Then, in Chapter Five, we change the perspective and turn our focus to the entrepreneurial team that builds and leads an impact enterprise. We argue why visions, plans, and models are important, and we provide some guidelines for practitioners. An even more decisive and challenging task is building an effective team at the top and an organization that can sustainably deliver both impact and financial results, as well as enable the navigation of operations through ups and downs (including crises).

Finally, in the sixth chapter, we address the issue of how to sustain impact and ongoing innovation. Effective governance and supervisory boards are critical in this regard and are often an underappreciated component. Systematically monitoring, measuring, and managing impact is another element − one where elea has invested substantially from the outset − that is needed to establish a common language and to optimize both the impact capital allocation as well as the setting and controlling of objectives. While these elements work at the level of single organizations, at the macro level, we increasingly see ecosystems (i.e., several organizations that have joined forces) being used as a means of addressing global challenges in a sustainable way. We then conclude with an expression of optimism that the momentum created by social entrepreneurship and impact investing will lead to convergence across private-corporate, civil-society, and public-sector organizations in making our economies more impactful and capitalism more inclusive.

We would like this book to be practical and easy to use so that readers can apply the concepts and ideas examined in each chapter to their "real life" situations. For this reason, we will conclude each chapter with a "your point of view" section that comprises learning objectives, reflection questions, and an invitation to think about various dilemma situations.

Global Covid-19 Crisis

As we are writing these lines in the spring of 2020, the global health and economic crisis that resulted from the spread of Covid-19 is in full swing. It is, thus, impossible to say at the moment how it will affect the geopolitical and geo-economic context, as well as the organizations and people described in this book. What is clear, though, is that the consequences in the short and long term are likely to be massive and multidimensional. This crisis has the potential to substantially disrupt and alter the course of the globalization megatrend. It is also already evident – which is sadly and unfortunately typical in such situations – that the most vulnerable people and the weakest organizations living in those countries with weak institutions and incompetent governments will suffer the most.

The demand for what elea has to offer is huge. Almost all elea enterprises have immediately switched to crisis mode. How severely they have been – and will be – affected by the Covid-19 pandemic depends on the country, the field they are active in, the characteristics of their business model, the capacity of their organization, their financial strength, and – above all – the quality and effectiveness of their entrepreneurial leadership. Beyond ensuring mere survival through adapting their operations, adjusting their models, and – often – downsizing their operations, several of them were quick in realizing new opportunities from the crisis, such as providing relevant information and goods to affected people at the base of the pyramid.

elea moved to home-office mode already before it was required by the Swiss government to do so. Since then, it has been in almost daily contact with its elea entrepreneurs around the globe to understand local situations, share experiences, help develop scenarios, think through solutions, and often just to empathetically listen to their many and serious concerns. Within a week, elea put together a significant emergency funding facility to make money available on flexible terms in typical investment structures, within a short period of time, and by means of a structured – but streamlined – decision-making process. The conditions to qualify for funding include a high conviction that the business model is resilient enough to survive the crisis, a plausible plan for relaunch and growth after the crisis, and a funding approach that is also carried by other external investors (besides elea).

After just a few months of having experienced this crisis modus operandi, it has already become evident that elea's model of combining financial and professional support is even more useful in such times. Both entrepreneurs and elea associates have been able to leverage the strong and trust-based personal relations built before the crisis to engage in deep and challenging dialogue about how to rethink and adjust models and aspirations and how to protect unique strengths and advantages. Thereby, elea encourages impact enterprises to address challenges along two dimensions: type and time frame. The focus and measures discussed should cover both short-term tactical and long-term strategic considerations to defend and further expand these impact enterprises. Two strong elea convictions have been confirmed over and over again during this crisis: people make the difference, and impact results from entrepreneurship.

Let us now begin our journey by taking a deep dive into four specific examples from elea's investment portfolio, with the objective of exploring entrepreneurial qualities.

Notes

1. Any author today will find it challenging to do justice to the task of considering all genders equally while keeping a text legible. We have addressed this challenge by switching gender perspective from time to time throughout this book, thereby avoiding undue burden on the reader by striving for complete linguistic gender correctness.
2. At elea, we define absolute poverty as daily income below USD 3.00. The World Bank differentiates between extreme poverty (daily income below USD 1.90) and the next poverty threshold at USD 3.20 in daily income (The World Bank, 2018).
3. See (Wuffli, 2016), sections 2.4 and 3.4.
4. See (Siedentop, 2014): Siedentop makes a convincing case that the focus on liberty in Europe started much earlier than traditional history stated, with its narrative of reformation and enlightenment as the cradle of freedom after the "Dark Middle Ages".
5. See (Dennett, 2017): Dennett describes the journey of human consciousness on the path of evolution as involving both the modification of (biological) genes and (cultural) memes.

References

Dennett, D. C. (2017). *From Bacteria to Bach and Back: The Evolution of Minds.* London: Penguin.

Hayek, F. A. (2006 (first published in 1960)). *The Constitution of Liberty.* London: Routledge Classics.

Judt, T., & Snyder, T. (2012). *Thinking the Twentieth Century.* London: Penguin.

Keynes, J. M. (1920). *The Economic Consequences of the Peace.* New York: Harcourt Brace.

Reinert, S. A., & Fredona, R. (2017). Merchants and the Origins of Capitalism. *Harvard Business School Working Paper, No. 18-021.*

Siedentop, L. (2014). *Inventing the Individual: The Origins of Western Liberalism.* London: Penguin.

The World Bank. (2018). *Nearly Half the World Lives on Less than $5.50 a Day.* Press Release. Washington. Retrieved October 14, 2019, from https://www.worldbank.org/en/news/press-release/2018/10/17/nearly-half-the-world-lives-on-less-than-550-a-day

The World Bank. (2020, 16 April). *Poverty.* Retrieved May 13, 2020, from https://www.worldbank.org/en/topic/poverty/overview

Wuffli, P. A. (2016). *Inclusive Leadership: A Framework for the Global Era.* New York, London et. al: Springer.

1

SEARCHING FOR ENTREPRENEURIAL QUALITIES

The first component of our new formula for capitalism is entrepreneurship, but what exactly is entrepreneurship? One of the most famous definitions of entrepreneurship comes from Professor Howard Stevenson, who holds the entrepreneurship chair at Harvard Business School. He said, "Entrepreneurship is the pursuit of opportunity beyond resources controlled" (Eisenmann, 2013). More specifically, "pursuit" indicates a singular, relentless focus, whereas "opportunity" points to the pioneering, innovative characteristics of entrepreneurship. "Beyond resources controlled" means the constant condition of resource constraint under which entrepreneurs operate. We like this definition, as it points to the mindset, role, and task of an entrepreneur rather than to his formal or institutional positioning. Entrepreneurs can be found in any organization and at many levels.

Related to this is the concept of social entrepreneurship, which was launched by Bill Drayton (the founder of Ashoka) as a primary force for social change. Ashoka (www.ashoka.org), which was founded in 1981, systematically identifies and supports social entrepreneurs (i.e., Ashoka fellows) to mobilize a global network of changemakers and enable learning from their innovations. Ashoka has likely inspired many other similar global initiatives and platforms that identify, evaluate, acknowledge, and support social entrepreneurs. Examples of this include the Skoll

Foundation, the BMW Foundation, and the Schwab Foundation for Social Entrepreneurship at the World Economic Forum.

What distinguishes social entrepreneurs from other, more commercially minded entrepreneurs? Professor Filipe Santos, Dean of the Catolica-Lisbon School of Business and Economics, argues in his article "A Positive Theory of Social Entrepreneurship" that social entrepreneurs predominantly focus on value creation by seeking sustainable solutions to problems, whereas other, more commercially minded entrepreneurs are primarily driven by value appropriation (i.e., extracting profits), which is based on a desire to secure a sustainable competitive advantage for their organization. According to this theory of social entrepreneurship, value is seen in a holistic way, without differentiating between economic and social value, and it extends beyond single organizations to include positive externalities, such as improved education or better living conditions for underprivileged people. Santos says: "Value creation from an activity happens when the utility of society's members increases after accounting for the resources used in that activity. Value appropriation from an activity happens when the focal actor is able to capture a portion of the value created by the activity" (Santos, 2009, p. 8).[1]

1.1 elea entrepreneurs in the limelight

Now let us review four long-term success stories from elea's investment portfolio, which illustrate the motivations, mechanisms, and results of creating impact and innovation. In the remainder of this book, we will frequently come back to examples either taken from these four investments, from other investments in the elea portfolio, or from other organizations that we have gotten to know over the years.

1.1.1 Angaza: Pay-as-you-go (PAYG) makes socially impactful products affordable[2]

The problem

One important aspect of absolute poverty is the shortage of cash. Whenever a poor household has an excess of cash, there are powerful forces at work that tend to immediately lead to consumption, thereby reducing the amount left for any meaningful savings. Satisfying immediate and diverse needs of family members, such as compensating for insufficient income, solving health problems, or coming up with money for school expenses, will always compete with saving cash for even very small investments into impactful goods or risk cushions. This makes it very difficult for families to acquire socially impactful products that could substantially contribute to reducing poverty. Take for instance solar panels and lamps, which provide reliable and clean energy for lighting and could enable access to educational offerings or income-generating activities at night in the world's many off-grid areas – where still over one billion people have no access to electricity. However, although many lamps with robust and suitable technologies were developed to address this problem, sales in areas with very low incomes are often disappointing because of a lack of affordability.

The solution

Angaza deploys pay-as-you-go (PAYG) technology in solar products and other electronic devices. PAYG is a mechanism by which customers pay in small affordable amounts in proportion to how much they use these products/devices. Angaza's solution consists of three components: 1) metering and monitoring technology that is embedded into devices by their manufacturers to control payments and unlock the device if sufficient cash is available, 2) a mobile app that allows sales agents to offer and manage consumer financing for their solar device using mobile money, and 3) a cloud-based back-end solution that allows manufacturers and distributors to monitor the products sold and their usage, as well as the respective payments. As a business to business (B2B) solution, at the end of 2019, Angaza partnered with more than 25 manufacturers and over 200 distribution partners. Its products are integrated with over 40 mobile-payment platforms and are available in over 50 countries, reaching more than 1.8 million customers. Thanks to Angaza's technology, people who could previously not afford solar products now have access to electricity and light.

The entrepreneurs

Lesley Marincola, founder and CEO of Angaza, grew up in Phoenix, Arizona. She comes from an entrepreneurial background without being conscious of it. Her father created his own computer software business, and her mother, a medical doctor, built a successful private practice in pulmonology. Her older brother Bryan would later join Angaza and become its Chief Technical Officer. Lesley's fascination with emerging markets started in middle school. She spent her summers volunteering, living, and working in emerging countries, mostly in Latin America. This was her first taste of living in off-grid rural communities.

Early on at Stanford University, having completed her undergraduate degree in product design and a master's degree in mechanical engineering, Lesley discovered her interest in product design and engineering. In the "Design for Extreme Affordability" Master Class at the Hasso Plattner Institute of Design (the d.school) at Stanford University, Lesley combined her interest in emerging markets with engineering. While at university, she worked on a student project with a solar-light manufacturer. Her task was to make solar energy affordable for emerging-market consumers. To achieve this, Lesley built a solar concentrator that increased the power output of solar panels. Although she did not walk away wanting to start her own company, the project opened her eyes to the scale of opportunity for energy access. She learned through personal experience how wonderful rural life is and how tight-knit these rural communities are. Even though these communities are remote, they are often plugged into the global digital economy, and increasingly so. With regard to product design and engineering, Lesley has developed a passion for building things with her own hands and taking them from point A to point B. She likes to see the things she is working on and to understand the basics, such as gears and linkages, and how those come together to form physical products.

After graduation, Lesley began working at a design consultancy in Mountain View, California. She considered this as her dream job, because she had always wanted to be a product designer. She worked on projects spanning consumer electronics and automotives to medical devices. However, Lesley continued with the d.school project in her free time. The summer after graduation, Lesley travelled to Tanzania to test her solar-energy ideas on the ground and continue prototyping. Even after starting work, Lesley would spend evenings and weekends working on her ideas. Finally, after a year and a half of juggling her job and her passion, Lesley knew she had to make a choice. Having a full-time job meant that she could not move the project in Tanzania as fast as she wanted to. She thus decided to quit her job and concentrate fully on her solar project.

Looking back, she does not recall being apprehensive about quitting her full-time job in Silicon Valley; for her, it was so normal to be an entrepreneur and to take that leap of faith, and Stanford University had fostered this mindset in their students as well. She had some savings that allowed her to pursue her passion, and she also had faith that she would be able to find a job if things did not work out.

elea's investment

As a result of a scouting tour to East Africa, elea got to know Angaza in 2012. As a Silicon Valley start-up that targeted poor customers, particularly in Africa, the company did not appeal to Silicon Valley venture capital firms at that time. Consequently, elea became the first institutional investor in Angaza and provided advice to them on many levels, such as strategy, organizational development, marketing and sales effectiveness, and leadership development. In 2013, elea made a sizable investment in a convertible note issued by Angaza. At the time, Angaza employed five people and had invested less than USD 750,000 from friends and family, angel investors (i.e., successful individuals who invest small amounts in promising start-ups to promote entrepreneurship), and prize money from competitions and grant-giving non-governmental organizations (NGOs).

Impact, innovation, and financial returns

Initially, Angaza just planned to produce another solar lamp with a PAYG mechanism. The company's strategic move from a lamp manufacturer to a PAYG technology provider, which was substantially influenced and supported by elea, planted the seed for global industry leadership in this field and for a great impact story. After a substantial financing round in 2015, Angaza closed another financing round of USD 10.5 million in 2017, which was led by Laurene Powell Jobs' Emerson Collective (a social change organization) and was joined by Rethink Impact, Salesforce Ventures, Social Capital, and the Stanford StartX Fund. Only one year later, Angaza reached an important milestone when it became evident that more than 5 million people in over 50 countries had benefited from their technology since inception. East Africa accounts for 60% of the company's sales, but the company has expanded rapidly by entering markets in West Africa and South America. At the end of 2019, Angaza employed 70 people, and current expectations are that the company will experience a tenfold growth in revenue and a threefold growth in personnel over the next four to five years. In light of this growing success and social impact, Angaza recently broadened its vision by positioning the company as a "software provider that powers businesses to the last mile."

While the principle of PAYG is ages old, the innovation of Angaza's model was in coming up with a very robust, cost-effective technical solution that combines hardware and software and considers both economic and technical conditions in poor countries. In addition to servicing a well-established, installed base of customers, Angaza also collects a huge and highly valuable amount of data on the household behaviors and consumption patterns of people at the base of the pyramid.[3] Achieving broad acceptance for this approach was by no means easy. Angaza invested a lot of effort in awareness building, training, and educating distributors and users. This investment has not gone unnoticed. In 2018, Lesley Marincola received global recognition for her work. She received both the Ashden Award and the Skoll Award, the most coveted prizes in the social-enterprise space. In addition, the elea Chair for Social Innovation at IMD created a case study on Angaza for MBA students learning about impact enterprises.

1.1.2 BagoSphere[4]: Wage-earning opportunities for provincial youth in the Philippines

The problem

In the Philippines, particularly in the provinces, a large part of the population lives at the absolute poverty level. Over the last decade, the country has developed a highly successful service industry (e.g., based on call centers and business-process outsourcing) that provides employment for well over one million people. Paradoxically, although there is strong demand for labor, young people do not receive an education that would give them the qualifications needed to obtain employment and earn decent wages in the formal economy. Furthermore, individual companies typically lack the staff and experience needed to identify, recruit, and train human talent in significant numbers.

The solution

BagoSphere offers short and focused intensive trainings in the Philippines to carefully selected poor youth who have the potential and appetite to enter the formal labor market at wages that are at least three to five times higher than at present and up to 8 to 10 times higher than those that they would achieve as a day laborer in the fields or with other irregular activities (e.g., a daily income of USD10–USD12 versus USD1–USD2). The training programs are centered on relevant professional and practical skills (e.g., IT skills, spoken and written language skills) as well as life skills, such as self-awareness and confidence, goal development, and work ethics. BagoSphere systematically links graduates with employers and measures success in terms of the number of students employed, rather than the number of completed programs or skills certificates. More recently, BagoSphere has begun to offer enterprise trainings; that is, customized offerings for companies in the services sector, to improve the effectiveness and efficiency of the onboarding process for new employees.

The entrepreneurs

Zhihan Lee, co-founder and CEO of BagoSphere, was born and raised in Singapore. During his childhood, his maternal grandmother played an important role. He remembers going with her to find a job in Chinatown when he was a small boy; she became a dishwasher in a Korean restaurant. Five years later, when Zhihan was 10, she died of lung cancer. This experience of death at a young age confronted him with very existential questions about his purpose in life and laid the groundwork for his passion to become a social entrepreneur. In high school, he enrolled in the military band and became a member of its leadership team, for which he was regarded by younger colleagues as a role model and a mentor. When thinking about this experience, he recalls being motivated by achieving impact through leadership, which was also the case when he was caring for his younger twin sisters. During his adolescence, Zhihan's father lost his job as a salesman for a large international diesel engine company and decided to become independent by setting up his own company. This would later inspire Zhihan to follow in his father's footsteps and become an entrepreneur himself.

So when Zhihan began his studies in mechanical engineering at the National University of Singapore (NUS), he had already reflected deeply on his life's purpose and realized the impact he could achieve in a leadership role. He was also motivated by his father, who was a role model for entrepreneurship. While studying at NUS, he was able to spend a year in Stockholm working for a start-up company in biomedical devices and, on another occasion, to work as a volunteer on social projects in Laos and Thailand. Both experiences motivated him to work for some time at an Indian impact enterprise called Head Held High, which turned out to be the blueprint for BagoSphere, offering programs for poor rural kids to become trained as data-entry typists. Together with his two co-founders, Ellwyn Tan and Ivan Lau, he started a pilot project in the Philippines in 2010 called BagoSphere, which he joined on a full-time basis a year later.

elea's investment

elea became BagoSphere's first international institutional investor in 2014 and has been very active ever since, continuously providing strategic and operational support as a member of the supervisory board. It has likewise helped BagoSphere to challenge and refine its business model and growth strategies, and it maintains a close connection to the senior management in a mentorship and advisory role on a broad range of leadership topics. Additionally, elea was instrumental in closing the most recent funding round in 2018 by providing matching funds for investments from the Philippines and the wider Asia–Pacific region.

Impact, innovation, and financial returns

In 2019, BagoSphere had over 2,000 alumni and trained over 700 students, of which over 80% found employment within 30 days after graduation. By then, it had also created crucial partnerships that gave students access to funding for their courses through both loans and scholarships. In that same year, approximately 1,800 young adults participated in company-focused trainings organized by BagoSphere, which resulted in the retention rate of newly hired employees increasing from 25% to 75% in these companies. BagoSphere also began to expand its business to Iloilo, a major location for business-process outsourcing, which has similar characteristics to the city of Bacolod, Philippines, where the organization was founded.

BagoSphere is a highly innovative company. Its holistic model not only emphasizes training but also recruiting and placement (in equal measure), which sets it apart from many traditional vocational skills building efforts. Its explicit focus on both professional skills and life skills in its training curriculum is another distinctive factor around which BagoSphere has developed a particular, human-centric way of interacting with students, which was perceived as quite unique in the Philippine context. Furthermore, the hybrid model that the company uses to fund commercial activities with philanthropic elements is also considered very innovative and particularly suitable for educational initiatives that involve poor people. In recognition for his contribution as a changemaker, Zhihan Lee became an Ashoka fellow in 2017.[5]

With regard to financial returns, the initial pilot operation in Bacolod achieved positive cash flow in 2018. BagoSphere was set up as a for-profit company but has always pursued its social mission with the aim of simultaneously building a commercially viable operation. In that same year, BagoSphere decided to give growth substantial preference over profitability. Consequently, it decided to found a new non-profit entity alongside its for-profit operating company to raise philanthropic capital for its educational content and to expand its business. This structure allowed BagoSphere to close a funding round with a combination of grants and convertible funding, thereby bringing in several new fund providers from the Philippines and Asia-Pacific, and from around the globe. Besides operationally generated cash flows and increases in its capital base, BagoSphere has succeeded in attracting substantial amounts of philanthropic capital to finance scholarships for its program participants as well.

1.1.3 Coffee Circle: Reliable income opportunities for smallholder farmers[6]

The problem

Coffee is the most consumed beverage in the developed world, yet coffee farmers often operate at very small scale, have limited skills, face logistical and other challenges to access the global market, and do not receive a fair remuneration for their product. As a consequence, they often live in absolute poverty.

The solution

Established in 2010, Coffee Circle buys high-quality coffee beans directly from farmers in remote areas at fair prices, roasts those beans in its own roastery in Berlin, and sells them mainly through its own dedicated online shop to customers in Germany, Austria, and Switzerland. Additionally, for every kilogram of coffee sold, Coffee Circle invests EUR 1.00 into tailor-made projects that either improve the living conditions of farmers (e.g., schools, healthcare, clean water) or strengthen the coffee value chain. Through the reliable and growing demand for its products, Coffee Circle is able to deliver a predictable and fair income to smallholder farmers in Ethiopia, Colombia, and other countries where coffee farmers live in poverty. Together with specialized training organizations, Coffee Circle also undertakes programs for coffee farmers to systematically improve the skills that are relevant for growing high-quality coffee and for enhancing the quality and quantity of their production.

The entrepreneurs

Martin Elwert, CEO and one of the three co-founders of Coffee Circle, was born in Ravensburg in Southern Germany. He studied business and thereafter worked as a management consultant at a major global consulting company. He and the two other co-founders, Robert Bach und Moritz Waldstein-Wartenberg, came up with the idea of Coffee Circle during an extended stay in Ethiopia, where they were confronted with absolute poverty while helping to build an orphanage. At the same time, they recognized the huge potential for generating income from premium specialty coffee, and they saw an opportunity to fight absolute poverty with an entrepreneurial approach.

elea's investment

Alongside other institutional investors, elea invested equity capital in Coffee Circle in 2013, provided grants for a skills program that targeted smallholder coffee farmers, and received matching grants by an international development organization. elea then participated in two subsequent capital raising rounds with additional investments. It has held a seat on Coffee Circle's supervisory board since its first investment and has been instrumental in providing strategic advice, coaching the leadership team, navigating the company through a crisis and a restructuring effort, and contributing ideas and recommendations for scaling up the business and raising capital.

Impact, innovation, and financial returns

In 2019, Coffee Circle sourced coffee from approximately 25,000 farmers in Ethiopia and 10 other countries with a purchase price that was more than double the commodity market price. For several years now, Coffee Circle has regularly delivered a double-digit growth in revenues. In 2019, it achieved over EUR 12 million in income from sales, which is 30% more than the year before. Its growth has been achieved by investing in technology, improving the quality of its coffee, and developing strong relationships with coffee farmers, as well as by improving the consumer experience and social awareness. In addition, since inception, Coffee Circle has raised EUR 2.2 million (through the EUR 1.00 per every kilogram of coffee sold and by accessing other philanthropic funds) for projects that benefit approximately 130,000 farmers and their families.

In accordance with its mission of "improving lives by delivering out-standing coffee," Coffee Circle developed a unique marketing approach and brand profile early on that leverage both a growing demand for specialty coffee in Germany as well as a growing appreciation by society for responsible businesses. With the internet as its main distribution channel and a communication approach that constantly links its customers to the farmers at the origin of its high-quality coffee, Coffee Circle has successfully catered to the upcoming urban lifestyle of young, socially conscious, and sophisticated consumers. It continuously focuses on farmer impact by keeping direct contact with them and purchasing directly from them. It has also shown courage by expanding coffee sourcing into "difficult" areas. For example, in the Democratic Republic of Congo, it has established "coffee quality facilities," with training centers to improve coffee quality for a cooperative of around 2,400 farmers who are threatened by fighting among local rebels, militias, and the official military.

In 2018, Coffee Circle reached breakeven and became the largest specialty coffee provider in Germany. In 2019, it opened up its first "own" coffee shop in Berlin to further strengthen its brand with a first step into the offline world. Coffee Circle appears to be well on track as a fast-growing consumer-goods company with strong operating cash flows.

1.1.4 Dharma Life: Access for rural India through village entrepreneurs[7]

The problem

In India, approximately 25% of the 900 million people who live in rural areas are considered poor (https://data.worldbank.org/indicator/SP.RUR.TOTL?locations=IN) live in rural areas. These poor individuals have little access to goods and services that would help them to achieve better livelihoods.

The solution

Dharma Life recruits, trains, and leads "Dharma Life Entrepreneurs" (DLEs) in the selling of socially impactful products and services at affordable prices in remote areas in India. DLEs are respected personalities with business savvy and influencing skills in local settings, who are oftentimes active as microentrepreneurs in fields such as farming and shopkeeping. The company operates a complex logistics system used to deliver these goods and services throughout the country. Dharma has a clear commitment to achieving behavioral change by building awareness, and – as in the case of Angaza – the company collects a lot of meaningful data on specific behaviors at the base of the pyramid. Along its journey, it has come to rely mostly on women as agents for change.

Through its business activities, Dharma Life provides the poor rural population in India with clean and affordable energy solutions, goods that contribute to increasing hygiene and water safety, and everyday livelihood products, such as induction stoves, mobile phones, and sewing machines. More recently, Dharma Life has added family planning services and feminine hygiene products to its offering. The DLEs not only market the goods but also educate the users on how to apply these goods and services. Because of their broad reach in rural India, they are also called upon by global corporations and development organizations to support awareness campaigns in areas such as hygiene, water safety, and technology usage.

The entrepreneurs

Gaurav Mehta, co-founder and managing director of Dharma Life, was born in 1979 and grew up in an entrepreneurial family of the Indian diaspora in Düsseldorf, Germany. His ancestors were either landowners from Multan (Pakistan) or bankers, industrialists, and Sanskrit scholars from Lahore/Sialkot (Pakistan). The year in which India and Pakistan separated (1947) turned out to be dramatic for his ancestors, as his grandparents had to flee the country under the threat of death given the local riots. Luckily, his grandfather succeeded in being accepted to the Indian Foreign Service and later opened an India Trade Centre and Consular Service in Frankfurt. Both of Gaurav's parents are medical doctors: his mother grew up in Germany, and his father moved to Germany from India. When he was a child, Gaurav visited India together with his family every year. He tells a story about a seven-year-old street boy who asked him (he was 12 at the time) for 1,000 rupees to set up a shoe-cleaning business. He convinced his father to grant the boy this entrepreneurial opportunity, with good results.

After high school, Gaurav studied business, first in Maastricht and then in London. He was hired by a top-tier global investment bank to work in healthcare mergers and acquisitions and at the same time engaged in social programs focused on education in India. After this, he went to New York to work for a global private equity firm and was on track to become a successful financial executive. However, after Christmas dinner at a fancy restaurant in New York City, he fell ill and developed a serious liver abscess. He had to be hospitalized and vacillated between life and death for a few months. This traumatic experience made him fundamentally rethink what he was aspiring for in life. Still passionate about solving social problems in India, he quit his job and went to do an MBA at London Business School. During his time at business school, he decided to dedicate his professional energy to a venture that he developed together with a few classmates and friends; namely, Dharma Life.

elea's investment

elea invested in Dharma Life in 2014 and has not only provided financial means but it has also actively engaged at the supervisory board level and provided support in strategy development, organization building, and information technology. More recently, in 2018, elea helped the team to create a Results-Based Financing (RBF) facility to fund awareness campaigns that should result in onboarding 30% more DLEs by 2020.

Impact, innovation, and financial returns

Dharma Life's impact is achieved at two levels: First, it provides livelihoods for the 16,000 DLEs working in over 40,000 villages across 13 Indian states. Second, as of 2019, it has helped to improve the livelihoods of more than 13 million people since inception by providing them access to socially impactful goods and services at affordable prices and through awareness and behavioral change campaigns.

This impact is achieved through an innovative enterprise model that combines the commercial activity of distributing goods and services and a philanthropic arm for awareness campaigns, which is funded by philanthropy-minded organizations and global corporations. Another highly innovative aspect of this company is its focus on intense training as well as on recruiting and developing people with initial entrepreneurial qualities. An additional aspect of innovation is the increasing proportion of women among the DLE network. Although this network was 90% male-dominated in its early stages, more recently, 80% of the growth in the network has been female due to modifications in the recruiting and training process.

Dharma Life's development has been all but linear. It has had to modify its model several times and has been exposed to existential threats; for example, when the Indian government surprisingly "demonetized" the economy in 2016 by declaring all banknotes of 500 and 1,000 Indian rupees as no longer valid (see also context box 5.7). Yet Dharma has proved its resilience through various ups and downs. In 2019, it achieved full profitability for the first time in its history. Moreover, in 2018, Gaurav was recognized as a young global leader by the World Economic Forum,[8] and in 2020, he became "alumnus of the decade" of the London Business School.

1.2 Defining entrepreneurial profiles

The personalities of the entrepreneurs in all four of these elea investment examples make a decisive difference. That is why we have dedicated several paragraphs to describing their personal stories, sometimes even hinting at their family histories. To assess the quality of an investment proposal, a good understanding of the genesis and motivation of the basic idea behind it is critical. This quickly leads to a desire to grasp the underlying entrepreneurial profile, with its specific mix of characteristics, which has to do with ambitions and motivational drivers, talent and skills, role models, and values. Some of these characteristics are generic to any entrepreneur, while others specifically relate to the profile of an impact entrepreneur.

Taking this argument one step further, we have also observed that different types of impact attract distinctive entrepreneurial profiles. Take, for example, Kanthari, which is an institute for entrepreneurship education in Trivandrum, the capital of the Indian state of Kerala, in the extreme south of India. It was created by Sabriye Tenberken and Paul Kronenberg to provide entrepreneurship training and development for talented and driven people who have had to overcome adversity, like Sabriye herself. She was born and raised in Germany and became blind when she was 11 years old. The name "kanthari" comes from a small but very spicy chili plant with numerous medicinal values and different colors that grows wild in Kerala. This name appealed to Sabriye, as it expressed her feelings of what she calls "creative rage". While "rage" refers to the feeling of being discriminated against that Sabriye experienced when growing up as a blind young person in Germany, "creative" means building a solution that generates positive social impact (i.e., Kanthari).

Sabriye and Paul developed a concept that differentiates between distinctive categories of social impact and assigns a specific kanthari color to each of them. Green kantharis are impact entrepreneurs who want to create ethical social change by starting grassroots projects with innovative approaches. Yellow kantharis create new products, strategies, or concepts for social change. The goals of this group are either to improve the living conditions of marginalized groups or to protect the environment. Orange kantharis use business as a tool for sustainable social change. Red kantharis advocate for a world free of discrimination, negative attitudes, and harmful norms. Their goal is to provoke a change of mindset in their communities. Purple kantharis use their creativity and art as a tool for making a difference. They are artists who provoke a positive change in mindset through their work (see www.kanthari.org).

What can academic research contribute to a better understanding and evaluation of entrepreneurial qualities? In recent years, academic researchers have systematically analyzed what differentiates entrepreneurs from non-entrepreneurs, and they have started to explore what is distinctive about social entrepreneurs versus more commercially minded entrepreneurs. While they agree that there is no simple one-size-fits-all template to describe the "entrepreneurial persona", they found certain specific characteristics that prompt people to become entrepreneurs, as well as personal motivations and preferences that keep entrepreneurs on their chosen path. Indeed, research undertaken since the 1990s suggests that there are systematic differences between entrepreneurs and non-entrepreneurs. Indicators of an entrepreneur are higher levels of self-confidence, less bias to protect the status quo, preference for more autonomy, higher self-efficacy, and lower thresholds of risk aversion.[9]

Some researchers have studied the baseline personality traits of entrepreneurs through the use of coherent models. One such multi-dimensional approach that has been popular since the 1980s is the "Big-5" model (see Figure 1.1). It defines personality by measuring five factors: openness, conscientiousness, extroversion, agreeableness, and neuroticism. Along these dimensions, entrepreneurs are typically described as being more open to experience, more conscientious, similarly extroverted as

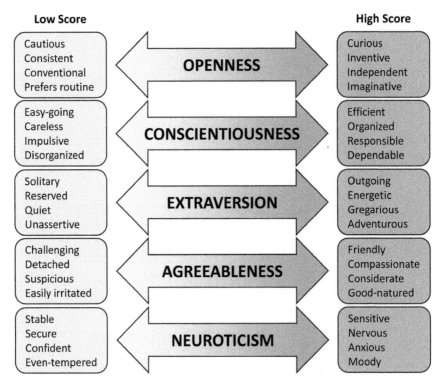

Figure 1.1 The "Big-5" model.

Sources: Openstax CNX Psychology, 2019; Young, 2018

compared to others, less agreeable, and less neurotic (Kerr citing [Zhao & Seibert, 2006]). Additional qualities that have become associated with the entrepreneurial personality in recent years include innovativeness, a locus of control, and the need for achievement (Kerr, Kerr, & Xu, 2018).

Turning to the differences between social and commercial entrepreneurs, in our practical experience, these are gradual rather than categorical. While social entrepreneurs – in line with Santos's Positive Theory – indeed tend to focus more on value creation, they also need to keep an eye on value appropriation in order to ensure that they can generate enough profits to care for their families and their future (after retirement). Moreover, there are many commercial entrepreneurs, for example in family businesses and among selected publicly listed corporations, who are intensely focused on long-term value creation, sometimes even more than on value appropriation.

A good understanding of entrepreneurial qualities is helpful for defining and evaluating the role and position of entrepreneurs relative to other actors and stakeholders as they seek to initiate and lead their enterprises. It can also provide clues about the specific skills, strengths, shortcomings, and development needs of entrepreneurs vis-à-vis the tasks and challenges they are facing. Consequently, it can help with the design of organizational solutions to entrepreneurial issues, for example, in terms of setting up suitable organizational structures and capabilities, determining the criteria for team composition, and establishing a promising executive modus operandi. As a result, a conscious consideration of the personal characteristics of entrepreneurs can contribute to strengthening the entrepreneurial and organizational effectiveness of the social enterprise being launched.

We will now describe four entrepreneurial qualities that contribute to sharper descriptions of entrepreneurial profiles. They refer to prosocial attitudes, the ability to sense opportunities, a differentiated approach to risk, and the ability to manage tensions between commercial objectives and social impact goals.

1.2.1 *Prosocial attitudes*

Taking into account the different dimensions of the "Big-5" Model, the mindsets of social entrepreneurs are typically marked by prosocial and communal orientations that include qualities such as altruism, tender-mindedness, trust, and modesty. As our examples show, the origins of such attitudes can lie deep within a person's personal history, in the way they were brought up and/or how they were touched by impressive role models. This may imply a higher level of sensitivity and a certain softness vis-à-vis other human beings than the widely perceived "toughness" of a typical entrepreneur, which is exactly in line with observations we have made when characterizing many elea entrepreneurs. Moreover, academic research has recently seen renewed interest in better understanding the role of emotion and passion in fueling a person's sense of entrepreneurship. Indeed, there is a range of emotions at play in entrepreneurship. Some are positive and empowering – such as the drive to achieve, to overcome obstacles and limitations, and to change the world by connecting to a higher good – while others stem from negative sources, like anger, fear of failure, or a sense of personal inadequacy.[10]

In academic literature, social entrepreneurship is seen as a powerful force that combines the passion and drive for forming new ventures with the prosocial attitude of aspiring to improve the well-being of a selected social group or segment. Through a review of the existing literature, Wendy Smith and colleagues found that companies set up by social entrepreneurs typically serve as a bridge for integrating the efficiency, innovation, and resources of profit-making entrepreneurs with the passion, values, mission, and concerns of non-profit organizations (Smith, Gonin, & Besharov, 2013).

Emotional qualities, such as passion and resilience, are highly relevant in our daily experience of working with social entrepreneurs. One of the elea entrepreneurs – representative of many others – describes her inner motivation as follows:

> I have an insatiable thirst deep down inside of me to use my life on this planet to make a positive difference for others, and due to this, I perceive every minute, every person I meet, every ecosystem I engage in as an opportunity to leverage to achieve this goal. It is not a feeling I can switch on or off. It is not something I learned. It is in my core.

Such passionate statements are a tremendously effective source of inspiration for all involved – and often a decisive factor for success – particularly during the inevitable ups and downs that occur when a social enterprise is being created and developed. At the same time, some complementarity between high levels of entrepreneurial emotionality and sobriety within the leadership team often contributes to its effectiveness.

One issue related to their emotional qualities that we sometimes face when working with elea entrepreneurs is that, like many entrepreneurs in general, social entrepreneurs often feel quite lonely in their roles. In addition, their roles are still considered as quite unusual within their local communities and families. They, therefore, appreciate being in communities with like-minded people all the more. At its ten-year anniversary in 2016, elea invited a dozen different entrepreneurs from its portfolio to Zurich for an extended weekend that included a series of workshops. While this community was as diverse as it can get, an immediate rapport was built among them, and lots of interesting connecting dots were explored. Based on this experience, elea decided to more actively organize ways to promote the development of this community of elea entrepreneurs. It, thus, started various platforms for regular exchange on topics of mutual interest.

A second issue that we are often confronted with when working with elea entrepreneurs is trust. Because of their prosocial attitudes, social entrepreneurs may at first trust other people more easily, given their altruistic intentions, but they are often disappointed when they experience failures of individuals or institutions in their respective countries. On the basis of such disappointments, many find it hard to extend trust beyond immediate family and close friends. This is particularly true in finance. Often, the founder entrepreneurs are themselves not financially experienced, but they also do not trust others to do it for them. Therefore, a frequent finding in elea's due diligence on future investments is the need to ensure that somebody of sufficiently high caliber will take care of the company's finances as a condition for investment by elea.

Having said all this, the combination of prosocial attitudes and emotional qualities makes elea entrepreneurs a group of wonderful people: while hugely diverse along many dimensions, they are deeply passionate about their mission, have high energy levels, and are curious and eager to learn and develop. They also show substantial resilience under adverse conditions and are typically fun to be with, and almost never boring. It goes without saying that they are also very scarce. In elea's experience, this is the most frequent bottleneck to sourcing attractive investments.

Finding the right entrepreneurs with the appropriate passion, commitment, and capacity, as well as a desire to learn to develop, is a challenging
and resource-intensive task.

1.2.2 A sense for opportunities

Opportunity recognition and intentionality are common entrepreneurial
qualities. Driven by their prosocial impact-seeking attitudes, social entrepreneurs recognize opportunities as they observe societal problems and gaps in
established supply-and-demand patterns. One example is Lesley Marincola
and her team at Angaza, who saw the lack of cash savings as a key impedi-
ment to purchasing socially impactful goods and, therefore, focused on pay-
as-you-go systems as a market opportunity. Then there is Zhihan Lee of
BagoSphere, who saw a massive opportunity through skills building in a
broken labor market, with its discrepancy between the incomes earned by
young, talented people doing irregular work in rural areas and the regular
salaries paid in formal labor markets for higher levels of skills.

It is the very nature of entrepreneurs, in general, that they have the
capacity to see opportunities where others see problems and to overcome
substantial hurdles that stand between reality and their entrepreneurial
dreams. This is even more true for social entrepreneurs. As the field of
fighting poverty with entrepreneurial means is still, in many ways, a
recent and untested area of expertise, their approaches and models are
typically highly innovative. Furthermore, they operate in countries with
far greater challenges (and more basic ones) than entrepreneurs who are
active in the developed world. Safety, rule of law, reliable infrastructure,
public service, functioning markets for basic goods and services – these
are all things that cannot be taken for granted.

The origins of this opportunity-oriented motivation vary. Some elea
entrepreneurs were brought to this path by specific experiences during
their youth, which could have been triggered by a health issue, as in the
case of Gaurav (Dharma Life), or by direct exposure to poverty, such as
with Zhihan (BagoSphere). Others adopted a more socially conscious
attitude when they were adults, sometimes after a successful career in
the corporate world. The result is an unwavering sense for realizing a
social impact opportunity and an ambition to build an organization that
makes a difference in the world, or as expressed in academic terms, a high
degree of intentionality. Studies looking into entrepreneurial motivations

show that social entrepreneurs share strong beliefs regarding their ability to tackle the different (and sometimes contradictory) aspects of a social venture's remit. They strive to produce and multiply social good, and they think of this quest as part and parcel of being an entrepreneur.[11]

1.2.3 A differentiated approach to risk

Creating value, which involves both social impact and financial sustainability, is a key dimension in understanding the concept of social entrepreneurship. The value creation opportunity has to be balanced against the perceived, or real, risks involved. Much of a typical entrepreneurial mindset is shaped by attitudes toward risk. As we will see in Chapter Six, the probability of meeting or exceeding impact expectations has been around 45% when we analyze elea's portfolio of 40 impact investments since inception. The return on an entrepreneur's investment – measured in monetary terms, but just as importantly in terms of the huge personal efforts, commitments, and sacrifices involved – may appear self-defeating.

Since social entrepreneurial opportunities often emerge from the contexts of perceived market failures, or where significant institutional voids exist, they are viewed as particularly challenging. The social entrepreneur must not only bear the risk of launching a new enterprise but also work to establish an infrastructure and new institutional pathways that support such an organization. In addition, an unclear relationship between impact and profit may add to the risks perceived. Moreover, as described in the aforementioned Positive Theory, and as we have experienced at elea, opportunities for value appropriation are very limited, which lowers the compensation that social entrepreneurs receive for the risks they take. Impact enterprises that operate in areas of absolute poverty, while striving for profitability, rarely generate substantial extra profits for entrepreneurs without achieving scale. For all of these reasons, one could argue that the risk profile of social entrepreneurs is higher than that of commercial entrepreneurs. In fact, predictions from existing theories on the social entrepreneur hypothesize that there is a positive relationship between prosocial motivation and risk tolerance.

To the contrary, Bird, Farber, and Reichert (2019) find that social entrepreneurs are less risk tolerant – that is, more risk averse as compared to commercial entrepreneurs – and that it is not prosocial motivation, per se, that alters a social entrepreneur's perception of risk. Rather, they pursue social entrepreneurial ventures because the utility they derive from the chance to create social value outweighs the disutility of the risk of engagement. For instance, social entrepreneurs are more likely to view nonexistent markets and institutional voids as opportunities rather than as threats. In doing so, however, they may underestimate the risks involved. In other words, a prosocial cost-benefit analysis may lead the social entrepreneur – even more so than a traditional entrepreneur – to fall prey to well-known cognitive biases; for example, a temptation to overoptimism and overconfidence. This mirrors elea's observations that very often both the estimates of social impact as well as the predictions of financial returns need to be downscaled to more realistic levels.

The notion of risk implies a certain level of knowledge. In other words, "when the probability of future states of the world is knowable, at least to a certain degree, risks can be priced and diversified away" (Kerr citing [Knight, 1921]) even if they are beyond one's control. By contrast, in the post Global Financial Crisis world, there has been a drastic increase in uncertainty, which has made it more difficult to describe what the future state of the world might be. Thus, risks are harder to identify and to quantify. This underlying trend encourages many social entrepreneurs to strengthen the resilience and agility of their organizations as risk mitigants (Kerr et al., 2018) (Knight, 1921).

1.2.4 *Managing the tensions between social and economic goals*

Social entrepreneurship takes many forms, from inclusive business models (with explicit social goals in addition to financial-return objectives) to cross-subsidization mechanisms (whereby profitable activities fund non-profit activities) up to hybrid structures (that combine both commercial and philanthropic entities). What these models have in common is an ambition that goes well beyond just reaping profits from a business and includes explicit, measurable benefits to society. While there are models where such benefits go hand in hand with generating profits, there are others where there is tension between the two. Such tensions need to be addressed by the entrepreneurs and their teams. Often, this entails experimenting and making adjustments to the design and implementation of the social enterprise, adapting to new organizational structures and decision-making processes, engaging in new types of alliances, and other factors. Producing social, economic, and environmental value at the same time can be a tough act to manage, as each of these types of value comes with its own principles, norms, and descriptors of success (Smith, Gonin, & Besharov, 2013).

Social entrepreneurs may, thus, face deep tensions and goal conflicts when combining business and philanthropic orientations. Indeed, social enterprises have frequently been classified according to the degree to which they adhere to a particular logic. In other words, a distinction is made between those that prioritize social-welfare logic and those that prioritize commercial logic (Smith et al., 2013; Grimes, 2010). While the ultimate and dominant goal of a social enterprise is the creation of social value, this is often not possible to achieve in a sustainable way without a commercially successful business activity.

Entrepreneurs, in general, and social entrepreneurs in particular, have to apply differentiated judgment calls regarding the mutual relationships between social impact goals and commercial success. For this, they must develop a deep understanding of the specific logic driving these activities. This calls for a pragmatic, learning-oriented approach in combining commercial and philanthropic solutions to optimize impact. Defining these balancing acts *ex ante* is often very difficult, because entrepreneurial journeys typically follow a nonlinear path of development. It sometimes turns out that problems that appear to be best resolved with market-based solutions are actually better served by more philanthropic ones, and vice versa. Examples are Dharma Life and BagoSphere. The potential for philanthropic capital that could be raised for Dharma Life's awareness campaigns was strongly underestimated at the outset, whereas, in the case of BagoSphere, the possibility to find commercial ways for providing scholarships to students in the Philippines was vastly overestimated.

1.3 Conclusions

1.3.1 Insights and takeaways

Individual personalities always matter in entrepreneurial activities. For companies at an early stage of maturity and institutionalization, such as the impact enterprises in which elea invests, they make a decisive difference. Ideas and models cannot be separated from the entrepreneurs in charge of driving their realization. Therefore, making a substantial effort to understand entrepreneurial characteristics and qualities is of utmost importance for the entrepreneurs themselves as well as for active investors.

In our tour d'horizon, where we reviewed both practical examples as well as academic research, we recognized that there are no simple formulas to describe and evaluate entrepreneurial qualities. Individual attitudes and behaviors, ambitions, and skills matter as much as the social, industry, and cultural context. Adding to the complexity are influences such as gender, education, and professional upbringing.

Nevertheless, the four categories of entrepreneurial qualities that we have discussed in detail can represent a starting point for a structured and informed dialogue, as entrepreneurs reflect on themselves and their colleagues, or as investors form a view during the due diligence process of a new investment opportunity. The result of such a dialogue should be a clearer profile of distinctive current strengths, future potential, and appropriate development measures. Over time, and with growing experience, such reflections can even evolve into a systematic approach to evaluate current and develop future qualities. This is particularly relevant for fast-growing impact enterprises where required entrepreneurial qualities rapidly change with the pace of development of the company. Qualities that are conducive to venture creation are typically very different from those that underpin the growth and long-term survival of an enterprise.

elea's experience in frequently – and often intensely – interacting on a personal level with its entrepreneurs suggests that significant value can be created from initiatives to understand and develop entrepreneurial qualities, despite their complexity. Learning not only from experience, both good and bad, but also from regular reflections on past performance and future aspirations, adds to their effectiveness and maturity as entrepreneurial leaders. Active and regular mentoring of entrepreneurs is, therefore, as important a task for elea professionals as is reflecting on development options for future leaders.

Interestingly, the capacity profiles of entrepreneurs in this field are typically very broad and diverse. World-class strengths (often recognized by important public platforms, such as Ashoka, the Skoll Foundation, and the Schwab Foundation for Social Entrepreneurship at the World Economic Forum) contrast with a lack of certain relevant experience and skills. Many entrepreneurs are excellent in articulating their story and making their case. They have learned to excite investors and negotiate resources for impact. Given that the part of the social entrepreneurial ecosystem that involves platforms of awards and recognition is quite developed, it can happen that elea entrepreneurs have already been in dialogue with world leaders in both government and business. Ironically, several of them are better at raising philanthropic capital than capital from professional impact investors, because the social impact element of the equation more strongly appeals to them than does the element related to the potential of the enterprise becoming an economically viable, sustainable business organization. One of the key drivers for the partnership between IMD and elea in creating the elea Chair and Center for Social Entrepreneurship was, indeed, the need to address specific skills gaps and strengthen the overall capacity of impact entrepreneurs.

1.3.2 *Your point of view*

We will typically begin these pedagogical sections at the end of each chapter with a few learning objectives. These are statements that define the expected goal of each chapter in terms of verifiable knowledge or skills that will be acquired by the reader as a result of reading the chapter. The learning objectives are then followed by reflection questions, which are designed to help readers to contemplate what they have learned and think more deeply about what they have read based on their own specific experience and knowledge. We believe that reflection is an important part of the learning experience. Additionally, we challenge the critical thinking of our readers with a debate on dilemma situations where there is no right or wrong answer.

Learning objectives

After studying this chapter, you should be able to

1. get a sense of how broad and diverse the field of impact entrepreneurship is based on the four elea investment examples;
2. identify the motivations, intentions, and values that can lead to the creation of a successful social/impact venture;
3. understand the entrepreneurial qualities that philanthropic impact investors look for in a successful investment; and
4. distinguish how impact entrepreneurs differ from other entrepreneurs.

Reflection questions

1. Based on your own experience, which characteristics and qualities describe entrepreneurs in general, and which traits are unique to the profile of an impact entrepreneur? What makes impact entrepreneurs different? Please explain.

2. Put yourself in the role of Lesley Marincola, Zhihan Lee, Martin Elwert, and Gaurav Mehta: which entrepreneurial qualities allowed them to succeed in leading an impact enterprise?

3. Do you identify with any of the impact entrepreneurs analyzed in this chapter? Which specific aspects do you identify with? Which ones do you not identify with?

4. Evaluate yourself in terms of the profile and qualities of an impact entrepreneur. Are there any specific traits that you feel need development?

5. Put yourself in the role of elea. Which entrepreneurial qualities would you look for in an impact entrepreneur? Which entrepreneurial qualities of Lesley Marincola, Zhihan Lee, Martin Elwert, and Gaurav Mehta captured your attention? Please explain.

6. If you were starting your own philanthropic impact investment organization, which entrepreneurial qualities would matter the most to you? Identify the professional development needs of social entrepreneurs you are familiar with. What are promising measures that could be taken to strengthen their effectiveness as entrepreneurial leaders?

Right vs. right dilemma: Business acumen vs. social passion

Designing, developing, and running an impact enterprise is extremely challenging. It requires the right passion, values, and mindset and also calls for a variety of critical experiences and skills in areas such as analysis and planning, people leadership, organization building, decisiveness, getting things done, etc. It is impossible to find all of these qualities in a single person, or even in a small team.

Often, impact entrepreneurs were social activists in their youth and feel passionate about social justice. They sometimes chose educational offerings (e.g., history, philosophy, sociology) with little relevance to building businesses. For example, their careers may have involved employment in public or private development aid agencies or in civil society. So they found their passion early on and then developed business acumen at a later stage. Meanwhile, other impact entrepreneurs enter with significant experience in business analysis and leadership. They may have an educational background in business, engineering, or law, and they often express a desire "to give back to society" after an accomplished first phase in their more traditional business careers. So they started by acquiring deep business expertise and then developed a passion for societal goals later on. Both types of profiles can become outstanding impact entrepreneurs. In many cases, these two types of profiles are coupled together and form a team to start up a social venture.

What are the advantages of a socially oriented founder versus a founder with a more commercial mindset? Which advantages might the commercially oriented founder have over one coming from the public or non-profit sector? What kind of tensions do you think are likely to emerge when these two types of profiles are both on the entrepreneurial leadership team? By contrast, how might they complement each other during venture creation? Debate the pros and cons of alternative profiles as you put together (or evaluate) an entrepreneurial leadership team.

Notes

1. We do not like the terms "social entrepreneur" and "social enterprise" very much. They disqualify all those entrepreneurs who are not given this label by implying that they do not produce social impact, whereas the vast majority of regular enterprises create massive social impact by offering useful products and services, providing income through employment, and contributing – through taxes – to state financing for public goods, such as education and social welfare. We have the same concern regarding the term "commercial entrepreneur," as there are many entrepreneurs with a commercial mandate that demonstrate outstanding social characteristics. We will therefore use the terms "social" and "commercial" when we refer to academic literature. Our preference is to use the terms "impact enterprise" and "impact entrepreneur" or "elea enterprise" and "elea entrepreneur" for those who lead the enterprises in elea's investment portfolio. Admittedly, these terms also have their definitional challenges (implying that "normal" entrepreneurs or enterprises have no impact), but they are at least parallel to the term "impact investing."

2. See www.angaza.com.
3. The term "bottom of the pyramid" (which we refer to as the "base of the pyramid") goes back to a paper written by C.K. Prahalad together with Stuart Hart in 1998, which highlights the business opportunity hidden in the fact that billions of people at the low end of the income scale were underserved (see the book that later appeared: [Prahalad, 2004]). Since then, this thinking has continued to inspire both corporations and social enterprises. One key aspect of this theme is the challenge of the last-mile distribution of basic goods and services to remote areas and at affordable prices.
4. The name "BagoSphere" is derived from Bago City, a small town close to Bacolod in the Philippines, which is one of the enterprise's main sites today and where the initiative originally started. See www.bagosphere.com.
5. https://www.ashoka.org/en-ch/fellow/zhihan-lee
6. See www.coffeecircle.com.
7. See www.dharmalife.in.
8. (Hussain, 2014); (MacKenzie, 2019)
9. (Kerr, Kerr, & Xu, 2018); (Palich & Bagby, 1995); (Busenitz & Barney, 1997); (Camerer & Lovallo, 1999); (Burmeister & Schade, 2007); (Douglas & Shepherd, 2002); (Xu & Ruef, 2004); (Benz & Frey, 2008); (Krueger & Dickson, 1993); (Forlani & Mullins, 2000); (Hvide & Panos, 2014)
10. (Fayolle & Liñán, 2014); (Kerr, Kerr, & Xu, 2018); (Zhao, Seibert, & Lumpkin, 2010)
11. (Fayolle & Liñán, 2014); (Frese, 2009); (Krueger, 2017); (Smith, Gonin, & Besharov, 2013); (Stephan & Drencheva, 2017); (Zahra & Wright, 2016)

References

Benz, M., & Frey, B. S. (2008). The Value of Doing What You Like: Evidence from the Self-Employed in 23 Countries. *Journal of Economic Behavior & Organization, 68(3-4)*, 445–455.

Bird, M., Farber, V., & Reichert, P. (2019). *Value Capture, Risk and Autonomy: Opportunity Evaluation Decisions of Social and Commercial Entrepreneurs.* Working Paper.

Burmeister, K., & Schade, C. (2007). Are Entrepreneurs' Decisions More Biased? An Experimental Investigation of the Susceptibility to Status Quo Bias. *Journal of Business Venturing, 22(3)*, 340–362.

Busenitz, L. W., & Barney, J. (1997). Differences between Entrepreneurs and Managers in Large Organizations: Biases and Heuristics in Strategic

Decision-Making. *Journal of Business Venturing, 12(1)*, 9–30. doi: 10.1016/S0883-9026(96)00003-1

Camerer, C., & Lovallo, D. (1999). Overconfidence and Excess Entry: An Experimental Approach. *American Economic Review, 89(1)*, 306–318.

Douglas, E. J., & Shepherd, D. (2002). Self-Employment as a Career Choice: Attitudes, Entrepreneurial Intentions, and Utility Maximization. *Entrepreneurship Theory and Practice, 26(3)*, 81–90.

Eisenmann, T. R. (10. January 2013). Entrepreneurship: a Working Definition. *Harvard Business Review.* https://hbr.org/2013/01/what-is-entrepreneurship

Fayolle, A., & Liñán, F. (2014). The Future of Research on Entrepreneurial Intentions. *Journal of Business Research, 67(5)*, 663–666.

Forlani, D., & Mullins, J. W. (2000). Perceived Risks and Choices in Entrepreneurs' New Venture Decisions. *Journal of Business Venturing, 15(4)*, 305–322.

Frese, M. (2009). Towards a Psychology of Entrepreneurship: an Action Theory Perspective. *Foundations and Trends® in Entrepreneurship, 5(6)*, 437–496.

Grimes, M. (2010). Strategic Sensemaking Within Funding Relationships: The Effects of Performance Measurement on Organizational Identity in the Social Sector. *Entrepreneurship Theory and Practice, 34(4)*, 763–783.

Hussain, S. (2014). Dharma Life: Making Profits through Rural Entrepreneurs. *Forbes India.* Retrieved May 4, 2020 from https://www.forbesindia.com/article/work-in-progress/dharma-lifes-making-profits-through-rural-entrepreneurs/38116/1

Hvide, H. K., & Panos, G. A. (2014). Risk Tolerance and Entrepreneurship. *Journal of Financial Economics, 111(1)*, 200–223.

Kerr, S. P., Kerr, W. R., & Xu, T. (2018). Personality Traits of Entrepreneurs: A Review of Recent Literature. *Foundations and Trends® in Entrepreneurship, 14(3)*, 279–356.

Knight, F. H. (1921). *Risk, Uncertainty and Profit.* New York: Schaffner and Marx.

Krueger, N. F. (2017). Entrepreneurial Intentions Are Dead: Long Live Entrepreneurial Intentions. *In Revisiting the Entrepreneurial Mind: Inside the Black Box: An Expanded Edition.* Cham: Springer.

Krueger, N. F., & Dickson, P. R. (1993). Perceived Self-Efficacy and Perceptions of Opportunity and Threat. *Psychological reports, 72(3 suppl)*, 1235–1240. doi: 10.2466/pr0.1993.72.3c.1235

MacKenzie, A. (2019). Changemakers: Gaurav Mehta. *London Business School Review.* Retrieved May 4, 2020 from https://www.london.edu/think/changemakers-gaurav-mehta

Openstax CNX Psychology. (22. October 2019). From Trait Theorists. Retrieved May 4, 2020 from https://cnx.org/contents/Sr8Ev5Og@4.100:Vqapzwst@2/ Trait-Theorists

Palich, L., & Bagby, D. (1995). Using Cognitive Theory to Explain Entrepreneurial Risk-Taking: Challenging Conventional Wisdom. *Journal of Businesss Venturing, 10(6)*, 425–438. doi: 10.1016/0883-9026(95)00082-J

Prahalad, C. K. (2004). *The Fortune at the Bottom of the Pyramid: Eradicating Poverty Through Profits.* Wharton School Publishing.

Santos, F. (2009). *A Positive Theory of Social Entrepreneurship.* Fontainebleau: INSEAD Social Innovation Centre.

Smith, W. K., Gonin, M., & Besharov, M. L. (2013). Managing Social-Business Tensions: A Review and Research Agenda for Social Enterprise. *Business Ethics Quarterly, 23(3)*, 407–442.

Stephan, U., & Drencheva, A. (2017). The Person in Social Entrepreneurship: A Systematic Review of Research on the Social Entrepreneurial Personality. *The Wiley Handbook of Entrepreneurship. Chapter 10.*

Xu, H., & Ruef, M. (2004). The Myth of the Risk-Tolerent Entrepreneur. *Strategic Organization, 2(4)*, 331–355.

Young, S. (17. August 2018). *Acts of Leadership: Exploring Leadership Issues, Thoughts and Ideas.* Retrieved October 22, 2019 from http://www.samyoung .co.nz/2018/08/the-big-five-personality-test.html

Zahra, S., & Wright, M. (2016). Understanding the Social Role of Entrepreneurship. *Journal of Management Studies, 53(4)*, 610–629.

Zhao, H., & Seibert, S. E. (2006). The Big-Five Personality Dimensions and Entrepreneurial Status: A Meta-Analytical Review. *Journal of Applied Psychology, 91(2)*, 259.

Zhao, H., Seibert, S., & Lumpkin, G. T. (2010). The Relationship of Personality to Entrepreneurial Intentions and Performance: A Meta-Analytic Review. *Journal of Management, 36(2)*, 381–404.

2

IMPACT INVESTING ON
THE RISE

The second component of our new formula for capitalism is capital. Over the last decade, the rise of impact investing has been the most significant trend in this respect. By the end of 2019, approximately 1,340 impact funds across the globe oversaw an estimated USD 500 billion of accumulated committed capital (according to the Global Impact Investing Network, www.thegiin.org). One of the pioneers of impact investing is Andrew Kuper, the founder and CEO of LeapFrog Investments. LeapFrog (www.leapfroginvest.com) was created in 2007 (the same year in which the term impact investing was coined) with a strong ethical foundation and a clear intention and commitment to combine profit with purpose. Its funds, which have attracted over USD 1.5 billion, invest equity in private companies that are domiciled in low-income countries (targeting areas with a daily income below USD 10). LeapFrog specializes in the financial services and healthcare sectors and makes investments of USD10–USD50 million in companies that have a strong commitment to purpose and impact, while ambitiously seeking to grow these businesses. As of early 2020, LeapFrog's companies served over 200 million people across Africa, Asia, and Latin America and helped to create almost 130,000 jobs. It has a staff of 60 people and maintains expert advisory capacity in the following fields: strategy and governance, products and pricing, sales and distribution, core operations, human resources and talent management, as well as technology and data.

How is "investing" defined? This term comes from the Latin word *investire* ("to clothe," or in the case of finance, "to give one's capital a new form") and means "to put money, effort, time, etc. into something to make a profit or get an advantage" (Dictionary.cambridge.org, 2020). The essential idea of investing is that an initial resource level, whether financial or non-financial capital (e.g., human capital, such as expertise, advice, and personal energy), is made available with the expectation that this will start a process of increasingly self-sustained activities. In the case of social impact investing, such investments are made with the intention of achieving beneficial consequences in terms of poverty alleviation and positive economic development. In this chapter, we will look at the origin and driving forces of this trend as well as its scope and the underlying motivations and intentions of investors.

2.1 The birth of impact investing

The term "impact investing" goes back to a report prepared by the Shell Foundation and published by Foundation Strategy Group (FSG) (a social enterprise dedicated to advancing the practice of philanthropy, social investment, and corporate responsibility) in 2006. In this report entitled "Investing for Impact," a framework for how proactive social investment can help to stimulate business-based solutions to social problems, was developed based on several case studies (Foundation Strategy Group [FSG], 2006). Subsequently, in 2007, Antony Bugg-Levine (then Managing Director of the Rockefeller Foundation) invited leaders in finance, philanthropy, and development to their Bellagio Center in Italy to discuss the creation of a new global investment industry that strives for positive social and environmental impact (Höchstädter & Scheck, 2015).

In a certain way, this idea was a variation of the "Big Push" theme launched after World War II, which was based on a belief that international resource transfers would facilitate economic development. This resulted in massive financial flows to poor countries in the context of public-sector development aid. While there are indeed some cases beyond the reconstruction of Europe and Japan after World War II (such as in South Korea and Taiwan) where international resource transfer was key to development success, other outstanding development achievements after World War II (such as Singapore and Botswana) were homegrown and resulted from a combination of strong state leadership, effective institutions, widespread entrepreneurialism, and accumulated capital. Consequently, significant controversy developed around how to balance capital transfers versus other factors in driving economic development (see Context Boxes 2.1 and 2.2 for an overview on the history of development aid and a summary about the debates related to it). Within this debate, impact investing emphasized the need for capital while also challenging conventional wisdom around aid. In particular, it called for different actors and different forms of aid: it should be executed primarily by private-sector actors rather than public-sector organizations, and it should come predominantly in the form of equity and debt investments rather than multilateral or bilateral aid or private charitable giving.

CONTEXT BOX 2.1: THE HISTORY OF DEVELOPMENT AID

Except for efforts to help citizens and rebuild destroyed economies after World War I, before World War II, the idea of transferring resources from wealthy to poor countries for the sake of their economic development had only little appeal. Poverty was widely seen as a matter of destiny. Resource transfers happened mostly within colonial structures and predominantly bilaterally – in both directions – between colonies and motherlands. This all changed with the successful reconstruction of Europe after World War II, which provided courage and raised expectations that the same could be possible for the entire underdeveloped world.

In his inauguration speech on January 20, 1949, U.S. President Harry Truman stated the fourth objective of his foreign policy as follows:

> We must embark on a bold new program for making the benefits of our scientific advances and industrial progress available for the improvement and growth of underdeveloped areas. More than half the people of the world are living in conditions approaching misery. Their food is inadequate. They are victims of disease. Their economic life is primitive and stagnant. Their poverty is a handicap and a threat both to them and to more prosperous areas. For the first time in history, humanity possesses the knowledge and skill to relieve [the] suffering of these people. The United States is preeminent among nations in the development of industrial and scientific techniques. The material resources which we can afford to use for [the] assistance of other peoples are limited. But our imponderable resources in technical knowledge are constantly growing and

are inexhaustible. (Source: Yale Law School. Link: https://avalon.law
.yale.edu/20th_century/truman.asp)

With these sentences, the 33rd U.S. President launched one of the most
ambitious initiatives that humankind has seen to this date. It was about
nothing less than lifting the world out of poverty. Interestingly, President
Truman highlighted the importance of technical knowledge before financial resources.

A year before, in 1948, in the context of the Marshall Plan, the U.S. had
started to transfer financial resources to Western Europe for reconstruction
after World War II. Between 1948 and 1951, USD 13 billion were provided to
the United Kingdom, France, Italy, the Federal Republic of Germany, and
the Netherlands. This early example of "impact investing" helped nurture
economic growth in postwar Europe and served as evidence that economic
growth could indeed be achieved based on external financial support.

The thinking behind this idea of a massive international resource transfer to boost economic development goes back to Paul Rosenstein-Rodan,
an Austrian economist, who wrote the founding article of development economics in 1943 (Rosenstein-Rodan, 1943). He called for large-scale externally
financed investment in Eastern European industry, because the required funds
would not spontaneously emerge from the private sector within this region.

Truman's world development agenda, combined with the positive experience of postwar European reconstruction, led to an approach that was seen
as applicable to the problems of all "Third World" economies and came to
be known as "The Big Push" (Easterly, 2005). The goals of this initiative,
which was launched by the U.S. and later adopted by other countries, was
to fight poverty, create commercial opportunities for the West, and – above
all – promote liberal capitalism and reduce the influence of communism.

The Bretton Woods institutions (initially the International Monetary Fund
[IMF] and the International Bank for Reconstruction and Development [IBRD],
later called the World Bank) were increasingly serving this agenda to support the economic development of poor countries. In 1956, the International
Finance Corporation (IFC) was founded and constituted possibly the first
dedicated institutional impact investor with its mission "to promote sustainable private-sector investment in developing countries, helping to reduce
poverty and improve people's lives" (www.ifc.org). The regional branches of
the World Bank, the Inter-American Development Bank (1960), the African
Development Bank (1964), and the Asian Development Bank (1966) later

followed. In addition, in 1961, President John F. Kennedy bundled several U.S. development agencies into one powerful organization, the United States Agency for International Development (USAID).

During the 1960s and 1970s, development economists argued that governments should take the leading role in economic development. In 1972, this concept was launched under the umbrella of the OECD in the form of "Official Development Assistance" (ODA). It was stipulated that developed countries should spend, on average, 0.7% of their GDP as ODA, a target that up to 2019 was met by only a very small number of individual countries. A particular focus was on large-scale infrastructure projects. Development aid was seen as a political instrument in the Cold War against the Soviet Union, at least as much as an element of economic policy for development. In the 1980s and 1990s, prevailing development paradigms started to suggest that markets, rather than state interventions, should be given the central role in development. The focus, therefore, shifted to policy frameworks that would emphasize the role of private enterprise and capital flows as an engine for development, while public aid programs (e.g., for infrastructure) were increasingly seen as complementary to market-friendly policy reforms (See: [Nowak, 2014] for an overeiw).

CONTEXT BOX 2.2: DO INTERNATIONAL RESOURCE TRANSFERS HELP ECONOMIC DEVELOPMENT?

Fifty years and an estimated USD 2.3 trillion worth of aid transferred from wealthy to poor countries later, a renewed debate emerged around the idea of "The Big Push." Controversies around the effectiveness of aid for sustainable economic development had started right from the beginning. Even the specific contribution of the Marshall Plan to the growth of Western European economies was challenged. U.S. President Eisenhower called for "Trade, not aid." The persistence of poverty in many countries, particularly in Africa, despite decades of massive international resource transfers, led the UN to take a new resolve at the turn of the millennium. In 2000, it agreed on eight Millennium Development Goals (MDGs) that were to achieve substantial progress in reducing hunger and poverty and in improving health, education, gender equality, and sustainable ecological development by 2015. Development economist Jeffrey Sachs was mandated by the UN to oversee progress on the realization of these aspirational objectives. In his book *The End of Poverty*, he identified a poverty trap for those (primarily African) countries that seemed stuck in absolute poverty. He encouraged rich countries to invest enough in the poorest countries so that they could overcome the trap and get their foot on the first rung of the ladder of economic development (Sachs, 2005).

His idea was challenged by more market-oriented development economists, such as Peter Bauer, William Easterly, Paul Collier, and – more recently – Dambisa Moyo and Nobel Prize winner Angus Deaton. Easterly, in particular, analyzed the relationship between public investment, development aid, and productivity growth in 22 African countries between 1970 and 1994. These countries spent USD 342 billion on public investments, while donors gave the governments of these same countries USD 187 billion in aid over this period. Yet per capita economic growth during this period in these countries was zero (Easterly, 2005, p. 8). Moyo even goes as far as saying that "Millions in Africa are poorer today because of aid; misery and poverty have not ended but have increased" (Moyo, 2009). One of the underlying reasons for this, according to Moyo, is that governments that receive aid respond more to the demands of donor governments than to the needs of their citizens and are, therefore, driven by the wrong incentives, besides caring mostly for their own interests. If taxes were an important income for them, they would have an interest in supporting a healthy and growing domestic economy and complying with the rule of law rather than focusing on negotiating attractive aid packages with governments or multilateral aid organizations. More recently, Angus Deaton provocatively argued that foreign aid to poor countries often hurts rather than helps the fight against poverty, particularly because it can undermine effective governance (Deaton, 2013).

Such critical authors see the problem less in terms of a disproportion between the needs of the poor and the level of aid resources and more in terms of the disappointingly small impact of the aid funds transferred. In their view, public-sector transfers often have negative side effects, as they encourage corruption, create longer-term dependence, destroy entrepreneurial incentives, remove the pressure from inefficient governmental bodies, and cement dysfunctional structures rather than reform them (see also: [Wuffli, 2016, p. 62 ff]).

In 2018, the McKinsey Global Institute conducted a study on 18 developing economies that averaged at least 3.5% per capita GDP growth over 50 years, or 5% annual growth over 20 years. They called these countries the outperformers. Eight ASEAN countries (Indonesia, Malaysia, Singapore, Thailand, Cambodia, Laos, Myanmar, and Vietnam) were among these 18.

In their analysis, McKinsey concluded that this exceptional performance was supported by a pro-growth agenda of productivity, income, and demand that featured steps to boost capital accumulation, including forced savings and the growth of financial institutions. In addition, large companies – those with annual revenue of at least USD 500 million – contributed substantially to these countries' outperformance in per capita growth (McKinsey Global Institute, 2018). The international transfer of financial resources was not mentioned as a factor driving growth outperformance in this study. However, it is most probably not a coincidence that many of the winners identified by McKinsey are countries that are strongly influenced by the Chinese diaspora, a notoriously entrepreneurial people with thousands of years of learning culture, cohesive values (particularly at the family level), and a long tradition of savings propensity.

Historically, by far the most spectacular success in economic development, which lifted hundreds of millions of people out of absolute poverty over just one generation, is of course the reemergence of China as a dominant world economy. Economists attribute this enormous success primarily to changes in mindset and economic policy that, in essence, go back to General Secretary Deng Xiaoping, when he famously said that it did not matter whether the cat was black or white, as long as it caught mice (e.g., [Shahid, 2009]). He, thus, sent the signal to Chinese people that pragmatism should supersede communist dogma and that making profit from economic activity is okay.

Two other outstanding, yet smaller-scale, economic development stories that are unrelated to international resource transfer are Singapore and Botswana. In both cases, state leadership was at the heart of success. When the founder and long-time leader of modern Singapore, Lee Kuan Yew, turned ninety years old, his closest aides published a book about their experiences with him (Jayakumar & Sagar, 2014). The following qualities, which were conducive to catapulting Singapore from a poor country to its current level of prosperity in less than fifty years, were mentioned again and again in this book:

- Charismatic personal leadership (thoughtfulness, courage, pragmatism, hands-on approach).
- Consistent enforcement of the rule of law.
- Strong focus on policy implementation.

- Excellence in recruiting, developing, and retaining talented people for public service.
- Emphasis of tolerance within a multiracial society.

Botswana is widely seen as an exemplary case of economic development in Sub-Saharan Africa. Instead of giving credit to international aid programs, this success is often attributed to the exceptional leadership quality of Sir Seretse Khama, Botswana's first president after independence, and to a traditional system of inclusive rather than extractive institutions (Williams, 2006). One of the remarkable features of Botswana was that it effectively provided public goods to its citizens (Wimmer, 2018).

More generally, the quality of political institutions and the existence of a vibrant, engaged civil society is increasingly seen as a major determinant of positive economic development (see e.g., [Acemoglu & Robinson, 2013], [Wimmer, 2018]).

Where does this debate stand today? Initially nurtured by ideological tensions between free-market liberals and state socialists, more recently there are clear signs of a more empirical discussion that is focused on what works and what does not. While the quality and effectiveness of governments and political institutions are decisive factors, there is often not much that can be done about respective shortcomings in the short term. Therefore, targeted initiatives, either in the humanitarian field (based on charitable contributions) or in the service of sustainable economic development (based on impact investing), are promising fields of action with increasing empirical track records.

In 2009, the Global Impact Investing Network (GIIN) was created, and a year later, J.P. Morgan published a study in collaboration with the Rockefeller Foundation and GIIN that explored the potential of impact investments as an emerging asset class with a view to making it accessible to institutional investors as well. According to J.P. Morgan, impact investments are defined as "investments intended to create positive impact beyond financial return ... as such, they require the management of social and environmental performance (for which early industry standards are gaining traction among pioneering impact investors) in addition to financial risk and return" (Morgan, 2010, p. 5).

According to this study, an asset class is described as a category of financial investments that is supported by a unique set of investment/risk-management skills; specific organizational structures to accommodate such a skills set; the creation of an ecosystem in the form of support from industry, associations, and education; and finally, standardized metrics, benchmarks, and/or ratings. The main investable sectors identified for impact investing include housing, water, health, education, and financial services. Other guide books added agriculture and environment to the list of investable impact areas (e.g., [Balandina Jaquier, 2011, p. 14]). In 2010, J.P. Morgan expected that the total capital investment potential in these sectors would reach between USD 400 and USD 1,000 billion by 2020. Of these, the largest opportunities, by far, were seen in housing and financial services (Morgan, 2010).

According to GIIN, impact investments since 2010 have increased at an estimated annual growth rate of some 13% and represent one of the fastest growing investment segments.

Currently, a broad and hugely diverse range of investor types is potentially interested in impact investment opportunities. There are wealthy entrepreneurs and their families who − either directly through their family office and/or through professional intermediaries, such as banks or wealth management advisors − want to align their financial investment strategy with their family ethics and values. Furthermore, pension funds, life insurance companies, and other institutional investors are taking steps to engage in this field to expand the proportion of assets managed in line with SRI (socially responsible investing) or ESG (environmental, social, and governance) criteria. For example, foundations want to align their investment approach to their principal mission, and corporations see it as a way of underlining their commitment to corporate social responsibility (CSR). And finally, some government entities may pursue such investments as an element of their national or international economic development policy agendas.

2.1.1 Driving forces

What have been the major drivers nurturing the development of this trend toward impact investing? We have discovered three: liquid wealth from globalization; a new, more inclusive capitalism; and low-yielding financial markets.

Wealth from globalization

Globalization and the development of financial markets over the past 30–40 years have created a tremendous amount of real assets and liquid wealth, both institutional and private. In addition, progress in healthcare and the resulting increase in living expectations has fostered an institutional need for financial capital accumulation and increasingly professionalized investment management. Individual savings plans have shifted to collective vehicles, such as pension funds, life-insurance schemes, and mutual funds. At the same time, structural changes within financial markets have created opportunities for entrepreneurial families to liquefy their assets by selling entire companies or issuing bonds or shares, thus providing an additional boost to the development of financial markets. Whereas in previous generations many owner entrepreneurs and their families had been rich only on paper, having reinvested all of their profits back into their companies, new generations of wealthy families have emerged that can actually deploy and spend their wealth at a relatively young age (see also [Wuffli, 2016, p. 18 f.]), and more and more of them seek to invest this wealth in instruments that prioritize the benefits to society.

New, more inclusive capitalism

A second driver of the impact investing trend has to do with the heightened awareness of the need to address pressing global challenges against the background of an evolving view on the role of capitalism. In the years following the Global Financial Crisis of 2007/2008, the somewhat fuzzy term "new capitalism" emerged. While there was no consensus on how to clarify this term, it did imply that there was an "old capitalism" that needed renewal. Old capitalism often refers to a quote in Milton Friedman's classic book *Capitalism and Freedom* where he stipulates, "There is one and only one social responsibility of business ... to increase its profits ..." (Friedman, 1962 [reprint 2002], p. 133). A shorter version of this thought ("the business of business is business") was used by Ian Davies, a former managing director of McKinsey & Company (Davies, 2005, p. 106).

New capitalism, by comparison, invokes higher levels of social consciousness and responsibility and says that the relationship between the economy and society should be redesigned; that is, the former should serve the latter, not the other way around. One important contribution in this debate is a book by Yale professor and Nobel Prize winner Robert Shiller, entitled *Finance and the Good Society*, in which he made a plea for better alignment between financial capitalism and societal goals. With a particular focus on financial firms, Shiller asked: "How can finance promote freedom, prosperity, equality, and economic security?" and "How can we democratize finance, so as to make it work better for all of us?" (Shiller, 2012, p. 2).

A review of available literature – both academic and practitioner – indicates a certain ideological tension between the advocates of old and those of new capitalism. The former believe that profitable business is strictly separated from charitable giving, whereas the latter see the value of hybrid models that productively integrate both business and philanthropic dimensions within a social enterprise (Bannick & Goldman, 2016).

Even though published long before the Great Financial Crisis (in 1998), a quote from Muhammad Yunus's autobiography, entitled *Banker to the Poor*, provides a possible meaning for how new capitalism could become more inclusive:

> Somehow we have persuaded ourselves that the capitalist economy must be fueled only by greed. This has become a self-fulfilling prophecy …, If you are a socially conscious person, why don't you run your business in a way that will help achieve social objectives? I profoundly believe, as Grameens' experience over twenty years has shown, that greed is not the only fuel for free enterprise. Social goals can replace greed as a powerful motivational force. Social-consciousness-driven enterprises can be formidable competitors for the greed-based enterprises. (Yunus, 1998, p. 215)

In recent years, more and more corporations have become much more serious about sustainability and social impact at a strategic level rather than at a more marketing-oriented level where CSR is used as an instrument for positive reputation management. Meanwhile, consumers are developing a clearer understanding about the products and services they buy, particularly about the environmental and social conditions under which they are manufactured. Talented professionals – if they seek employment at all – want to work for organizations with a clear societal purpose. Moreover, investors, at a minimum, seek compliance with SRI or ESG standards and look more and more for impact investment opportunities where a positive correlation between the strategy and activities of a business and clearly defined societal benefits can be plausibly illustrated (see also [Henderson, 2018]). It can be assumed that the experience of the Global Covid-19 Crisis will further strengthen this trend.

Low-yielding financial markets

A third driver behind the momentum favoring impact investing originated from the challenges to traditional investment thinking that arose over the first decade following the Global Financial Crisis. As a result of extremely low interest-rate levels, many investors adjusted their appetite for risk toward riskier and more volatile investments. At the same time, standard hierarchies of risk-return relationships – ranging from less risky assets (e.g., government bonds) to more and more risky assets (e.g., corporate bonds and equity) – were challenged by the financial-crisis experience. Such "disorders" in the risk-return relationships of traditional financial assets may have paved the way for the acceptance of elevated and uncommon risk profiles that typically characterize impact investment opportunities. A recent empirical study actually confirms that a low-yield environment can induce investors to accept higher risks (Lian, Ma, & Wang, 2018).

2.1.2 The scope of impact investing

In recent years, a rich and diverse discussion among practitioners and academics has evolved around the definition and scope of impact investing. Authors typically agree on two key elements that constitute the definition of an impact investment; namely, the need for intentionality on the side of the investors (which will be discussed in more detail later on in this chapter), combined with some analytical concept for impact measurement (which will be dealt with in Chapter Six) (see e.g., [Allman, 2015]; [Grabenwarter & Liechtenstein, 2011]; [Balandina Jaquier, 2011]).

The scope beyond these two definitional criteria is controversial and in a state of flux: many authors and practitioners see impact investing occurring primarily through private equity and debt structures, whereas other authors also include public instruments, such as social impact bonds and green bonds, among impact investments. The broader the scope, the more difficult it becomes to differentiate impact investments from the SRI and/or ESG criteria pursued by more and more "regular" public and private investor markets.[1]

Indeed, there are clear signs of convergence between large global corporations and the impact focus stipulated in these pages. IMD strategy professor Thomas Malnight (among others) considers purpose to be a fourth driver of strategy, in addition to creating new markets, serving broader stakeholder needs, and changing the rules of the game. Based on his work with corporations, he recommends putting purpose at the core of the strategy, as this promises three specific benefits: more unified organizations, more motivated stakeholders, and a broader positive impact on society.

One example of such a purpose-driven approach is the Finnish oil-refining firm Neste (www.neste.com). This company fundamentally transformed its business, which was focused almost entirely on crude oil. Under the leadership of its CEO Matti Lievonen, over a period of seven years Neste established itself as the world's largest producer of renewable fuels derived from waste and residues (Malnight, Buche, & Dhanaraj, 2019).

Another example is Royal DSM, a traditional Dutch coal mining company that underwent a 10-year transformation process to specialize in nutrition, health, and sustainable living, with the goal of creating brighter lives for all. Its CEO Feike Sijbesma firmly believes that "we cannot be successful, nor can we call ourselves successful, in a society that fails," and characterizes DSM's approach as purpose-led and performance-driven. He explicitly orients DSM's corporate strategy toward the UN Sustainable Development Goals and even abolished the term corporate social responsibility (CSR), as it indicates a field at the margin, not at the center, of their strategy (www.dsm.com).

OCP Group, based in Morocco, is a third example. It is a leading global fertilizer producer with almost a century of history in serving the phosphate industry and agriculture. During a multiyear transformation process, its CEO Mostafa Terrab adopted a holistic approach to sustainable development based on the four pillars of a circular economy: phosphate resource preservation, sustainable production, smart consumption, and waste recycling. With farmers at the core of OCP Group's strategy, OCP also leverages its capacities to boost local entrepreneurship and farming-related projects, as well as social-impact-oriented projects, thereby creating a local entrepreneur ecosystem (www.ocpgroup.ma; see also [Croset, 2014]).

It is helpful to think about the scope of impact investing as being within a range that goes from one extreme (that of "financial only") to the other (that of "impact only"), as presented by Bridges Fund Management (formerly Bridges Ventures), one of the pioneers in the field of institutionalized investment firms. They were founded back in 2002, with a special focus on sustainability and impact (see Figure 2.1).

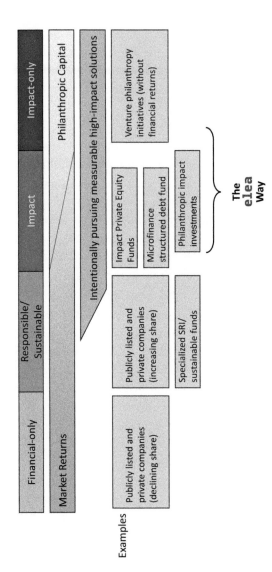

Figure 2.1 Models of impact investing.

Source: Bridges Fund Management, 2015

The positioning along this spectrum is determined to a large extent by the type of investors as well as their level of available means. For instance, many intermediaries acting in a fiduciary capacity on behalf of their beneficial owners (e.g., pension funds, life insurance companies, and mutual funds) will position themselves in the field of "financial only" or, depending on their governance mechanisms, will increasingly choose categories with more explicit sustainability criteria, such as SRI or ESG (see the "Responsible/Sustainable" fields in the chart). Private investors who have regular incomes and are in average wealth brackets will also be found more often in these zones, because they will shy away from the higher risks and the lower liquidity associated with impact investing. The Impact" and "Impact only" fields, on the other hand, will be primarily favored by wealthy individuals, family offices, and foundations that apply more of a philanthropic angle, such as elea.

2.2 Investor motivations and intentions

As intentionality is one of the defining criteria for impact investing, the question arises as to how intentions can be better understood, described, and classified. Improved knowledge of impact investors' motivations as a basis for analyzing their intentions and their criteria for investment decisions is an important priority for academic research, as was revealed in a 2017 study by Roundy, Holzhauer, and Dai entitled "Finance or Philanthropy? Exploring the Motivations and Criteria of Impact Investors":

> Furthermore, it is not known what motivates individuals to become impact investors. Nor is it clear what criteria they use to evaluate ventures (or entrepreneurs) when making investments. These issues represent important omissions in management, entrepreneurship, and finance literatures because without a firm understanding of what is unique about this category of investor, and why and how they invest, it is not clear if impact investors represent a new type of market actor and what role they play in society. It is also difficult to discern the extent to which prior theories and findings derived from the study of either traditional investors or philanthropists can be used to understand the behaviors of impact investors. Moreover, without a deeper understanding of the phenomenon, concrete recommendations cannot be made to

practicing impact investors, policymakers seeking to encourage impact investment, or entrepreneurs seeking resources from such investors. Finally, it is important to understand how impact investors think and analyze investments because, as an increasingly large pool of investors, if they prefer to invest in certain categories of firms (e.g., green energy or social enterprise), then this may shape the development of these industries and markets. (Roundy, Holzhauer, & Dai, 2017, p. 4 f.)

In their study, which was based on interviews with 31 impact and non-impact investors, the authors differentiated between three types of investors with different intentions: venture capitalists (individuals or funds), impact investors, and angel investors. Whereas venture capitalists seek profit maximization, impact investors always have a dual motivation: achieving financial returns and benefits to society. For their part, angel investors (who typically invest in early stage start-ups) seek profitable investments but also consider motives beyond purely financial returns, such as helping good entrepreneurs or contributing to building an effective start-up ecosystem.

2.2.1 *The trade-off debate*

One way to categorize the motivations and intentions of impact investors is to look at the relationship between desired financial return and impact. Are impact investors looking for "impact first" or "financials first"? Is there a trade-off between the two, and if so why and with what implications? Is it due to the nature of these investments that the achievement of impact requires some sacrifice of financial return, or is it the other way around; namely, that true impact investments do not require trade-offs?

There is a difference in perspective between practitioners and academics with respect to this relationship between financial return and impact. Many practitioners (often impact investors themselves) adhere to the "no trade-off" camp for obvious reasons. Combining financial return and socially responsible environmental impact without trade-offs would encourage commitments from a broader number of investors and could, thus, mobilize higher amounts of capital. Academics, on the other hand, aspire to establish definitional clarity with analytical rigor. The authors of an empirical study among 60 active impact investors (mostly family offices) stipulate that "true impact investing" should be strictly separated

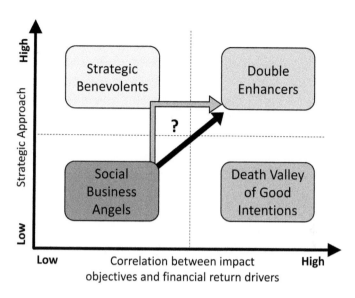

Figure 2.2 Social impact/financial return trade-offs.

Source: Grabenwarter & Liechtenstein, 2011

from all investments with a trade-off between impact and financial return, because "any business model in which every unit of social/environmental impact has a cost in terms of financial return is, therefore, inevitably a disguised form of philanthropy" (Grabenwarter & Liechtenstein, 2011, p. 11). Based on this "purist" understanding of impact investing, they go on to describe different types of investors that make different investment choices based on two sets of criteria; namely, a low versus high strategic approach in choosing investments and a low versus high correlation between impact objectives and financial return drivers (see Figure 2.2).

In practice, the relationship between impact and financial return critically depends on the economics of a chosen model. Hence, transparency in analyzing purely "commercial aspects" (i.e., those based on market-related revenues and expenses) versus hidden philanthropy, as advocated by Grabenwarter & Liechtenstein, is helpful. In some impact enterprises, impact goes hand in hand with financial returns. A social business that targets consumers at the base of the pyramid with affordable, basic consumer goods will make more money as it reaches more customers while proportionally increasing its social impact. In other businesses, externalities that are prevalent in poor countries require some level of financial expense that would not be needed in the developed world and, therefore, represent examples where financial return must be sacrificed in favor of impact. Examples of such externalities include the need to educate farmers for fair-trade agricultural production, or the special requirements in developing life skills for disadvantaged young people as they take part in employable skills building programs.

Depending on the level of strategic approach and the type of economic model, impact investors can be categorized in four ways. Double enhancers, according to Grabenwarter & Liechtenstein, are "true impact investors" who seek out business models where there is a strong correlation between impact and financial performance. Strategic benevolents, on the other hand, are those investors with a clear strategic framework who focus on models where the correlation between impact and financial performance is not linear. Impact investors with an opportunistic, rather than a strategic, approach often lack experience in the field and end up in the "death valley of good intentions" with a high likelihood of disappointments. Social business angels are opportunistic investors that navigate between "true impact investment" and more hybrid models (Grabenwarter & Liechtenstein, 2011, p. 25 ff.).[2]

2.2.2 *The principle of additionality*

Another way to categorize the motivations and intentions of impact investors is to understand whether their investments are intended to make a difference as compared to more traditional investments. Where does impact investing end and traditional investing begin? This is a particularly relevant question for investments with a positive environmental impact: Are wind farms in the European North Sea or solar energy plants in Australia impact investments or just traditional renewable energy investments in the infrastructure asset class? What about gas turbines that complement solar plants in California to absorb peak electricity consumption in the two hours after sunset? Would they be considered as impact investments too? Extrapolating this thinking, it becomes hard to draw a line between a fundamentally innovative way of investing versus a traditional investment approach with an attractive marketing label attached.

An important academic contribution that helps to provide an answer to this question is the principle of additionality. According to a thought piece by Stanford Professor Paul Brest and others, the defining criteria for impact investing is whether a certain social outcome would have otherwise occurred without this investment; that is, whether such an investment was "additional" and, therefore, made a real difference. If such a difference is not realized and a certain impact outcome results from traditional investments, then the impact label would neither be justified nor necessary (Brest & Born, 2013).

An interesting example is the development of mobile phones in emerging economies. There are few investments that have had greater social impact in poor countries than those that have led to a high penetration of mobile phones in countries such as Kenya and many other countries. They have contributed to higher levels of local empowerment in rural areas (e.g., through price transparency), better skills (e.g., through the text-messaging-based education of farmers), and more efficient and secure payments (through mobile money). However, these investments were made by global telecommunications companies without an explicit impact intention in mind and, thus, lack the additionality component.

Following the principle of additionality, impact can be achieved at three levels; namely, at the enterprise level (i.e., the investee company), the investment level (i.e., the investment company), and at the level of the entire ecosystem beyond these two. Whereas enterprise impact can relate to products (e.g., affordable goods that target the base of the pyramid) and/or operations (e.g., hiring staff from slums or poor rural areas), investment impact looks at the special methods of investing (e.g., sourcing, selecting, and monitoring impact investments). Non-monetary impact beyond that means the positive consequences that result from, say, improving the enabling environment for social enterprises and investors or from aggregating capital and providing investment services (Brest & Born, 2013). The "additionality principle" encourages investors to differentiate and prioritize specific impact categories at the enterprise and investment level and beyond, thereby helping them to concentrate their investments where they can make a difference and thereby contribute to an optimized capital allocation.

2.2.3 Ethical roots

What exactly is impact? Ultimately, impact is rooted in ethics. Yet, formal logical frameworks often refer to impact as the consequence of mission, objectives, inputs, activities, output, and the outcome of a given intervention, rather than make an explicit link to ethics and values (Allman,

2015, p. 27 ff.). From a more content-oriented perspective, there have been extensive discussions about what impact is in specific fields. For example, in the fields of economic development and poverty economics, much progress in terms of articulating impact has recently been achieved (e.g., based on work done at the MIT poverty lab of Nobel Prize winners Abhijit Banerjee and Esther Duflo [Banerjee & Duflo, 2011]). In terms of a broader and more aggregated understanding, impact definitions typically do not go beyond the reference to a desire for either social and/or environmental benefits to society. Furthermore, academic researchers who are committed to a positive rather than a normative scientific approach are understandably reluctant to take a stance on ethical questions around impact, as can be seen in the following quote:

> Different impact investors have different goals – to prevent malaria in Africa or to improve children's nutrition, foster energy efficiency, or promote community development. Investors' goals may sometimes compete with one another ... In short, the range of possible objectives for impact investing is virtually as broad as the range of those in philanthropy. From a moral point of view, one can argue that some objectives are more important than others and that some are reprehensible. But these questions, which philosophers have debated for centuries, lie beyond the scope of this article. For better or worse, whether an activity has impact in achieving a specified goal is essentially a technical, value-neutral question. (Brest & Born, 2013, p. 3)

At elea, however, we strongly believe that practitioners (e.g., entrepreneurs, impact investors, and entrepreneurial philanthropists) should articulate and justify their stance on desirable impact goals within the context of ethics and values. This is needed to clarify the choice of specific impact goals and the relationship between them. One might ask, "Do social goals take precedence over environmental priorities?" Sometimes, these two goals are in conflict with each other. For example, creating better livelihoods for human beings can go against ecological sustainability goals. In such cases, is human dignity preferable to planetary health or the other way around? And for what reasons and under what conditions?

Within these two broad impact areas, one could then ask questions about the priority of specific objectives, which would give hints about whether an impact-driven asset allocation methodology is being used: Does social housing provide more impact than health or education? How about financial inclusion or access to affordable consumer goods? Furthermore, how do specific investment opportunities compare in terms of their social impact; for example, debt versus equity instruments, public companies versus private equity investments, or individual stocks within or across industries?

Answering such, admittedly complex, questions is not only needed to make individual investment decisions. It is also necessary to construct investment portfolios in a systematic, rather than an opportunistic, way. This matters particularly when intermediaries act on behalf of beneficiaries, as opposed to wealthy individuals investing their own money. Should portfolios, for example, diversify into different impact themes and risk-return profiles to gain broad exposure to different sectors and to minimize risks? Or should they, rather, concentrate on investments within one impact theme to gain deep insights on different roles within an ecosystem that possibly strengthen each other, thereby maximizing the overall impact?

The 17 Sustainable Development Goals (SDGs) adopted by the UN in 2015 (see Figure 2.3) are a good starting point for such a positioning, as they express broadly accepted global ethical values. While they do not offer any indications about how to prioritize them and how to manage the trade-offs between them, they represent a comprehensive set of global impact objectives that are legitimized by the most global governance mechanism that exists, the UN. They also permit investors to localize their investment decisions relative to their contributions in closing gaps between SDG objectives and the current situation. SDG500, an initiative that was launched in January 2020 at the World Economic Forum in Davos, is an example of such an approach. Different actors (including UN agencies, development finance organizations, a non-governmental organization [NGO], and an impact fund) have joined forces to mobilize USD 500 million in blended-finance impact capital to help close the funding gap in realizing the SDG ambitions (www.weforum.org).

Another example is PG Impact Investment (PGII) (www.pg-impact.com), which is the impact investment organization of Partners Group, a global leader in private-markets investing domiciled in Switzerland. This institutional impact investment company explicitly links its impact objectives to selected SDGs and is able to benefit from the investment expertise and

Figure 2.3 UN sustainable development goals (SDGs).

Source: United Nations – https://www.un.org/sustainabledevelopment/
The content of this publication has not been approved by the United Nations and does not reflect the views of the United Nations or its officials or Member States.

global infrastructure of Partners Group.[3] At the end of 2019, PGII managed over USD 200 million. Its investment approach combines social impact goals and market-level financial-return expectations. The reference to specific SDGs permits the quantification of the resources needed to close the gaps between the current status and targets stipulated by the SDGs. PGII estimates this to be approximately USD5–USD7 trillion annually through 2030.

Examples of such gaps include

- 2 billion people lack access to savings, credit, pension, and insurance services.
- 1.4. billion people do not have access to electricity and are using unsafe and environmentally unfriendly energy solutions.
- 1 billion people lack access to healthcare, clean water, and sanitation.
- 1.2 billion people live in crowded, inadequate, and/or unsafe housing.
- 800 million people, a majority of whom are subsistence farmers, are affected by food insecurity.
- 363 million children and adolescents are without access to a quality, affordable education.

2.3 Conclusions

2.3.1 Insights and takeaways

This brief overview of the impact investing trend shows its potential as well as its challenges. Impact investing has emerged as an asset class of its own and is growing faster than most other asset classes within the universe of financial assets worldwide. As a result, the diversity of impact themes and single investment opportunities is expanding and, over time, a secondary market will evolve that will provide the necessary liquidity for trading opportunities. This is good news for both impact investors and impact entrepreneurs. Impact investors will obtain more choices for making investments that meet their intentions, and they will increasingly be able to develop distinctive portfolios with specific impact goals, financial return targets, and risk parameters. Particularly with the development of a secondary market, they will receive more data points regarding the market pricing of such investments, which will allow for signals that facilitate portfolio optimization.

At the same time, impact entrepreneurs will be able to tap into deeper and more differentiated pools of capital to support their development needs from a financial perspective. As investor intentions proliferate, they will have more choice in terms of selecting those investors that can be most helpful to them, possibly including non-financial advice in the form of expertise and experience-sharing. And as a secondary market develops, they will be able to receive more information on market prices as well as a clearer sense of the (financial) value of their enterprise. Consequently, they will be in a better position to explore and evaluate alternative exit opportunities.

However, on this path toward a large, liquid, and more diverse impact investing market, several challenges will need to be overcome. As we have seen, knowledge about the motivations and intentions of investors is still very limited. More clarity about which impact themes investors are focusing on, and why, would help. Also, a better understanding of the relationship between impact objectives and financial risk/return profiles could likely contribute to improved investment decisions and better portfolio construction. As an example, impact enterprises often apply hybrid models in which financially profitable activities (such as the sale of impactful goods and services) cross-subsidize unprofitable areas (such as the education of farmers or awareness campaigns for poor people). Consequently, impact investment firms (or individual investors) need a clear idea about their appetite for sacrificing potential profit in favor of social goods for which there is no market. This depends on how their impact goals are rooted within an ethical framework, as well as on their preferences with regard to financial risk/return profiles.

Ultimately, investors should have a clear idea about where and how they would like to make a difference: Is it at the level of a single impact enterprise or an ecosystem of enterprises focused on one impact theme? Or is it at the level of an investment organization with a distinctive investment approach? And what kind of a difference do they want to make, with what purpose in mind, and with what underlying theory of change? These are all complex questions, but both practitioners from pioneering organizations as well as academic researchers can contribute to expanding the knowledge base and facilitating learning opportunities in this regard. In the following two chapters, we will look at the approaches that elea has adopted to address and overcome such challenges – at least to some extent.

2.3.2 *Your point of view*

Learning objectives

After studying this chapter, you should be able to

1. identify those characteristics that distinguish impact investing from more traditional asset classes;
2. describe the key elements and scope of an impact investment;
3. identify the main drivers of an impact investing strategy using a purpose-driven approach (e.g., according to [Malnight et al., 2019]);
4. recognize the link between the motivations and investment decisions of impact investors; and
5. define intentionality and additionality, give examples of both criteria, and explain their relevance on investment decisions.

Reflection questions

1. What are the essential elements that define impact investing?
2. Put yourself in the role of an investor. Where would you invest considering the spectrum defined by Bridges Fund Management, and why? Do you think you would face a trade-off between impact and financial returns? Why, or why not? How would you deal with a potential trade-off?
3. Put yourself in the role of an impact investor. What would be your main intention when investing for impact? Justify.
4. Where do you stand on the "additionality debate"? What are the pros and cons of additionality as an investment criterion?

Right vs. right dilemma: Social vs. environmental objectives

How does an investor choose specific impact goals? Should social goals take precedence over environmental priorities? Investors will eventually face an ethical dilemma by having to choose between two possible options, neither of which is absolutely acceptable from an ethical perspective. For example, consider the case when social and environmental goals may be in conflict with each other, such that creating better livelihoods for human beings can detract from ecological sustainability goals. In such cases, is human dignity preferable to planetary health, or the other way around? For which reasons, and under which conditions? Likewise, consider the case when investors have differing preferences regarding the priority of specific social or environmental objectives. Does social housing provide more impact than health or education? Answering these questions is not only required to make individual investment decisions, but it is also necessary in order to construct portfolios in a systematic, rather than an opportunistic, way. Ultimately, investors are "responsible" for their decisions, and they need to think through the ethical dimensions of their impact investing approach.

Construct a "real-life" dilemma situation and debate the pros and cons of alternative choices.

Notes

1. For an overview on this debate, see (Höchstädter & Scheck, 2015, p. 459). According to GIIN, which follows a rather rigorous definition, approximately 60% of impact investments were made through private-equity or private-debt vehicles, whereas the rest were executed through public instruments, real assets, or other vehicles (GIIN, 2018).
2. See also a useful framework developed by the Omidyar group, a leading impact investment organization, which provides clear criteria for determining under which conditions trade-offs between impact and financial returns should be accepted (Bannick, Goldmann, Kubzansky, & Saltuk, 2017).
3. PGII is a subsidiary of the Partners Group Impact Foundation (PGIF), a non-profit organization under state supervision. The net profits earned by PGII are distributed by PGIF to organizations in the field of philanthropic impact investing. Peter Wuffli was a board member of Partners Group Holding from 2009 to 2019, and he has been a member of the board of trustees of PGIF since 2016. Andreas Kirchschläger (CEO of elea) has been a board member of PGII since 2016.

References

Acemoglu, D., & Robinson, J. (2013). *Why Nations Fail - The Origins of Power, Prosperity and Poverty*. New York: Currency.

Allman, K. A. (2015). *Impact Investment*. New Jersey: Wiley.

Balandina Jaquier, J. (2011). Guide to Impact Investing For Family Offices and High Net Worth Individuals: Managing Wealth for Impact and Profit.

Banerjee, A. V., & Duflo, E. (2011). *Poor Economics: A Radical Rethinking of the Way to Fight Global Poverty*. New York: PublicAffairs.

Bannick, M., & Goldman, P. (2016). *Moving Beyond the Tradeoff Debate*. Omidyar Network.

Bannick, M., Goldmann, P., Kubzansky, M., & Saltuk, Y. (Winter 2017). Across the Returns Continuum. *Stanford Social Innovation Review*, pp. 42–48.

Bridges Fund Management. (2015, November). *The Bridges Spectrum of Capital: How we Define the Sustainable and Impact Investment Market*. Retrieved January 12, 2020, from https://www.bridgesfundmanagement.com/wp-content/uploads/2017/08/Bridges-Spectrum-of-Capital-screen.pdf

Brest, P., & Born, K. (2013, August 14). Unpacking the Impact in Impact Investing. *Stanford Social Innovation Review*. https://ssir.org/articles/entry/unpacking_the_impact_in_impact_investing

Croset, P. (2014). *Ambition at the Heart of Change - A Lesson in Management from the South*. Malakoff: Dunod.

Davies, I. (2005). What Is the Business of Business? *The McKinsey Quarterly, Number 3*, pp. 105–113.

Deaton, A. (2013). *The Great Escape*. Princeton: Princeton University Press.

Easterly, W. (2005, October). Reliving the 50s: The Big Push, Poverty Traps, and Takeoffs in Economic Development. *NYU Development Research Institute Working Paper No. 15*.

Foundation Strategy Group (FSG). (2006). *Investing for Impact - Managing and Measuring Proactive Social Investments*.

Friedman, M. (1962). [reprint. In 2002]). *Capitalism and Freedom*. Chicago: The University of Chicago Press.

Global Impact Investing Network. (2018). Annual Impact Investor Survey.

Grabenwarter, U., & Liechtenstein, H. (2011). *In Search of Gamma: An Unconventional Perspective on Impact Investing*. University of Navarra: IESE Business School.

Henderson, R. M. (2018, February 12). *More and More CEOs Are Taking Their Social Responsibility Seriously*. Harvard Business Review.

Höchstädter, A. K., & Scheck, B. (2015, December). What's in a Name: An Analysis of Impact Investing Understandings by Academics and Practitioners. *Journal of Business Ethics, 132(2)*, 449–475.

Lian, C., Ma, Y., & Wang, C. (2018, August 22). *Low Interest Rates and Risk Taking: Evidence from Individual Investment Decisions. Review of Financial Studies.* doi: 10.2139/ssrn.2809191

Jayakumar S., & Sagar, R. (2014). *The Big Ideas of Lee Kuan Yew.* Singapore: Straits Times Press Pte Ltd.

Malnight, T. W., Buche, I., & Dhanaraj, C. (2019)., September-October). *Put Purpose at the Core of Your Strategy. Harvard Business Review.*

McKinsey Global Institute (2018). *Outperformers Maintaining ASEAN Countries' Exceptional Growth.*

Morgan, J. P. (2010). *Impact Investments - An Emerging Asset Class.* New York: J.P. Morgan.

Moyo, D. (2009). *Dead Aid: Why Aid Is Not Working and How There Is a Better Way for Africa.* New York: Farrar, Straus and Giroux.

Nowak, W. (2014, May). The Evolution of Development Assistance. *Journal of US-China Public Administration, Vol. 11, No. 5,* 454–462. Retrieved October 22, 2019, from http://www.davidpublisher.org/Public/uploads/Contribute/552e1af02b368.pdf

Rosenstein-Rodan, P. (1943, June-September). Problems of Industrialization of Eastern and Southeastern Europe. *Economic Journal,* pp. 202–211.

Roundy, P., Holzhauer, H., & Dai, Y. (2017, August). Finance or Philanthropy? Exploring the Motivations and Criteria of Impact Investors. *Social Responsibility Journal, 13(3).*

Sachs, J. (2005). *The End of Poverty: How We Can Make It Happen in Our Lifetime.* London: Penguin.

Shahid, Y. (2009). *Development Economics Through the Decades - A Critical Look at 30 Years of the World Development Report.* The World Bank.

Shiller, R. J. (2012). *Finance and the Good Society.* Princeton: Princeton University Press.

Williams, S. (2006). *Colour Bar: The Triumph of Seretse Khama and His Nation.* London: Penguin.

Wimmer, A. (2018). *Nation Building - Why Some Countries Come Together While Others Fall Apart.* Princeton: Princeton University Press.

Wuffli, P. A. (2016). *Inclusive Leadership: A Framework for the Global Era.* New York, London: Springer.

Yunus, M. (1998). *Banker to the Poor: The Story of the Grameen Bank.* London: Aurum Press.

3

elea's FOUNDATION AND OPERATING MODEL

Having explored entrepreneurship and capital in more general terms, we now focus on elea as one possible way in which our formula "Entrepreneurship times Capital equals Profit and Impact" can be brought to life. After discussing the founders' motivations and intentions in creating elea, we show how it is rooted in an ethical framework that we call "liberal ethics." We reveal how this ethical framework, with its guiding virtues, shaped some of the important initial design decisions and then elaborate on how elea works today. Philanthropic impact investment management, which is at the core of its operating model, is the process by which new investment opportunities are sourced, evaluated, and selected, and thereafter supported over 7 to 10 years, until elea eventually exits the investment. In addition, our philanthropic investors' circle ensures elea's sustainability in terms of its funding, and our professional development program facilitates the critical resources required to support its portfolio companies with non-financial support in the form of expertise and knowledge-sharing.

3.1 Founders' motivations and intentions[1]

elea was founded by one of the two co-authors of this book, together with his spouse, following a long career in consulting and banking. The process of creating elea was not straightforward. It took approximately three years of deep reflection, as well as debates within the family and with friends. The three main motivations for creating elea were,

1. gratitude for being born and raised in one of the wealthiest, most beautiful, and safest countries on earth, Switzerland, and for the possibility of having a successful professional career;
2. passion for poverty and development economics that was already nurtured as an economics student while at university; and
3. capacity in terms of both life energy and financial means (his family's long-term financial needs were covered, and there was still a meaningful surplus of money available for investment), given that he was able to enjoy an accelerated executive career at a young age.

The main intention behind the creation of elea was to provide access to globalization opportunities to those individuals who have not been able to benefit from them. More specifically, its purpose is to fight absolute poverty with entrepreneurial means in order to contribute to the world's greatest challenge; namely, "to end poverty in all its forms" (according to SDG1).

3.1.1 *Access to globalization opportunities*

As mentioned above, the key initial idea that led to elea's creation was related to globalization, which has been (and still is) the most powerful megatrend of our generation, as its full name "elea Foundation for Ethics in Globalization" indicates. It offers many benefits, but also many challenges, all of which have become much more apparent in recent years as compared to the time when elea was created. Globalization is understood as the process by which the fragmented world view of the 1970s, with its three-tier structure,[2] has transformed into a perception of the world as one entity that is characterized by huge international flows of goods, services, people, capital, and information, as well as by intense and multifaceted cross-border interconnectedness across different geographies, societal sectors, and types of organizations. It has enabled massive benefits, such as lifting hundreds of millions of people out of poverty, primarily in China and India. Furthermore, it has created universal awareness about the great challenges that our planet faces. Persistent absolute poverty and environmental damage, both of which threaten the sustainability of planet earth, are two of the major challenges that have already been addressed twice by the leading global governance mechanism, the United Nations (UN). In 2000, the UN had agreed on and established eight Millennium Development Goals (MDGs) for 2015. These have since been replaced by the previously mentioned 17 Sustainable Development Goals (SDGs) for 2030 (agreed on in 2015).

On the negative side, however, the globalization process has led to disorientation, uncertainty, and uneasiness due to its accelerating pace, increasing complexity, and unknown risks. Take for instance modern technology, which provides us with universal access to instant and effective information but makes the differences in income, wealth, and livelihoods among individuals and countries even more evident. This has fostered the worrying notion that the benefits of globalization are unevenly distributed and that globalization is producing both winners and losers. It was exactly this asymmetrical distribution of globalization's benefits that the founders had in mind when creating elea. They wanted to help others benefit from globalization as they have.

3.1.2 Fighting absolute poverty with entrepreneurial means

Along with the motivational factors driving the thought process for setting up elea in the years 2004–2006, the founders also had to determine its specific purpose. "Fighting absolute poverty with entrepreneurial means" turned out to be the essential phrase describing elea's purpose, its very reason for existence. Why?

Historically, poverty has been regarded as a fateful destiny that is structurally determined. In the 1970s and 1980s, efforts to understand and fight poverty were mostly seen through highly ideological left-wing/right-wing lenses that were shaped by the Cold War and were, therefore, more often than not politicized. Since then, the focus has shifted to a much deeper understanding of the root causes of poverty and to debating what works and what doesn't in practice in terms of impact and results. At the macroeconomic level, the work of Acemoglu and Robinson looked at the crucial role of political institutions with regard to the origins of poverty, which is in opposition to more traditional theories that look at geography, climate, or colonial history. They analyzed areas that have very similar characteristics, with the exception of their political institutions (such as the region around the U.S.-Mexican border), and concluded that the single most significant factor explaining the difference in prosperity between the Mexican and American sides of the border was the effectiveness of institutions, such as government administration or rule of law (Acemoglu & Robinson, 2013).[3]

At the microeconomic level of households and individuals, Esther Duflo and Abhijit Banerjee (two MIT economists who, together with their colleague Michael Kremer, received the 2019 Nobel Prize in Economics) published the book *Poor Economics*. This book summarized their insights in analyzing poverty, and highlighted factors such as lack of knowledge, skills, and expertise, as well as deeply held misperceptions and rigid norms, as factors leading to poverty that were at least as important as a lack of financial resources. For example, health problems often arise because people do not have the most basic knowledge of the critical importance of clean water and hygienic practices (e.g., washing hands) or because they blindly trust unqualified doctors who prescribe expensive, yet ineffective, medication. Skills levels are often low because teachers are absent or do not have the necessary qualifications. Furthermore, a lack of productivity and income generation in agriculture is often caused by a lack of understanding about how to deploy fertilizers or by insufficient price transparency, which leads to dependency on the middleman (Banerjee & Duflo, 2011).

In recent years, there has been a quantum leap in the depth of knowledge about poverty, with growing evidence that poverty can be effectively and systematically reduced. In addition to the progress achieved in China, which has made the greatest contribution to lifting people out of poverty globally (i.e., the proportion of Chinese people living in extreme poverty was reduced from 60% to 12% between 1990 and 2010), some other examples are

- **India**: Extreme poverty (i.e., less than USD 1.90 in daily income) was reduced from 38% to 13% from 2004 to 2015, thanks to robust economic growth (The World Bank, 2019).
- **Peru**: The share of the population that is poor fell from 55% in 2001 to 21% in 2016 (The Economist, 2018). An important factor for this success was a policy that favored open markets while keeping monetary stability based on a strong, independent central bank.

- **Bangladesh**: From 2000 to 2016, the number of people living in extreme poverty declined from 46 million to 24 million (The World Bank, 2019), driven by an economic growth rate of approximately 5% and public-policy measures that supported a balanced distribution of the benefits of growth. Some examples include measures and initiatives to encourage family planning, which empowered women and drove down birth rates; productivity improvements in agriculture; and a thriving civil society. Two civil society initiatives have had a tremendous impact in the field of microfinance; namely, Grameen Bank and BRAC (The Economist, 2012).
- **Ethiopia**: Extreme poverty fell from 56% in 2000 to 31% in 2011, driven mainly by agricultural growth (The World Bank, 2015).

Of the more market-oriented, capitalist-driven strategies to fight poverty, the success story with the longest track record to date is, indeed, microfinance. One of the microfinance initiators was Muhammad Yunus, who founded the Grameen Bank in Bangladesh in 1983 and received the Nobel Peace Prize in 2006 for his life's work. By supporting entrepreneurial independence and self-employment through the development and distribution of repayable microcredits (above all among women), Yunus's organization may possibly have helped some tens of millions of families to escape absolute poverty. Since then, the concept has become mainstream and has inspired thousands of development organizations worldwide.[4]

While we appreciate all of the controversies around differences in effectiveness among alternative strategies, distinctive ideological stances, and various perspectives, two things are clear: poverty is no longer an inescapable fate as it was perceived to be until deep into the 20th century (i.e., it can be successfully defeated), and there is much evidence that entrepreneurially driven market solutions can effectively help to reduce poverty levels. These two insights at the time of creating elea have been continuously reconfirmed with successful examples from our own work and from observing many other initiatives. It has also led to a strong and unwavering commitment to this purpose and, over time, to the perception that impact investing is one of the most effective and sustainable mechanisms for putting this purpose into practice.

elea's purpose, to fight absolute poverty with entrepreneurial means, is intricately interwoven with its underlying ethics. Poor people lack access to many basic goods and services, such as housing and healthcare, electricity for lighting, education for employability, and mobility. They are not able to accumulate any significant cash surplus, because they have a multitude of pressing needs. Therefore, if anything adversarial happens, such as a bad harvest, an accident, a work conflict, or an illness, it means catastrophe and an existential struggle. In short, poor people do not have the liberty to shape their lives and to realize their potential. Liberty is, in fact, at the center of elea's "liberal ethics" framework.

3.1.3 Liberal ethics[5]

Our global era challenges conventional ethical thinking and calls for new answers to the age-old ethical questions: What is a good life? What is responsible behavior? What is just/fair among people? So how can these questions be answered? Among secular ideologies, we distinguish between two categories of responses: an individual one and a collective one. Either an individual, in exercising her freedom, is concerned about leading a good and responsible life and behaving fairly, or this duty is assumed by a collective entity, such as a state or another type of organization. Both categories exist, both can be justified, and in the real world they usually do not appear in black or white but rather in varying shades of grey.

elea's stance favors the individual dimension: we describe it as *liberal[6] ethics*. The starting point is individual liberty, with both its negative and positive meanings. In its negative connotation, liberty is about protecting individuals from unwanted interference by governments or society. Positively viewed, liberty represents the freedom of individuals to be their own masters and fulfill their own potential, including the possibility to choose their own individual ethical concepts. Classical political liberalism has focused on negative liberty. However, we believe that our global era in particular, with its multiple new opportunities that could not even have been imagined by previous generations, demands a focus on positive liberty. In other words, people should be encouraged to explore the world with all of its breadth and depth to find and shape a good life (see [Berlin, 1969, p. 131] for the most prominent discussion of negative and positive liberty).

While this sounds rather theoretical, it is of eminent importance in elea's daily work. In our efforts to source new impact investments, we look for outstanding individual impact entrepreneurs on-site, who see opportunities and are willing and able to dedicate large parts of their life's energy to building an impact enterprise. While we do, from time to time, work with official aid organizations to benefit from matched funding opportunities, we are rather skeptical of projects initiated by public development aid and carried out by employed functionaries.

The ethical companion of liberty is responsibility, which relates to the second age-old ethical question of "What is responsible behavior?" Peter Drucker, one of the most influential thinkers and writers on the subject of management theory and practice, once said, "Freedom is not fun, it is responsible choice" (Drucker, 2004, p. 49). As opportunities and possibilities for individuals have expanded in our global era, so have global challenges, vulnerabilities, and risks. Responsible people and organizations should, therefore, accept and live up to differentiated thresholds of responsibility, depending on the number of positive liberties that they have, in the broadest sense of the word; that is, not only in terms of their command over financial and physical resources but also their ambitions, energy, expertise, and capabilities. This ethical thinking was at the heart of the decision to create elea. The founders concluded that their contribution to meet a high threshold of responsibility would be to share the opportunities from globalization with those who, up to now, have not had access to them.

When does the liberty of some negatively affect the liberty of others, and what can and should be done about it? These are issues related to the third ethical question: "What is just/fair among people?" The British philosopher Isaiah Berlin famously observed that freedom for the wolves has often meant death to the sheep. This question is likely the most controversial of the three to answer, and it is the one where those with an individualist stance on ethical thinking are usually in opposition to those with a collectivist one. At the core of the debate is the type and degree of equality between people that is considered to be acceptable from a justice/fairness point of view. The interest of economists, philosophers, and politicians in this topic has been increasing recently, given evidence of growing material inequality in several Western countries (particularly in the U.S.).[7]

For most liberal thinkers, the equality of opportunity is at the forefront of concerns. Particularly when applying a world perspective, which is warranted in our global era, the biggest source of inequality of opportunity – and the one that people can do the least about – is where one is born; that is, in which country, in which family, and under which conditions. Whereas the topic of inequality within and between countries has been controversially debated for a long time, research on global equality among individual people on the earth is still in its infancy. An obvious starting point for any liberal to answer this third ethical question is to focus on ways to eradicate absolute poverty, thus providing at least some equal opportunity to those at the very bottom of the pyramid.

Ethical virtues for day-to-day guidance

In line with the liberal ethics framework, we consider a few practical ethical virtues to be important and helpful in guiding us in our daily work. They are integrity, humbleness, engagement, and partnership.

Integrity manifests itself when somebody expresses his ideas, ambitions, and intentions in a clear and reasoned way, and when his concrete actions are in line with this. In other words, when saying what we are doing, why we are doing it, and then actually doing it are consistent. Integrity is a combination of identity (clarity on what and who we are) and authenticity (consistency in our convictions and between what we say and what we do). This concept goes much deeper than a superficial call for honesty and consistency. It is a very basic prerequisite for relationships based on trust. As many elea activities are centered on relationships – with entrepreneurs, investors, and other investment organizations, as well as among elea colleagues – we apply high thresholds of integrity to our own behavior as well as in how we expect others to behave.

Humbleness is another virtue that is critical, particularly in light of elea's great global ambitions. In some ways, its journey has been a humbling experience. It takes substantial resources and hard work on a daily basis to achieve impact. Sometimes, efforts fail or are undone by external factors, such as political instability that results from bad governance practices. People with less engagement in this area often challenge our work by asking, "Is it not a drop in the ocean and therefore meaningless?" The principle of humbleness requires two things: accepting that some things are challenging and that there are no quick fixes, and recognizing that it takes continuous creativity and persistence to continue on the road to create impact despite all the roadblocks. This means being rigorous in finding and selecting new investment opportunities and showing flexibility and resilience when things go differently than planned. It also means enjoying those moments where new perspectives are created and where an intervention makes a real difference in people's lives.

Mastering the challenge of achieving impact requires active **engagement**. To be actively engaged means identifying and pursuing appropriate ambitions and seeing them to fruition, and it involves setting appropriate goals and priorities and being disciplined about their implementation. It is also about leveraging opportunities based on one's capabilities, motivations, and contextual factors. The term "engagement" is closely related to the term commitment. Founding and building elea and continuously supporting its development was a possible way of engagement for its founders to meet a high responsibility threshold commensurate with the available resources.

Finally, there is **partnership**, in the sense of peer-level relationships both within our organization as well as with external partners that are rooted in mutual understanding, respect, and trust. Both official development aid and paternalistic philanthropy often suffer from asymmetrical, hierarchical relationships between donors (who play the active, powerful role) and receivers (who are more on the passive side of things). At elea, we actively practice partnership principles in our daily work and occasionally reflect among ourselves, or together with investees, on how we are living up to our promises in reality (see Chapter Five for a discussion of these principles in more detail). Fostering partnership principles and behaviors is an uphill battle given a history of hierarchy in society that goes back several thousand years. Take the example of Confucian philosophy, according to which hierarchy between superiors and subordinates (men and women, old and young alike) shaped relationships and dominated thinking and acting. Despite the fact that large parts of our "new" world across various sectors still adhere to a hierarchical mindset, we nevertheless believe that there is no alternative to a horizontal partnership approach and that this form of collaboration is gaining ground and will eventually become the dominant pattern of how humans work together.

3.1.4 Key design decisions

In addition to defining elea's purpose and ethical framework, there were other important decisions that needed to be made during its design phase and thereafter. One was whether to build a new organization or to partner up with an existing one. elea opted in favor of building a new organization, to create a platform where expertise could directly be combined with capital, where knowledge and experience could be developed and protected in an institutionalized way, and where potential additional philanthropic investors who are interested in contributing to the cause could be attracted in order to achieve sustainability for elea itself.

Another issue was whether to focus on philanthropic impact investing only or to combine it with a financial-return-focused impact fund structure within the same organization. Looking at examples where this was done, there was a concern about having to confront difficult conflicts of interests and about the risk of a drift in purpose resulting from a hybrid approach to philanthropy. In the end, the decision was taken to focus on philanthropic impact investing, as this field of investing seemed to be in higher need of additional capacity and required undiluted focus. Furthermore, the founders were encouraged by friends with more experience in the field to concentrate on certain geographies. However, they decided in favor of a thematic rather than a geographic focus to underline the global scope and to allow for and learn from different approaches to similar problems across geographies.

There was also a discussion whether consulting services should be offered to help other philanthropists in similar fields to establish themselves, in order to leverage elea's growing expertise and experience (e.g., in impact measurement, management, and how to organize and govern an entrepreneurial, innovative foundation). In the end, the decision was taken in favor of an approach that strongly aligns elea's external capital providers with its investment organization. More specifically, this approach allows third-party philanthropic investors to invest alongside elea's capital while avoiding conflicts of interest and difficult debates around investment purpose, theme, and criteria.

Choosing the name was another important decision because of its strong signaling effect. The founders searched for an attractive name under the condition that it should not be linked to their family name. While, of course, the founders derive tremendous personal satisfaction from the creation and ongoing positive development of elea, they prefer to remain unrecognized. elea is the name of an ancient city in Southern Italy (called Velia today), which is 140 kilometers south of Naples and was founded by the Greeks around 540 B.C. Besides operating a port, it was also the domicile of a pre-Socratic school of philosophy, the "Eleatics." It seemed to be a good symbol for the ups and downs of globalization and for the importance of a solid philosophical underpinning.

All of these decisions were taken with guidance from several principles that are ultimately underpinned by liberal ethics. Among the most important ones were

- **Additionality**: elea aims to make a difference in the field of philanthropic impact investing, a field that was at a nascent stage of development when elea was founded and still, today, does not yet have established principles and best practices. With the privilege of a greenfield start and the possibility to take risks, we believed that elea should make an effort to contribute not only to the beneficiaries of its investments but also to the expansion and development of entrepreneurial philanthropy more generally. A specific consequence of this thinking was an initial commitment to build up a professional team of specialists inside of elea to develop and apply impact-oriented expertise in sourcing, evaluating, and supporting investment opportunities. Later on, this fundamental belief led to the creation of the elea Center for Social Innovation at IMD, which seeks to inspire and encourage leaders in business, civil society, and government to create social innovation in their respective fields. While elea is not a formal member of the effective altruism movement that was launched in 2016, it has very much adopted the same mindset of reviewing its philanthropic endeavors with self-critical skepticism and a high aim for effectiveness (see: www.effectivealtruism.org).

- **Justifying tax deductibility**: A particular aspect of additionality is a continuous attempt to justify elea's activities as a tax-exempt foundation under Swiss state supervision. In other words, elea aspires to at least meet and eventually to exceed the threshold set by the government regarding the alternative use of its tax savings as Swiss public expenses. Given that Switzerland has one of the world's most effective and efficient governmental administrations, this threshold is high. For example, it can be met by focusing on those innovative, high-risk investments with substantial potential benefits for society for which the public sector is structurally not able, or is less well equipped, to undertake.[8]

- **Engaging with professional credibility**: Along the lines of the additionality principle, elea chose its fields of engagement according to its distinctive profiles and skills. The professional backgrounds of its staff are mostly economics, business, and law. Therefore, investment themes were selected where these skills would make a difference, and areas where elea lacked professional credibility were discarded (e.g., healthcare, where solid medical expertise is essential).

- **Analytical, systematic decision-making**: While all decisions clearly have strong emotional and intuitive aspects, at elea we uphold high standards of transparency, conscientousness, rationality, and honesty in our decision-making processes. That is why we joined forces with McKinsey & Company at the beginning, to help us become more familiar with the sector and to guide our thought process. We were as conscientious as possible in our decisions. As an example, when we defined "Fighting absolute poverty with entrepreneurial means" as our purpose, we constructed a decision tree to systematically identify and evaluate alternative options for deciding on our purpose (see Figure 3.1). Furthermore, we made a commitment already then to create a systematic approach to measuring and managing impact (which later turned into the elea Impact Measurement Methodology; see Chapter Six).

- **Alignment with ethics**: As we strongly believe in ethics and values, we checked all of our decisions thoroughly in terms of their fit with our liberal ethics framework (the starting point of which is individual liberty) and our guiding virtues to avoid basic inconsistencies that challenge our integrity. One example is our decision to focus on individual entrepreneurial initiatives rather than on collective public-policy measures as drivers of impact. Moreover, we make investments step-by-step with tangible and measurable progress, allowing continuous learning and improvement, given our humble realization that changing the world radically in just one generation is simply not a realistic undertaking.

These critical reflections, which were made at the time of elea's creation and initial development stage, have been regularly reviewed in acknowledgment of the fact that philanthropy oftentimes does not face the same level of scrutiny that is faced by politicians or business executives. Only

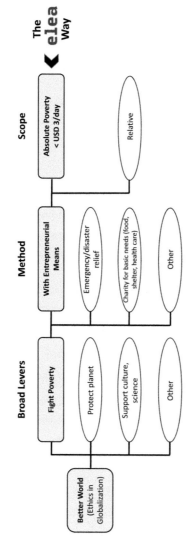

Figure 3.1 The elea decision tree.

Source: elea

recently, with the spectacular donations made by Bill and Melinda Gates and Warren Buffett into the Bill and Melinda Gates Foundation, and the subsequent public appeal for a billionaires' "Giving Pledge," has philanthropy received higher levels of attention in public debates. This has led Professor Rob Reich at Stanford University to call for levels of regulatory and media scrutiny within philanthropy comparable to those that are applied to the public sector and the corporate world. In his view, a higher level of scrutiny would mitigate the risk of abuse by donors who gain substantial influence by donating large amounts of wealth to philanthropic institutions. He also advocates that if philanthropy is properly structured, then it will support a strong liberal democracy (Reich, 2018).[9]

At the time, we saw elea's development very much within the context of the debate around an emerging "new capitalism" following the Global Financial Crisis of 2007/2008. Innovative trends, such as microfinance, impact investing, and social entrepreneurship, inspired elea's thinking and nurtured its vision to realize its purpose by aspiring to be a role model organization with charisma in the field of entrepreneurial philanthropy. As a professional and active investment manager, we create measurable, long-lasting social impact and strive to be the partner of choice for social entrepreneurs and philanthropic investors, as well as provide an attractive platform for ambitious, talented professionals (see www.elea-foundation.org).

3.2 Operating model

This vision also defined elea's operating model, which we will discuss now. While elea has the legal form of a tax-exempt charitable foundation, its operating model looks rather like an investment organization (see also [Wuffli & Kirchschläger, 2017]). The model has three major components that mutually reinforce each other like a flywheel. At the core is philanthropic impact investment management (the process of finding and optimizing investments). This is nurtured by a philanthropic investors' circle, which refers to a group of personalities and organizations that enable elea's activities through their financial and non-financial support. The third component is its professional development program, which describes the way in which elea recruits, motivates, develops, and retains its professional staff. As elea makes new, impactful investments, it reinforces the appetite of existing investors and attracts new philanthropic investors. Furthermore, a growing capital base helps to win and fund its professional staff, which in turn is instrumental in sourcing and evaluating new investments. Important additional layers supporting this model are elea's knowledge base, such as the elea Impact Measurement Methodology (eIMM) and the insights gained from collaborating with the elea Center for Social Innovation at IMD, and the community of elea entrepreneurs, investors, and team members (including alumni) (see Figure 3.2).

3.2.1 Philanthropic impact investment management

Identifying and evaluating new investments and managing the existing portfolio of investments for maximum impact value creation is at the heart of what it takes to realize elea's purpose. Therefore, processes, methods, and tools that relate to this key component of elea's operating model enjoy the highest priority.

During elea's initial founding period, we took substantial time to explore, experiment, and learn from both our good and bad experiences in making philanthropic impact investments and supporting their development. At times, we worked with large development organizations that were more accustomed to implementing projects on behalf of public-aid agencies than working with a small, young, and entrepreneurial foundation like ourselves. We also supported individuals who, sometimes, found our standards of professionalism and ethics to be quite challenging. While, in hindsight, we could possibly have taken shortcuts, overall it was a necessary and valuable journey to gradually refine our areas of investment, sourcing methods, investment criteria, and ways of contributing to impact creation through partnering with the entrepreneurs of the companies in our growing portfolio.

By and large, we followed advice based on other people's experiences, such as Julia Balandina Jaquier's *Guide to Impact Investing: For Family Offices and High Net Worth Individuals,* where she makes the following recommendations based on case examples:

- Analyze and manage investments with rigor as a key to success in impact investing.
- Use a step-by-step approach, starting by segregating a portion of wealth for venture investing or investing in safer areas and taking time to increase [the] percentages of impact investments across various asset classes.

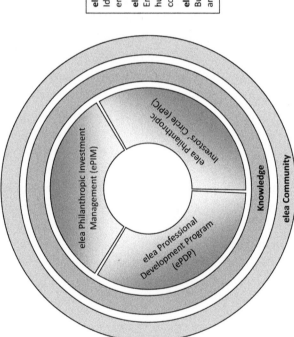

elea Philanthropic Investment Management:
Identifying, evaluating and supporting
entrepreneurial assets for poverty alleviation

elea Philanthropic Investors' Circle:
Engaging philanthropic capital (financial and
human) from individuals, institutions, and
companies

elea Professional Development Program:
Building and developing a high-performance
and passionate professional team

Figure 3.2 The elea model.

Source: elea

- Collaborate with other impact investors to leverage their experience, skills, and resources.
- Be prepared to take some risks and make some mistakes.
- Analyze and measure your impact.

We also experienced some of the common mistakes that she summarizes, such as falling into the "mission trap" (i.e., getting carried away by the promised impact, while underestimating the risks of an investment), underappreciating the cultural challenges related to the traditional divide between social good and making money, and prioritizing values and integrity over skills in a partner (Balandina Jaquier, 2011, p. 15ff).

Sourcing and screening investment opportunities

What have we learned on our journey to date, and how do we actually source and evaluate investments as well as manage our portfolio for maximum impact value creation? There is no one best way, and the sourcing options we have used are quite diverse. Angaza came on our radar screen during a scouting tour in East Africa. Founder Lesley Marincola had developed a keen interest in elea, as she found it very challenging to raise patient philanthropic impact investment capital in Silicon Valley. Both Dharma Life and Coffee Circle were introduced to us through our network (i.e., the responsible leaders' circle of the BMW Foundation). BagoSphere was also identified during a scouting tour that included the Philippines.

Our experience in sourcing investments through the years has been characterized by a mix of systematic and opportunistic approaches, with a clear trend toward more proactive, analytical methods. Scouting tours play a major role. These entail a visit to two or three countries by one of elea's associates to systematically identify potential investments based on diligent preparation. Preparation activities include carrying out thorough desk research that leverages the relevant information available on websites and in social media, making use of elea's network, and accessing diverse information sources, such as the Swiss embassy, executives from global corporations, local incubation initiatives, and business-plan competition platforms.

During an initial phase of building elea, clear criteria for identifying a promising investment still had to be defined and continuously adjusted. Furthermore, the desired portfolio characteristics — in terms of risk, geographical mix, and the diversity of themes – were still at an early stage of development. Over the years, two things have changed: (1) elea has sharpened its focus and continuously refined its criteria based on accumulated experiences, with both successful and less successful investments, as well as growing professional capacity, and (2) the impact entrepreneurship movement has gained such momentum on a global scale that the number of potentially attractive investment opportunities has exploded. Along with this trend, there has been a step change in visibility: nowadays, most impact enterprises already have a company website describing their vision and ambition, and they have an active presence on social media. Frequently, they begin to market their purpose long before they are in a position to offer products and services to clients.

As a result of this evolution, and because the effectiveness of sourcing, to a large extent, determines the potential for impact creation, elea made a major resource commitment to this task and adopted a systematic, proactive methodology. The principle upon which this methodology is based is to search for what we would like to invest in rather than to evaluate what is brought to us. While we still regularly look at a number of unsolicited proposals, the core sourcing engine starts with desk research, where promising opportunities are identified by theme and geography and prescreened along defined criteria. The criteria either relate to individual organizations or to an emerging new ecosystem or industry of impact creation.

Peer-to-peer lending in agriculture was such a theme that emerged with the progress made in financial technology and addressed a key problem facing farmers in poor countries; namely, the frequent lack of access to affordable working capital. elea wrote a *white paper* on this emerging opportunity and then systematically researched individual enterprise activities in this field with the intention of picking two to three of those with the most promising models for doing deeper analysis. In this strategic approach, which aims to understand entire impact ecosystems and the specific role of individual impact enterprises within them, we see ourselves aligned with a concept developed by Professor Alnoor Ebrahim at Tufts University in his book *Measuring Social Change* (Ebrahim, 2019). This concept differentiates among impact-seeking strategies depending on the level of uncertainty regarding cause/effect and on the intended control over outcomes. Those strategies with complicated cause-effect relationships and high-impact ambitions should be analyzed as entire eco-systems of social change that extend beyond single organizations in order to then identify attractive individual impact enterprise models.

After elea has gradually reduced the number of potential investment opportunities from thousands to hundreds, it organizes research nights with the entire team in an effort to further reduce the number of candidates. This is done by means of an internal competitive pitching effort among small groups, which is followed by exploratory calls on high-potential candidates. The result is a few dozen potential investments that are then further screened, possibly on the occasion of an on-site visit. At some stage, the team forms a positive view and comes up with a preliminary investment recommendation (PIR), which lays out why a certain investment could be attractive and what further analysis should be undertaken to develop an investment recommendation for the board of trustees.

More recently, this process was enhanced by an additional element. As elea has been involved with certain enterprise developments that have continued on a very solid course of success for several years (e.g., our four lead cases: Angaza, Coffee Circle, Dharma Life, and BagoSphere), we naturally built on our growing confidence in their capabilities to leverage capital by offering them add-on investments. For example, we participated in follow-up financing rounds for Coffee Circle and Dharma Life to fund further growth. We also provided match funding for BagoSphere's efforts to raise local funds, thereby helping them to create a philanthropic arm for their business that provides students access to financing for their training programs.

Due diligence, investment decisions, and contracting

Once there is sufficient support for a PIR, elea's team then embarks on a due diligence effort. At elea, due diligence is a crucial and challenging task that we take very seriously and involves a significant effort. The complete process for an investment candidate of medium complexity can easily consume three to five person-months, and elea carries out between 5 to 10 due diligence efforts, on average, per year. Often, targeted entrepreneurs express surprise at how deeply we get involved, and mention that this is rather unusual in our sector of philanthropic impact investing.

Many early stage investors shy away from such an intense due-diligence effort and address the risk of failure by investing smaller, diversified amounts rather than carrying out a thorough analysis, understanding, and assessment.

However, as we are looking for intense, multiyear partnerships in our model, shortcutting due diligence is simply not an option. Besides creating support, alignment, and excitement for an investment internally, due diligence is often the first step to building knowledge, respect, and trust with the leadership team of the impact enterprise that could potentially become part of our investment portfolio. The due diligence process, thereby, serves as the foundation for effective future collaboration, for it provides great insights about the people and their modus operandi, as well as about the current and intended status of strategies, models, and plans, which is an important due diligence finding in and of itself.

The criteria we are looking for at the board level when deciding on an investment recommendation are straightforward. Essentially, three questions need to be satisfactorily answered:

1. Does an investment promise a realistic path to significant social impact and financial sustainability, and is it in line with elea's purpose, vision, and values?
2. Are we confident that we can engage with the leadership team of an investee company in a long-term productive collaboration along mutually agreed principles of partnership?
3. Can elea contribute to impact value creation by leveraging its professional expertise beyond its financial capital investment?

So what were some of the key attractions at the time that encouraged us to pick Angaza, Coffee Circle, Dharma Life, and BagoSphere? Angaza, which was initiated by an American entrepreneur with a science background, was our first investment in the digital solutions space. We recognized the massive impact potential of the pay-as-you-go technology, which removed one of the biggest bottlenecks in last-mile distribution initiatives, and we were impressed by the innovative, yet robust, technical solution that Lesley and her brother had developed. An additional factor was that the team seemed open to being challenged on the design of the business model and the strategy to be pursued.

Coffee Circle was our second major investment in the global-agricultural-value-chain investment theme. Prior to this investment, we had already made a successful investment in Pakka (www.pakka.ch), an impact enterprise that imported organic and fair-trade-labelled cashew nuts from India (and other agricultural products from other poor countries) into German-speaking Europe with great success. We could, therefore, already demonstrate substantial know-how on how to cope with the typical challenges facing early stage agricultural trade investments, such as balancing sales and production, organizing affordable working capital, and complementing founder personality skills with professional executives that have relevant experience in the field.

Dharma Life was a particularly appealing investment opportunity because of its huge impact potential to address poverty in rural India by means of a highly innovative model. Having already been exposed to several last-mile distribution initiatives (e.g., through an effort to improve the effectiveness of mom-and-pop shops in Bolivia), we could contribute substantial expertise about the opportunities and barriers of serving base-of-the-pyramid customers with socially impactful goods.

Finally, BagoSphere was especially interesting because of its success rate in procuring employment for poor youth from rural areas in the Philippine provinces based on its holistic approach – from selection of students to training and finding employers. This approach was in contrast to many less-than-successful attempts, where European vocational skills development models were adopted in poor countries without sufficiently considering characteristics and constraints within the local context.

Many steps that are used to perform due diligence within the field of philanthropic investing are common to the evaluation of an investment opportunity in any field. However, when assessing philanthropic impact investment candidates, there are some specific aspects unique to impact investing that make due diligence particularly challenging and deserve special attention. In our experience, there are at least four major differences as compared to common due diligence practice.

First, factual information as a basis for due diligence is usually thin, not well documented, and difficult to obtain. Often business plans lack a substantial analysis of facts, and sometimes even the most basic financial statements are not available or are of poor quality. Much of this is related to the early development stage of these enterprises, the lack of professional resources, and sometimes also a lack of experience in handling institutional capital. Therefore, an important part of any due diligence effort is to work together with the entrepreneurs and their leadership teams to build a factual base of relevant and plausible data – a task that is time-consuming and calls for extended on-site visits.

Second, the founders are key. Much impact value at this stage is embedded in their personality traits. What drives their motivation? How committed are they to their ambitions? How do they balance social impact and financial return goals? What is their skills profile in terms of strengths, development needs, and gaps? And, most importantly, what are their values and how ready are they to embark on an intensive, multiyear partnership with elea based on complete mutual openness, respect, and trust? To gain deep, possibly evidence-based, insights into these complicated questions is another reason why elea never invests in companies without extended on-site visits by at least one member of our professional team. In addition, a top-level dialogue between the entrepreneurs and the CEO and/or Chairman of elea is a mandatory element of every due diligence process.

Third, finding the right balance between what the enterprise is like today and what it aspires to become in the future is essential. Of course, the hockey-stick shape of business plans is a common phenomenon in any due diligence that involves expected future opportunities. However, because the enterprises often do not have much history, in philanthropic impact investing the emphasis is even more forward-looking. Thus, a common challenge for the elea team while working on a due diligence is how to get a sense of what are ambitious, yet somewhat realistic, objectives for the company, and what would the worst case scenarios look like?

Finally, because the elea team is so deeply involved in due diligence – working together with the entrepreneurs and their leadership teams to understand the current situation and get a sense for the mix of ambition, potential, and realism of their future plans – managing expectations is a major challenge. Sometimes, business models need to be questioned and changed or investment proposals need to be rejected altogether. This can occur either because of surprising new facts being uncovered or for reasons that have nothing to do with the individual company; for example, due to portfolio concentration aspects or the lack of available capacity to fund and mentor an investment (see Figure 3.3 for a complete list of questions to be addressed at the board level as part of elea's comprehensive due diligence package).

1. Are vision and values aligned with elea's perspectives?

2. Is the overall current situation sufficiently promising?

3. Is the potential for growth attractive enough?

4. Is the environmental footprint acceptable?

5. Are the financials transparent and solid?

6. Can we legally protect our investment?

7. Can we productively work with the leaders?

8. Do we have the required financial and professional capacity?

Figure 3.3 The eight elea due diligence questions.

Source: elea

To address all of these important and difficult aspects of the philanthropic impact investing due diligence process with the necessary sophisticated and subtle judgment, discussions on each and every potential investment take place at three levels at elea: within the due diligence team, led by a senior team member; within elea's leadership team, led by the CEO; and at the level of the board of trustees (for final approval), led by the Chairman, who is also one of the founders.

Investment instruments

Besides the basic "go/no go" decision on an investment recommendation, a crucial question to address is how much and what type of capital should be invested and under what conditions regarding governance and legal terms. As a general guideline, elea looks at what is most helpful for the development of an enterprise given its special circumstances in terms of maturity, financial versus non-financial needs, and business-model requirements. We seek to invest several hundred thousand Swiss francs and to have a positioning as a minority shareholder among a small handful of external investors – beyond founders, friends, and family – that is meaningful and distinctive but leaves the founders in the driving seat. We also try to avoid the risk of becoming a "shareholder of last resort."

Regarding the type of capital, elea, overall, targets a balanced mix between equity and equity-like investment, debt instruments, and grants. The choice of which instrument is determined primarily by the specific requirements of this investment. In principle, elea invests through four forms:

1. **Non-financial support only**: At an early stage, or in a complex situation that involves restructuring, the best support is sometimes advice; for example, on strategic direction, organizational development options, alternative legal and governance structures, or capital-raising strategies. Such support, however, is always given with the expectation of making an investment in the near future.

2. **Grants**: elea is a tax-exempt foundation and, as such, is also in the position to provide grants. Grants are typically given in two circumstances: either to fund those elements of hybrid structures that have a more philanthropic character (e.g., skills development programs for coffee farmers that supply Coffee Circle or student-financing facilities for BagoSphere) or to act as one element in a pre-investment financing structure so as not to overburden a portfolio company's balance sheet or dilute initial ownership at an early stage. These grant cases are always linked either to very clear milestones or results. (We rather shy away from repayable grants, as they can be a substantial drag on the liability side of our investee's balance sheet.)

3. **Debt instruments**: Loans or convertibles are used in situations where the type of capital raising has not yet been defined (e.g., for bridge financing) and/or in countries where foreign ownership is restricted. The key benefit of convertible structures is the possibility to compensate the convertible bond holders for the risk they take at this early stage by granting interest and/or discounts at the time of conversion (e.g., equity raise events), while avoiding unproductive discussions on valuation at early enterprise development stages.

4. **Equity**: Once companies have already reached or plan to reach a certain stage of maturity, equity is the natural way for elea to become engaged. If it is too early for a regular equity investment, SAFE arrangements (i.e., simple agreements for future equity) can take the

place of convertibles, thereby avoiding unnecessary legal complexity as well as the placement of a burden on our investee's balance sheet.

The guiding principle according to which elea chooses the amount and structure of an investment is based on a balanced perspective about the future development of an enterprise. We are not focused on short- and medium-term interests as an investor but rather on the long-term ones. We, therefore, do not seek to leverage our trusted relationships with the entrepreneurs to achieve unreasonably low valuations, nor do we recommend overloading the balance sheet with excessive debt (including repayable grants), because this could jeopardize future fundraising rounds. We look for fair arrangements in the spirit of an aligned partnership with the entrepreneurs in favor of social impact and long-term financial viability rather than in the spirit of an overly greedy approach that emphasizes maximum upside.

elea has never had to take an entrepreneur to court (nor has it been taken to court by an entrepreneur), and we will continue to do our best to avoid this in the future. However, we do insist on comprehensive contractual frameworks with three benefits in mind: contracts help define collaboration mechanisms (e.g., in the form of supervisory board seats or other advisory roles), enable solutions to protect minority rights (e.g., against financial dilution or the dilution of social purpose), and allow thinking through alternative scenarios for future development (including different exit options).

Impact value creation

Often, already during the due diligence phase, and certainly after the closing of the investment agreement, strategies for maximizing impact value creation are discussed between the entrepreneurs and the elea team. Adding value to an investee company beyond providing financial capital has been a core principle at elea since inception. As our experience with individual companies – as well as within our investment sectors – increased, impact value creation initiatives evolved beyond the debates at board levels and began involving our junior talent as well. Currently, we dedicate substantial and growing resources to elea impact value creation, or, as we call it, eIVC. To ensure effectiveness and continuous learning in this field, elea regularly organizes internal eIVC luncheons, where examples of impact value creation initiatives are presented, best practices are documented, and relevant experiences are exchanged. This helps establish an institutional capability that not only contributes to maximizing impact with the companies in our portfolio but also adds to our credibility as we develop new investment opportunities.

Typical topics for such luncheon meetings include these:

- How to effectively align leadership teams and their supervisory boards around a social purpose, vision, and values.
- How to develop and execute growth strategies for scaling up a business.
- How to define an ambitious, yet realistic, five-year vision with consistency around social impact goals, financial objectives, required resources, and effective organization and leadership.
- How to strengthen marketing and sales effectiveness.
- How to navigate through crises.
- How to develop and implement capital-raising strategies.
- How to build effective leadership teams and governance structures.

These luncheon discussions, typically, lead to the documentation of a specific method or instrument for practical applicability, with real-life examples attached.

Exit planning and realization

Before elea enters into an investment agreement, options for exiting a commitment at some stage after several years are discussed, either together with the elea entrepreneurs and/or internally. Following the principle of additionality, elea should commit its financial and non-financial resources where it can make a difference, while avoiding long-term structural dependencies. As investee companies develop, grow, and mature, elea's potential to make a difference diminishes. Angaza and Coffee Circle are both examples where regular institutional investors could be attracted and where philanthropic impact investing is no longer at the forefront of their requirements.

While elea has had some successes in exiting its investments, realizing profitable exits out of equity stakes in impact enterprises, in particular, has proven to be challenging. As we hear from other investment organizations, we are not alone in this experience. Achieving profitable exits is not straightforward and typically takes longer than expected. In the early stages of elea's development, we targeted exits after 5 to 7 years. More recently, we rather look at a time horizon of 7 to 10 years. Why is it so difficult, and what needs to happen for a more favorable exit environment? One part of the explanation is the limited maturity of the sector. As impact investing is only a little over a decade old, a somewhat liquid secondary market has not evolved yet, and many more recently established impact funds concentrate on making primary investments. Another part is related to elea's close collaboration with the teams leading the companies in its portfolio, which creates intense mutual bonding. Breaking such bonds through an exit is emotionally hard. New investors take comfort from such close relationships and make a continued elea stake a condition for their becoming engaged. And, after all, it is not always rational to exit just at the moment where growth, and consequently impact as well as financial return, are accelerating.

Nevertheless, to remain in compliance with the additionality principle, exits are necessary at the moment when philanthropic capital is no longer required and more commercially oriented impact funds can be attracted. Therefore, as an active investment period progresses, it becomes increasingly important for elea to systematically develop those aspects of an investment that favor its ability to exit. This includes a strong track record of both impact and financial performance, as well as a strong and resilient leadership team, effective corporate governance, and a transparent organization and culture. With the increasing breadth, depth, and maturity of impact investing, a secondary market will evolve exactly as it happened a decade or so earlier when secondary buyouts became a rule rather than an exception in traditional private equity investing. Consequently, we have high confidence that the environment for profitable exits will significantly improve in the years to come. This will make the sector more attractive, as it enhances the effectiveness of capital deployed in impact investing.

3.2.2 Philanthropic investors' circle

When elea was created, the founding family committed CHF 20 million to finance the buildup and ongoing operation of the foundation. Given the appetite for philanthropic impact investments at the time and the founders' ambition to establish a professional team, they came up with a Plan A and a Plan B. Plan A foresaw that elea would succeed in attracting like-minded third-party investors for contributions of philanthropic capital, and who would become a long-term viable philanthropic impact investor, helped in part by reinvesting the financial returns of the most successful investments after exit. According to Plan B, elea would be liquidated after a period of, say, 10–15 years, having exhausted its capital resources and having, hopefully, made a number of socially impactful and financially successful investments. As we will describe in more detail in Chapter Six (Section 6.2.4), when we take a look at elea's lifespan going forward, we are pleased and proud that Plan A was successfully implemented and Plan B was shelved.

During the first few years, we did not accept any third-party capital. This was because we wanted to explore, experiment, learn, and adjust our model without putting external capital at risk. Only three to four years after launch, due to the growing confidence in our approach, did we start to systematically look for external capital providers who would become members of our philanthropic investors' circle. We had three target groups in mind. First, entrepreneurial families with similar characteristics to that of the founding family: a penchant for entrepreneurship, and an appreciation for a professional, analytically driven investment approach to addressing social issues, as opposed to more emotionally based, traditional charitable giving. Another target were foundations with a broader remit who would be prepared to outsource their activities dedicated to fighting absolute poverty to another foundation that specializes in this field. And, finally, companies who would consider a strategic partnership with elea as a meaningful component of their responsibility agenda.

Our investors' circle offering is straightforward: we want our external philanthropic investors to be completely aligned with our investment philosophy, impact aspirations, and process. We have, thus, stayed away from forms of cooperation that would compromise our investment philosophy and process. As an example, we would not search for investments for third parties against a finder's fee without being invested in the impact enterprise ourselves, and we would also not offer due diligence as a service. Moreover, wherever possible, we try to do co-investments with professional partners that we know very well and with whom we share similar investment philosophies as well as levels of professionalism and expertise.

That said, within the parameters of elea's current investment capacity, our external investors have the possibility to allocate their capital contribution to a specific selection of elea's investee companies, depending on their individual preferences in terms of themes, geographies, and specific enterprises. Thereby, they are able to combine a tax-exempt philanthropic donation with the idea of having a stake in elea's portfolio of direct investments. By far, the largest proportion of the committed amounts goes directly into funding single investments and the directly allocated cost of supporting them, while a small percentage is allocated to cover indirect investment expenses, particularly the efforts to find and evaluate new investments.[10] Our investors can also become personally engaged, depending on their appetite and capacity. Some of them have engaged with and supported their investments on-site (sometimes, together with their family as way of creating social awareness among their children), others have provided professional guidance on their specific area of professional expertise, while others are content with one annual briefing on the status and impact achieved within their subportfolio. For investors with a somewhat limited financial appetite, we have created a standardized package of investments with fewer opportunities for customized engagement.

Besides our annual impact performance reporting and additional informal ways of getting together, the investors' circle offering includes one formal event per annum. On this occasion, investors meet with elea entrepreneurs, staff, and fellow investors and thereby have the opportunity to exchange views and broaden perspectives. Over the years, the elea community – with its shared agenda on fighting poverty and an inspiring engagement among like-minded people – has evolved, grown, and become quite active. As of 2019, our philanthropic investors' circle had a sizable number of several dozen elea investors, and it had made contributions substantially in excess of the initial funds contributed by the founders' family. This circle is tremendously valuable, far beyond its crucial role in ensuring elea's medium- to long-term financial viability. It brings together a great and diverse group of distinct personalities and constitutes a great source of advice, encouragement, moral support, and critical feedback.

As elea completed the first decade of its journey in 2016 in healthy shape, and given the high level of excitement regarding opportunities to tap into during the second decade, in 2017 we embarked on a planning exercise to

create ambitious, yet realistic, scenarios for the future in order to establish
leadership priorities and better understand constraints.[11] One such constraint was the fact that our funding principle for direct and indirect costs
did not allow for building any reserves that were necessary to absorb risks,
extend the lives of our winning investments, or finance strategic initiatives. To address this, we contacted some of our most loyal philanthropic
investors and invited them to join an exclusive "Comité de Patronage."
We asked them for a significant capital contribution that could be used to
strengthen elea's balance-sheet capacity, with objectives such as funding
investments in elea's organizational strength (e.g., talent program), its institutional capabilities (e.g., knowledge base), or its risk absorption capacity
(e.g., setting up an emergency funding facility in response to the Global
Covid-19 Crisis). With this access to both investment-related philanthropic
capital and free equity, and with a solid perspective for financial returns
above cost at a number of our most successful investments after exit, elea
will be sustainably funded for the foreseeable future.

3.2.3 Professional development

In 2019, elea launched an annual talent program with the goal of attracting
young professionals who have an appetite to embark on a career in philanthropic impact investing. The pilot effort for this initiative was designed as a
two-year structured development journey, either targeting people between
their bachelor's and master's studies and/or at the start of their professional
careers. We positioned ourselves next to global consulting companies and
financial services firms at recruiting events with selected universities, and
we were overwhelmed by the success. Over 70 students showed interest,
many of whom have excellent qualifications. We ended up hiring four
junior talents, sometimes in a head-on competition with high-profile alternative employers. This experience showed us that our offering of highly
demanding professional work in a competitive environment with a clearly
meaningful purpose met an enthusiastic response.

Since the outset, the elea Professional Development Program (ePDP)
has been an important pillar of our work, which, in its significance,
goes far beyond just "administrative resources." The objective was to
create and accumulate expertise and know-how, share experiences, and
build an institutional memory in order to be able to become a learning

organization. elea has been fortunate to be able to attract great people and to retain them for a long time. As of 2020, its leadership team has an average tenure of 11 years with elea. We aspire to be the employer of choice for professionals who want to make a career in impact investing. In line with our commitment to additionality, our team adds value to the quality and distinctiveness of our portfolio through sourcing, evaluation, and ongoing monitoring and support. Thus, adding young talent to our team also serves to create awareness and enthusiasm among the younger generation for our understanding of inclusive capitalism, for ethics, and for engagement in finding solutions to very large societal problems.

For every Swiss franc that we invest in either a grant or the risk component of a loan or an equity stake, we invest another Swiss franc into our impact value creation efforts. This intensive and expensive focus on leveraging capital contributions with professional expertise is quite unique and sets elea apart from more traditional philanthropic and charitable work. After almost 15 years into our journey as philanthropic impact investors, we are more than ever convinced that this is the right way for the focus and model we have chosen. Philanthropic impact investing is highly challenging work. It is similar to venture capital and private equity investing, but with the added dimension of social impact. Such efforts require hard work, talent, skills, ambitions, and performance-driven attitudes that are comparable to those of any other professional services company in the consulting or financial services industry.

We have, therefore, structured our professional development program after the model of commercial professional service companies. It starts with a positioning in the talent markets that attracts ambitious, competitive, hard-working individuals with a strong foundation of ethics and values. The recruiting process is intense, always involves a significant number of our senior team members, and looks at different angles, such as motivational structures and backgrounds, ambition, and entrepreneurial drive and energy, as well as work ethics. It also tests intellectual curiosity, analytical skills, and comfort levels at solving real-life elea case examples. We are searching for young professionals, mostly with business, economics, legal, information technology, or science and engineering backgrounds, whose alternative target employers are commercial companies.

Working at elea is serving a higher purpose that goes far beyond just "having a job." Hence, compensation is not the most essential part of the entire package, even though we pay for performance and are guided by market practices in our compensation approach. Our team members are evaluated annually based on an analytical performance measurement and management system (PMM), which is centered on self-evaluation and takes into account our ethical beliefs about liberty and accountability. As our colleagues reach higher levels of achievement and competence, they can receive promotions, and we co-invest with them in their further professional education. We consciously attract young talent to develop them internally, so that they can professionally grow into the elea way of operating and behaving, to make a difference for both investees and for elea. In addition to our dedicated staff members, we also deploy seasoned professionals for specific temporary project assignments, or we ask selected philanthropic investors who have both an appetite for professional activity and the relevant experience to help us as senior advisors. In doing so, they contribute their expertise and help our young professionals to grow.

This development program is embedded in a culture characterized by strong partnership values and flat hierarchies, and that emphasizes learning, development, and contribution. elea has established accountabilities around the core components and processes of its operating model and encourages bottom-up initiatives and teamwork. The guiding thought is that elea associates should advance in their professional and personal skills development at least at a similar pace to their peers who opted for careers in commercial professional service companies. Besides the growth of individual colleagues, this systematic development program helps us to ensure that elea can grow as an organization.

3.3 Conclusions

3.3.1 Insights and takeaways

elea, like other philanthropic investment organizations around the globe, strives to make the world a better place. Its combination of ethical values, purpose, and distinctive operating model is a unique endeavor that is intricately linked to the founders' ideas, personalities, and way of doing things. By sharing our reflections, insights, and lessons – rather than providing a blueprint – we hope to inspire others to find and explore their own path. In our experience, learning can only take place when implicit assumptions behind decisions and developments are made explicit, so that they become open for debate and further improvement and development. In these pages, we have, thus, made room for extensive reflection on ethics and virtues, not because we believe that everybody should adopt liberal ethics and live by the same virtues, but rather to encourage others to likewise engage in deep thought about why they are doing what they are doing.

There is rarely a right or wrong answer when addressing such issues. Does a philanthropic initiative result from a specific experience during a crucial moment in one's life, or is it rather the outcome of an intellectual thought process? Does the chosen purpose follow an intuition that is related to a personal or family constellation, or does it address a universally recognized human need? Are decisions taken based on clear criteria and the analysis of facts, or are they rather based on gut feelings? We would argue that making the effort to reflect on deeper "whys" about how answers to such questions are derived can lead to higher levels of consciousness and consistency, and through that, possibly to higher levels of effectiveness and impact.

Transparency in decision-making also helps to sharpen the profile and identity of an investment organization. Our decision to define elea's purpose as fighting absolute poverty with entrepreneurial means enabled a clear strategic focus and direction, and it helped to identify the trade-offs with other possible statements of purpose, such as those in the field of environmental protection. Being clear about one's identity helps when finding out where and how an organization can make a difference in line with the additionality principle. While this all sounds clear and well thought out, we should, however, not succumb to the delusion that this was all rationally designed and planned. Much of elea's profile and identity today resulted from a learning journey that was exploratory and involved much trial and error.

3.3.2 *Your point of view*

Learning objectives

After studying this chapter, you should be able to

1. identify the motivations and intentions of elea's founders and analyze the drivers that led to the creation of elea;
2. describe elea's integrated approach using entrepreneurship and capital to drive social innovation;

3. differentiate traditional philanthropy from philanthropic impact investing;
4. explain elea's ethical approach to philanthropic impact investing;
5. summarize and describe the central attributes of elea's operating model (investment management, investors' circle, and professional development); and
6. evaluate elea's operating model (How do these components reinforce each other? Are there tensions between them?) and propose new features for expanding and leveraging the impact of such an organization.

Reflection questions

1. What is the link between elea's purpose to fight absolute poverty with entrepreneurial means and the ethical position of elea's founders (http:// www.elea-foundation.org/en/about-us/what-is-eleas-purpose)?
2. What are the most important differences between traditional philanthropy (i.e., charitable giving) and elea's approach to philanthropic impact investing?
3. Why are integrity, humbleness, engagement, and partnership practical virtues of an impact investor? Based on your experience, could you identify other virtues that are necessary to becoming an impact investor? If so, which virtues, and why are they important?
4. What are the advantages of elea's operating model? What are its main challenges? What can impact investors learn from it?
5. What advice would you give to elea's leadership team as the model is further developed? Suggest three ideas of how elea's operating model could be expanded and leveraged.
6. If you were part of elea's board, what three to five key performance indicators would you suggest to measure the success of elea's operating model? Justify.

Right vs. right dilemma: Crowding out vs. crowding in

The presence of both public and private capital providers to an impact investment can either encourage or deter private investors from investing, depending on the type of involvement. Two competing mechanisms explain this phenomenon: crowding out and crowding in. Crowding out suggests that public subsidies to a recipient organization displace the donations of private donors, because private donors (taxpayers) perceive government funding as a substitution for their investments.

In contrast, crowding in suggests that a government subsidy signals an organization's effectiveness and is, thus, used as a "quality stamp" that encourages private investors to provide additional funding. However, in situations where impact enterprises have earned revenues, public subsidies or private philanthropic investments can either crowd out or crowd in private commercial capital, depending on the circumstances. A similar mechanism is at work in the relationship between philanthropic impact investors and traditional charitable organizations. Channeling philanthropic funds to revenue-generating enterprises can cannibalize funding for more traditional, donation-oriented institutional structures that tackle social ills.

Debate the pros and cons of alternative funding strategies regarding the opportunities and risks of crowding out versus crowding in.

Notes

1. For more information, see also: (Wuffli, 2016) 2.1; 3.2.1; 3.3; (Wuffli & Kirchschläger, 2017).
2. In the 1970s, the world was structured into three tiers: The "First World" referred to capitalist, industrialized countries like the United States, Western European countries, and other industrialized countries like Japan, Australia, and New Zealand; it covered approximately 15% of the world's population and accounted for over 60% of global GDP. The "Second World" was the influence sphere of the former Soviet Union and was closed to all others, hidden behind the Iron Curtain. And the "Third World" – the only one of these three terms that is still occasionally used today, despite its obvious obsolescence – included everything else and was characterized by poverty, famine, war, and natural disaster. Large parts of Asia and Latin America, in particular, were looked at as hopeless in light of overpopulation and difficult climatic conditions, whereas there was more optimism about Africa, based on its wealth of natural resources.
3. See also (Wimmer, 2018), where the crucial role of civil society in its contribution to the well-being of states is analyzed.
4. As with most initiatives that target the fight against poverty, microfinance also has its controversial aspects. In their book *More Than Good Intentions*,

economist Dean Karlan and researcher Jacob Appel refer to a study in India which revealed that a high proportion of microcredits were being used to pay off other debts, rather than to make investments into new entrepreneurial ventures, and that the empowerment of women as a result was not all that clear (Karlan & Appel, 2012, p. 78ff.). The study concluded the obvious, namely that granting credit is a means, not an end, and that somebody does not automatically become an entrepreneur just by having money.

5. For this section see (Wuffli, 2016), 3.4, and 3.5.

6. Whenever we refer to "liberal" in this book, we mean it in the continental European sense (i.e., those who favor individual liberty, free markets, responsibility, and a limited scope of interference by the state).

7. For a perspective on this debate that is rooted in liberal thinking and argues that a deeper look into the causes and dynamics of inequality is warranted, see: (Deaton, 2013).

8. See also: (Reich, 2018). In his critical analysis of philanthropy in the U.S., Reich challenges why donations to schools in wealthy communities that essentially benefit the children of wealthy families should be tax deductible, as they do not benefit society overall. Quite the contrary, they help to increase inequality within the U.S. and, thus, fail democracy, in Reich's opinion.

9. For another recent and highly critical review of philanthropy, see: (Giridharadas, 2018). The author fundamentally challenges philanthropy for cementing the status quo rather than encouraging radical change in society. He argues in his book that donations by the wealthy help to maintain the status quo rather than encourage radical changes.

10. As elea does not engage in retail fundraising, and, therefore, spends very little on marketing, our administrative expenses are very limited.

11. Among the new initiatives launched as part of this effort was the creation of the elea Center for Social Innovation and the professorial elea Chair for Social Innovation (currently held by Professor Vanina Farber, who co-authored this book) at IMD.

References

Acemoglu, D., & Robinson, J. (2013). *Why Nations Fail - The Origins of Power, Prosperity, and Poverty*. New York: Currency.

Balandina Jaquier, J. (2011). Guide to Impact Investing: For Family Offices and High-Net-Worth Individuals: Managing Wealth for Impact and Profit.

Banerjee, A. V., & Duflo, E. (2011). *Poor Economics: A Radical Rethinking of the Way to Fight Global Poverty*. New York: Public Affairs.

Berlin, I. (1969). *Four Essays on Liberty*. Oxford: University Press.

Deaton, A. (2013). *The Great Escape*. Princeton: Princeton University Press.

Drucker, P. (2004). *The Daily Drucker*. New York: Harper Business.

Ebrahim, A. (2019). *Measuring Social Change - Performance and Accountability in a Complex World*. Stanford: Stanford University Press.

Giridharadas, A. (2018). *Winners Take All - The Elite Charade of Changing the World*. Alfred A. Knopf.

Karlan, D., & Appel, J. (2012). *More Than Good Intentions*. London: Plume.

Reich, R. (2018). *Just Giving - Why Philanthropy Is Failing Democracy and How It Can Do Better*. Princeton: Princeton University Press.

The Economist. (2012, November 3). Bangladesh and Development - The Path Through the Fields. The Economist. Retrieved October 15, 2019, from http://www.economist.com/news/briefing/21565617-bangladesh-has-dysfunctional-politics-and-stunted-private-sector-yet-it-has-been-surprisingly

The Economist. (2018, May 10). A Warning on Poverty from Peru. The Economist. Retrieved October 15, 2019, from https://www.economist.com/the-americas/2018/05/10/a-warning-on-poverty-from-peru

The World Bank. (2015). *Ethiopia Poverty Assessment 2014*. Washington D.C. Retrieved October 15, 2019, from https://openknowledge.worldbank.org/handle/10986/21323

The World Bank. (2019). *Poverty & Equity Data Portal - Bangladesh*. Retrieved October 15, 2019, from http://povertydata.worldbank.org/poverty/country/BGD

The World Bank. (2019). *Poverty & Equity Data Portal - India*. Retrieved October 15, 2019, from http://povertydata.worldbank.org/poverty/country/IND

Wimmer, A. (2018). *Nation Building - Why Some Countries Come Together While Others Fall Apart*. Princeton University Press.

Wuffli, P. A. (2016). *Inclusive Leadership: A Framework for the Global Era*. New York, London: Springer.

Wuffli, P. A., & Kirchschläger, A. (2017). Conscious and Ethical Investing - Investor Life Cycle and Investment Process. In C. Ter Braak-Forstinger, *Conscious Investing* (pp. 171–191). Petersfield/Hampshire: Harriman House

4

---

elea's INVESTMENT FOCUS

In the previous chapter, we reviewed the "why" of elea's creation and the "how" of its operations. In this chapter, we will discuss the "what" of its investment activities: At what development stage of impact enterprises does elea invest? What are the chosen impact areas and investment themes? What type of companies does elea prefer? And what had elea learned as it evolved toward these focus areas?

The required investment approach and the economics of investing vary depending on the development stage of a company. elea chose to focus on the period between the post-start-up phase and the period of early growth, as we saw a significant opportunity to make a difference in this challenging, yet decisive, stage. With regard to investment themes, elea focuses on areas that are meaningful and relevant for the fight against absolute poverty but also fit with elea's capabilities and skills profile. elea looks for innovative enterprises that have a potential for growth and large-scale leveraging of both entrepreneurial and financial resources. Size matters not only because of economics but even more so because the impact typically grows with the size of an enterprise as more people can be reached. As an enterprise grows, however, the risk of a drift in purpose occurring has to be closely monitored.

4.1 Impact enterprise development

On Monday, July 12, 2010, the jury of a global business-plan competition called "Solar for All" met in San Francisco to award the first prize of USD 250,000 (funded by Deutsche Bank) to a young firm called Greenlight Planet. Indian-based Greenlight Planet had a bold mission; namely, to provide the world with low-price off-grid electricity solutions in the form of solar lamps. "Solar for All" was initiated by Ashoka (a community of changemakers) and the Canopus Foundation, and several other impact organizations (including elea) joined in as well. It was meant to address one of the major challenges resulting from absolute poverty; that is, the absence of artificial light during the nighttime, which hinders education, income-generation opportunities, and more generally, the quality of social life for poor people. As a consequence, many of these poor individuals are driven to migrate to urban slums.

Today, Greenlight Planet is one of a small number of social businesses that has dramatically scaled up its operations. At the end of 2019, approximately 27 million people in over five million off-grid homes were using their lamps daily. It employs 800 people in 11 offices and serves over 60 countries globally (www.greenlightplanet.com). Already in 2012, they attracted institutional impact investors (e.g., the Oasis Fund), reached profitability, and were valued well above cost. elea did not invest in Greenlight Planet. However, based on the knowledge we gained through supporting this competition, elea was in a position to invest in Angaza shortly thereafter, which turned out to be another impressive success story (and a significant supplier to Greenlight Planet).

Greenlight Planet and Angaza are two examples of impact businesses that have substantially progressed on a road to growth and financial sustainability. Successful cases of this type are quite rare. Today, there are probably a few hundred of them, but not thousands or even tens of thousands. Many fail. Success and failure are, of course, typical for the process of enterprise creation that follows the theory of capitalism by the great liberal economist Josef Schumpeter. He called the process through which capitalism creates and destroys value "creative destruction":

> Capitalism … is by nature a form or method of economic change and not only never is, but never can be, stationary. The … process of industrial mutation … incessantly revolutionizes the economic

structure from within, incessantly destroying the old one, incessantly creating a new one. This process of Creative Destruction is the essential fact about capitalism. (Schumpeter, 1976)

The small number of successful examples is also explained by the patience that it takes to develop successful enterprises in a field that is still quite young and lacks entrepreneurial development ecosystems of a size and sophistication that characterize vibrant start-up scenes, such as the ones in Silicon Valley, Berlin, Tel Aviv, and Zürich/Lausanne. In many cases, it takes 8 to 10 years and beyond to go from prototyping and the early start-up phase to refining business models and developing organizations up to a level at which they have achieved proven growth trajectories and financial sustainability, which is a prerequisite for tapping institutional impact investment markets. On these journeys, which usually do not follow linear development paths but are rather characterized by phases of trial and error as well as progress and setbacks, the type and extent of support and the nature of the supporting ecosystem differ widely and must be customized for each investment during its specific stage of development.

A review of academic and practitioner literature offers a range of frameworks to distinguish between different development phases in the process of enterprise development. One example is a sequence of six phases depending on the degree of maturity and type of activities (www.coxblue.com/the-6-stages-of-a-startup-where-are-you/).[1] These phases include the following:

1. **Concept and research**: Conduct thorough research, then create a business plan and a mission statement.
2. **Commitment**: Create a prototype, develop a process, and start building a team. Secure funding.
3. **Traction**: This is the first year of a start-up. Begin to get the word out about your product and gain your first customers.
4. **Refinement**: This is year two. Continue refining your product or service.
5. **Scaling**: Scaling, or growing, starts from year two to three and lasts for years.
6. **Becoming established**: This is likely in year three or after, where you may see considerable growth.

Figure 4.1 The social enterprise development propeller.

Source: http://propelloradvisors.ca/wp-content/uploads/2016/03/social-enterprise-development-path.pdf

The most comprehensive framework we found in this research was a flywheel-like "propeller" that describes a social enterprise development path (see Figure 4.1). It visualizes different approaches and highlights that the path is not linear (which is very much our experience at elea).

4.1.1 A three-stage model

While these examples from academic and practitioner literature structure the process of enterprise development into different components, with their distinctive tasks and challenges, they typically do not link together entrepreneurial and investor perspectives with a view to combining processes, such as support mechanisms and funding approaches. For this reason, at elea we apply a three-stage model to impact enterprise development that is based on different types of interactions between entrepreneurs and investors in order to define our distinctive positioning. These three stages are

> **Candidate creation**: During this first stage, ideas for future enterprises are explored and developed with the aim of creating viable candidates. The intensity, scope, and time horizons of mutual commitments between entrepreneurs and investors during this stage are rather limited and small scale.
>
> **Enterprise development**: During this second stage, enterprise models are tested, refined, and implemented. This stage is resource

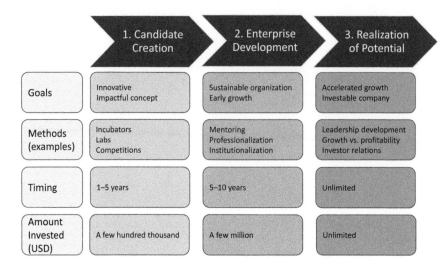

	1. Candidate Creation	2. Enterprise Development	3. Realization of Potential
Goals	Innovative Impactful concept	Sustainable organization Early growth	Accelerated growth Investable company
Methods (examples)	Incubators Labs Competitions	Mentoring Professionalization Institutionalization	Leadership development Growth vs. profitability Investor relations
Timing	1–5 years	5–10 years	Unlimited
Amount Invested (USD)	A few hundred thousand	A few million	Unlimited

Figure 4.2 The three stages of impact enterprise development.

Source: elea

intensive and requires a close partnership between the entrepreneur and the investor.

Realization of potential: During this final stage, the full market and impact potentials are realized.

Let us now dig deeper into each of these three stages: What are their specific objectives and desired outcomes? How are they different from each other? What are critical issues and enablers during each stage? What does it take to succeed? (see Figure 4.2)

Stage one: Candidate creation

At the beginning of any innovation process, there is an idea that is conceived, articulated, and owned by a single individual or a team. This is no different for social innovations than it is for any other innovation. There are, of course, many possible sources for new ideas. One of the established mechanisms in a market economy to systematically discover and evaluate new ideas is competition. Not surprisingly, therefore, start-up or business-plan competitions are a useful instrument in this respect, and they are often applied for social business ideas as well.

A highly visible example is the "YouWiN!" program (i.e., Youth Enterprise with Innovation in Nigeria), which was created by the Nigerian government and awarded USD 100 million to over 3,000 entrepreneurs between 2012 and 2015. David McKenzie, lead economist at the World Bank's Development Research Group, analyzed the results of 1,920 "YouWiN!" participants. He concluded that grant recipients were 37% more likely to survive the next three years and 23% more likely to grow beyond 10 employees than other entrepreneurs who did not participate in this program. McKenzie estimated that YouWiN! generated over 7,000 new jobs, and it cost the government only about USD 8,500 per job as compared to USD11,000–USD80,000 per job for job-creation programs introduced in other developing countries (McKenzie, 2015). Currently, in Africa alone, there are over two dozen business-plan competitions that are organized either by local organizations or international NGOs.

There is similar evidence regarding the effectiveness of business-plan competitions from Central America: TechnoServe, an international non-profit organization (and strategic partner of elea) that seeks enterprising solutions to alleviate poverty conducted a full-scale study of the 13 business-plan competitions it held in Central America in 2009. In general, entrepreneurs participating in the programs dramatically outperformed other start-up endeavors. They created two and one-half times more jobs over two years and generated twice as much sales growth in the first year, mobilizing nearly three times as much capital. All in all, these programs generated USD 3.70 in incremental revenue over three years for every U.S. dollar spent and one full-time job per USD 700 spent (TechnoServe, 2009). (Analyzing the difference between USD 700 per job and USD 8,000 per job in the above-mentioned example from the Nigerian government's YouWiN! Program would probably be worth another study …)

Interestingly, business-plan competitions are also favored by business schools to encourage practical learning by MBA students in a competitive environment and within a learning-oriented support structure. Dharma Life, for example, was conceived of by students of the London Business School during a business-plan competition. The business school at Chicago University likewise runs such competitions, whereby the focus is on learning opportunities, not on building viable business ventures. Besides tangible results in enterprise development and job/income creation, business-plan competitions also offer a series of intangible advantages in terms of skills and network development: they help the entrepreneurs and their teams to solidify business plans and align team members, as well as to gain self-confidence and acquire pitching practice; they contribute to building important networks in a relevant ecosystem and attracting both talent and capital; and they often provide access to professional mentoring opportunities, thus helping with skills transfer and experience exchange from more senior to more junior entrepreneurs. An empirical study covering 62 owners of new ventures who had participated in a business-plan competition showed that over half of them applied their experience by identifying new risks, clarifying new competitors, attracting business advisors, modifying products and services, developing an exit strategy, or developing distributions strategies (Thomas, Gudmundson, Turner, & Suhr, 2014). From the perspective of investing individuals and organizations, business-plan competitions create transparency about investment themes and business models, and they help in the selection and resource-allocation processes.

The practitioner literature on the "dos and don'ts" of business-plan competitions[2] cites disadvantages as well. Business-plan competitions tend to distract entrepreneurs from their focus on customers in favor of addressing the interests of investors. Sometimes, the total cost of application (including the opportunity cost of distraction) far outweighs the often modest prize money, which raises the question of whether more traditional efforts to search for individual angel investors are not superior. A certain hype, particularly in Africa, also favors the emergence of an almost specialized "business-plan competition industry" in which a certain group of applicants concentrates on capturing prize money from the different competitions without ever having the serious intention of building a business.

Our experience from seeing ideas evolve from business-plan competitions into impact enterprises suggests that the following factors contribute to their success:

- **Thematic focus versus shotgun approach**: One of the reasons why the "Solar for All" business-plan competition was successful was its thematic focus, which allowed for a clear identification of the target group of potential impact entrepreneurs and permitted the assembly of a specific group of organizations that could leverage this special expertise. Furthermore, its plausible purpose facilitated the raising of necessary funds, because it appealed to potential donors.
- **Comprehensive ecosystem**: Talking to the participants of business-plan competitions confirms the value of intangible benefits beyond the energizing kick from competitive peer pressure and the

value of the prize money. In particular, one key benefit is the possibility to tap into a relevant network of entrepreneurs, investors,
leadership coaches, and technical experts who can all contribute to
strengthening the proposal either by providing advice or guidance or
by challenging it. Impact entrepreneurs can also hugely benefit from
the experience of others on how to organize thinking, structure proposals, and pitch stories effectively.

- **Long-term commitment**: Even though the single business-plan
  competition from the eyes of an individual participant may look like
  a sprint, creating an organizational setup that is sustainably successful
  is more like a marathon. Whether a business-plan competition has
  made a substantial contribution or not will only become visible after
  the prize-winning impact enterprises have acquired many years of
  track record. It takes time to distinguish the winners from the losers, learn from flawed judgments made in the past, and accumulate
  expertise and wisdom in picking the right candidates. This calls for
  the supporting organizations to take a long-term perspective.
- **Content-driven passion over hyped marketing**: Above all, it takes
  a strong passion for the themes involved in order to inspire both participants and donors. Particularly in the field of impact business plans,
  there is a risk of hype at the expense of substance. Identifying and
  meeting young potential impact entrepreneurs is highly attractive for
  private and corporate philanthropists. Depending on the chosen geography, it adds to diversity, provokes intellectually stimulating debates,
  and demonstrates commitment and youthful energy – and all this at a
  rather modest cost. Yet the impact of interventions at this early stage of
  development is limited due to the low probabilities of success.

A promising candidate for the development of an impact enterprise can
obviously emerge from other mechanisms that help to crystallize ideas,
define aspirations, size up impact and financial potential, and develop
and test prototype products and initial concepts with potential clients.
However, all of these efforts typically reach their limits when the resources
from friends and family are exhausted and the dedicated commitment of
one or several individuals over a substantial time period (beyond a few
weeks and months) is required to make further progress. These moments
represent an important milestone for the life or death of a potential future
impact enterprise. The most telling way to determine whether an impact

enterprise has future potential is to see if there are one or more individuals with a strong conviction about the project's future success and a commitment to invest a decisive part of their life into turning their idea into reality. This typically concludes stage one, and then the hard part – the building of the enterprise – begins. It is at this stage of impact investing in which elea has chosen to focus its energy and resources.

Stage Two: Enterprise development

During the second phase of the journey to create a sustainable impact enterprise, the goal is to build an enduring organization. Unlike during the first phase of rather "light" personal and financial investments, efforts during this phase involve serious (i.e., multiyear) professional and personal commitments by key individuals, and substantial resources (in the hundreds rather than the tens of thousands of U.S. dollars). Investments at this stage, therefore, have a more elevated risk profile.

Despite high expectations that each individual impact enterprise will achieve both long-term financial success and social impact, a positive financial outlook across a portfolio of such ventures at this early stage is not realistic; their strategic and organizational viability is too uncertain, and their leadership structure is often unstable. Consequently, the risk of failure is high. In addition, the small size of an investment relative to the high cost of both sourcing and due diligence before an investment is made, as well as the advice and support provided during the active period of an investment, put an additional burden on expected net returns. Finally, according to our experience, successful ventures in our fields of activity will only outperform by a factor of, maybe, two to five times the invested capital, and not by a factor of a few hundred to a few thousand times, like, for example, in technology start-ups for developed countries. As a consequence, philanthropic capital is needed to fund such a portfolio of early stage ventures in order to complement cash flows from repaid loans and the successful sale of equity from those ventures that developed into successful companies.

Therefore, those claiming that you can "make money" with an impact enterprise often do so only after the success has been achieved; that is, with the benefit of hindsight and by focusing on the few highly successful survivors, thereby conveniently forgetting about all the efforts that were required to create that success. An often more accurate characterization

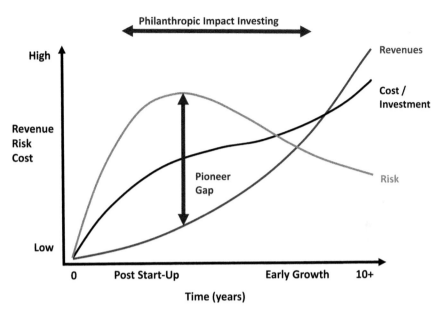

Figure 4.3 The pioneer gap in impact investing.

Source: elea

of this phase of enterprise building is the expression "pioneer gap" (also more depressingly described as the "death valley curve"). These terms are, sometimes, used in the venture capital industry to refer to the dangerous phase in enterprise development when risks are high, the visibility on a positive outcome is still low, and the negative cash flows from operations need to be funded (see Figure 4.3).

Stage Three: Realization of potential

The main characteristic of a stage-three investment is its attractiveness for institutional impact investors that are committed to delivering both impact and financial returns to their beneficiaries. This requires impact companies to have reached a certain size that allows them to absorb significant amounts of financial investments, either in the form of debt or equity. Typically, impact funds consider approximately USD 5 million to be a minimum threshold for a direct investment. The reason for this requirement is that the expenses incurred for sourcing, due diligence, and ongoing support cannot exceed a low single-digit percentage, to ensure that the investment delivers a positive net financial return to its beneficiaries. If the gross return of such an investment is around 5%–7%, it may be able to afford 2% (USD 100,000) to finance such activities and still provide a positive return of 3%–5%. In addition to having a convincing case for social impact and reaching the minimum size to qualify for investment by an institutional impact investor, stage-three impact enterprises need a certain level of strategic clarity, organizational efficiency, leadership stability, and governance effectiveness. These are required to show that they have a plausible investment thesis that is in line with positive financial return targets and limits the risk of underperformance. Given the growing momentum of the impact investing sector, an increasing number of impact enterprises has been meeting these requirements. One of elea's main ambitions in its support of enterprise development efforts is to be the last philanthropic investor in a company that is on its way into stage three.

Listening to commercial impact investors, a particular challenge that they face is finding good investments with attractive financial terms amidst intensive global competition. Government agencies and concessionary capital from development-finance organizations that benefit from subsidized cost of capital tend to push the asset prices of impact enterprises up and their financial-return potential down. The challenge that impact investors face from subsidized concessionary capital is well described by Keith Allman, a former banker who joined the Geneva-based impact investment firm Bamboo Finance:

> Difficulty in sourcing investments that met most investors' social criteria was a theme that echoed across my peers. This led to very competitive situations where some non-traditional investors took approaches that lacked rigor and led to inflated valuations. With costs of capital near zero for these entities, the problems could be sustained, but ultimately, it was no longer commercial investing at that point but a charitable intermediary. ... There are many publications available that have striking images of rural villagers using innovative technologies and compelling stories of impact-oriented companies, but these are largely motivational and show basis causality. It's the day-to-day tasks of impact investors – which involve accounting, corporate finance, valuation, statistical measurement, and social metric analysis – that are the most difficult, but the most important. (Allman, 2015, p. Viii)

He then goes on with his analysis of the sector in saying that "it is not easy to both create a profitable business that has a significant social impact and also scale that business so that it generates commercial returns for investors and continues to progress its social mission" (Allman, 2015, p. 1).

4.1.2 elea's focus on stage-two investments

Stage two is in many ways the most challenging of the three: impact enterprises are still small and often face significant uncertainties regarding their strategic direction and their organizational development, and their leaders more often than not lack experience in certain areas and, therefore, need substantial professional support in addition to financial capital. All of this makes investments at this stage risky and, due to the high transaction and support costs relative to their small size, expensive. So why did elea choose this focus area after having acquired some experience with stage-one projects (such as our contribution to the "Solar for All" business-plan competition)? The first reason is that stage two is critically important for the development and growth of the impact investing sector: without stage two, there is no stage three. Based on our experience, we have not come across development stories of impact enterprises that went directly from business planning to investable companies without first being exposed to all the risks, costs, and uncertainties of stage two for at least a few years.

The second reason is that this investment field is anything but crowded. While there are a few organizations with a similar focus, we could only name one or two dozen globally that follow such an approach.[3] This is underlined by the following quote by Marco Piñatelli, the founder and CEO of Inka Moss in Peru (one of elea's investments), which is an example for other anecdotal evidence of this type. He says,

> elea's willingness to invest equity into our social company is a godsend: we were looking for three years to find a provider of patient social capital. What we did find were organizations that gave us short-term credit for working capital, grants, or funds that were looking for investments of USD 10 million or more.

Third, while risky and expensive, stage-two investments fit with elea's hybrid character as a philanthropic organization with an entrepreneurial mandate. Its philanthropic funding provides elea with the required appetite for innovation and risk, and it allows for patience regarding financial returns. Furthermore, its professional setup makes it possible for elea to offer essential support beyond financial capital. This hybrid aspect is why we came to call what we do philanthropic impact investing,[4] which differs from both stage-one and stage-three investments. Apart from the investments of the start-up entrepreneurs and their families, as well as angels, stage-one investments are often charitable grants to develop an important, yet at the same time quite crowded, component of the impact investing ecosystem. Stage-three investments, on the other hand, do not require philanthropic capital; they are at a scale and have the institutional stability that makes them attractive for impact funds with both impact objectives and financial return targets.

To maximize the probabilities for success, elea looks for the following critical criteria before arriving at a positive investment recommendation:

- The business model of an impact enterprise should be sufficiently visible and tested to allow for a ballpark quantification of the targeted social impact. Without clarity about the mechanism for achieving social impact and some perspective on the range of varying quantities of impact that can be achieved, it is not possible to develop an investment thesis. In the case of Angaza, an in-depth technology assessment from the highly reputable German Fraunhofer Institute was crucial for a positive assessment of this investment. The assessment concluded that the pay-as-you-go technology would work in Kenya given its current mobile telecoms infrastructure, which is still largely based on conventional mobile phones that do not have smartphone functionality or internet access.

- A medium-term path to economic sustainability has to be plausibly articulated. On one hand, this means a view about market potential and current or future competitors that allows for a growing revenue and gross margin projection for the candidate in question. On the other hand, it requires an analysis of both one-time investments and regular running costs that allows for a plausible path to breakeven within 3 to 5 years. If it takes very aggressive assumptions to derive positive gross margins for the foreseeable future, or if initial investments are required of a magnitude that pushes the breakeven point far into the future, say 7 to 10 or even more years, then there is no case for impact enterprise development and other options should be explored; for example, finding a charity with ongoing investment income that is comfortable with sustainably funding a social activity.

- Good ideas, ultimately, only become reality if combined with entrepreneurial energy and relevant skills. Therefore, the third and most critical criterion is the existence of either an individual entrepreneur or an entrepreneurial team that has the essential intrinsic entrepreneurial qualities that are necessary to succeed. These include a plausible motivation that drives the social impact approach, full commitment over five to seven years, resilience, passion, partnership values, and integrity. In addition, the personal chemistry between the entrepreneurs and the elea team should be sufficiently strong to allow for a respectful, trust-based intense collaboration over the years to come. At elea, we talk in this context about the "beer test"; that is, after a full day of substantive work, would we still want to go out for a beer together, or would we feel that the common interest does not go beyond the professional aspect of togetherness.

After 7 to 10 years of more or less intense partnership – while hopefully achieving impact in the range of what was initially aspired to – considerations of exiting the investment become preeminent. elea's ambition is that its active investments reach stage three before exiting, so that elea is the last philanthropic investor during the development journey of an impact enterprise.

4.2 Choosing purposeful investment themes

How can elea's purpose to fight absolute poverty with entrepreneurial means be broken down into specific actionable investment themes? Let us first elaborate on how purpose leads to change and then discuss elea's four investment themes in detail.

4.2.1 Purposeful transformational change

On the world's journey toward a more inclusive capitalism, purpose is a crucial term with growing appeal and a sense of urgency. At the level of organizations, purpose means to clearly articulate and communicate the "why" of an endeavor in order to engage resources for its pursuit. Mere survival or maximizing of profit are no longer enough for a business enterprise to succeed and excite stakeholders who want to know what an organization stands for and understand why it exists.

This is particularly true for the people working for such an enterprise. They want the company's articulated business purpose to be meaningful, authentic, and realistic so that they are able to identify with it and are motivated to align their ambitions, energies, talent, and skills into making it a reality. At the level of individuals, purpose is an important motivational factor that refers to the extent to which somebody feels connected to or receives meaning from their work (Bundgaard & Roy, 2014). More generally, and beyond work, the purpose of life is to express an individual's unique gifts and make a difference in the world (Eisenstein, 2013). Contributing to making things purposeful inspires and energizes, for the human psyche has a fundamental need to find a sense of purpose in life – to transcend the self and connect to something larger. As the living standards of individuals have improved and they have climbed up the needs pyramid developed by psychologist Abraham Maslow, these perspectives have acquired more and more urgency.

Once organizations succeed in aligning their search for purpose with the goals of individual stakeholders, be it team members or investors, the chances that interests across society will be more harmonized will rise. What was found to be true for traditional profit-seeking business enterprises[5] is even truer for companies that are focused on social impact. A purpose that is rooted in a pressing social need may indeed prove to be more efficient in motivating both professionals and impact investors to search for meaning, as our daily experience at elea exemplifies.

Let's look at a few statements among companies in the elea portfolio that refer to their purpose:

> We create the technology that allows business to offer life-changing products to anyone, anywhere … Angaza technology empowers distributors to make life-changing products accessible and affordable to individuals in emerging markets, even those who live on less than USD 2.00 per day … (www.angaza.com)
>
> We transform lives around the world through sustainable training and employment programs that provide a path to lifelong employment and opportunity. (www.digitaldividedata.com)[6]
>
> We aim to make living easier, every day, by delivering underserved consumers and their communities the choice, convenience, and opportunity they deserve through a network of digitally enabled agents located close to their home. (Copia, www.copiaglobal.com)[7]

"Change" and "transform" are terms often used by companies when stating their purpose.[8] This is because purpose, particularly in a social context, frequently aims at innovation (e.g., new markets, products, and processes), and fundamentally transformed business models are often at the heart of making a difference in improving the status and livelihoods of poor people. Some organizations even put transformational change at the heart of their purpose. Ashoka, for example, defines social entrepreneurs primarily as agents of change. Similarly, the World Economic Forum (WEF), one of the best-known platforms for selecting and nurturing the leaders of tomorrow, is "committed to improving the state of the world," and IMD wants to "challenge what is and inspire what could be."

This is where the "Theory of Change" methodology comes in: it is a well-known concept applied in the non-profit and governmental sectors to describe the relationship between the intended impact of social initiatives and their eventual short-term, medium-term, and long-term outcomes.[9] The Theory of Change maps out a social initiative through six stages:

1. Identifying long-term goals (i.e., defining ambitions, objectives, and outcomes) is an important first step in the process.
2. Once long-term goals are identified, considering "what conditions must be in place for us to reach these goals." This includes backwards mapping and connecting the preconditions or requirements necessary to achieve these goals and explaining why these preconditions are necessary and sufficient.
3. Identifying basic assumptions about the context.
4. Defining the interventions that will need to be carried out as part of the initiative to create the desired change.
5. Developing indicators to measure outcomes to assess the performance of the initiative.
6. Writing a narrative to explain the logic of the initiative.

This methodology was derived from the work of Don Kirkpatrick, a professor at the University of Wisconsin who started developing a model for evaluating the success of education in the 1950s. This concept was then adopted in the 1990s by the Roundtable on Community Change of the Aspen Institute to evaluate comprehensive community initiatives. Since then, it has been refined and further developed and is being applied to a broad range of initiatives in the U.S. and globally. Typically, it describes a specific, measurable social-change initiative that forms the basis for strategic planning, ongoing decision-making, and evaluation. Several high-profile philanthropic foundations (e.g., the United States Agency for International Development [USAID], the Rockefeller Foundation, the Ford Foundation, the United Nations Development Program, the World Bank, Amnesty International, and Greenpeace) have adopted this formalized and highly structured methodology as part of their tool kit in impact measurement.

elea has not formally adopted the Theory of Change methodology, but its approach is highly aligned with the thinking behind that theory in terms of identifying and evaluating its investment themes at a systemic level as well as at the level of single investment opportunities. We look for impact models with tangible and highly plausible aspects of change and a high degree of innovation. Our journey has, thus, been an evolutionary process through which we have crystallized both our preferred form of investing – namely, taking stakes in companies rather than sponsoring development projects – as well as our four themes. As we will now elaborate on, these themes all have to do with access: i) access to skills for employability; ii) access to affordable, socially impactful goods and services; iii) access to cash income from global agricultural value chains; and iv) access to digital solutions for better livelihoods.

4.2.2 Access to employable skills building

One of the greatest challenges in fighting absolute poverty is how to equip young people with the necessary skills to earn a living for themselves and their families toward the end of their basic education in school, or afterwards. When young people have a job and earn a decent salary, this not only contributes to wealth creation but also to reducing the risks of political instability, violence, and war in the regions where they live.

With the launch of the UN SDGs and their emphasis on education and lifelong learning (SDG 4) as well as the need to provide decent working conditions for all (SDG 8), the theme of "skills for employability" (or, in World Bank terminology, TVET; i.e., technical and vocational education and training) has received more attention on the global agenda to fight poverty. This is against the background of TVET's rather bad reputation in many poor

countries (particularly in Africa). Indeed, vocational skills development programs face a number of hurdles, the most important of which are

- **Lack of demand:** There are often no companies that have the
  capacity to employ people with apprenticeship qualifications, or
  existing companies have not adopted a mindset that recognizes the
  value of investing in the skills development of young people, both
  for their company's long-term competitiveness and to contribute to
  the larger societal benefits of higher youth employment levels.
- **No effective public-private partnership-based ecosystem**:
  Vocational skills development systems should be embedded within an
  ecosystem of different actors from the private and public sectors (e.g.,
  companies, industry associations, educational institutes, and government departments) to be effective. In many developing countries,
  several pillars of such ecosystems do not exist either due to weak public or private-sector institutions, a lack of capabilities, or a shortage of
  funding. As a result, critical requirements, such as suitable expertise,
  curriculums, certification processes, training infrastructure, and student financing facilities, are often missing.
- **Insufficient employability**: People from poor backgrounds, who
  either grew up in urban slums or in destitute rural areas, often have
  not learned the most basic behaviors and attitudes that form the basis
  for employment in the formal labor market.
- **Lack of appreciation:** Parents, teachers, and opinion leaders in society at large often appreciate people with university degrees that may
  lead to government positions more than those with vocational skills
  qualifications that allow for income generation through craftsmanship.

elea chose this investment theme because of its obvious relevance in the
fight against absolute poverty and because of a need for innovative models
to overcome the challenges of youth unemployment. This theme is also
very close to Swiss DNA, as Switzerland has a centuries-long tradition of
providing apprenticeships for the acquisition of vocational skills based on
a dual system where companies and schools collaborate in effective pri-
vate-public partnerships. This is one of the reasons why Switzerland does
not experience significant youth unemployment. It is, thus, a natural area
where the Swiss Agency for Development and Cooperation (SDC) sees

opportunities to apply its expertise in developing countries (see Context Box 4.1).

CONTEXT BOX 4.1: KEY FACTORS FOR THE SUCCESS OF TECHNICAL AND VOCATIONAL EDUCATION AND TRAINING INITIATIVES (TVET)

The Swiss Agency for Development and Cooperation (SDC) provides a positive example of comprehensive vocational skills development programs. Having been active in this sector for over 60 years, the SDC acknowledges the role of TVET in the fight against poverty and has stepped up its commitment in this field. This agency currently works together with 30 partner countries toward an inclusive, more effective approach to vocational skills development (Swiss Agency for Development and Cooperation [SDC], 2016). The SDC was inspired by the vocational skills development system in Switzerland (VPET = Vocational Professional Education and Training), which has evolved over centuries and is widely seen as a success. It is characterized by the following factors:

- Close cooperation between the public and private sector and their different stakeholders.
- Dual-track approach based on real workplace learning as a complement to classroom training.
- Qualifications developed according to labor market needs.
- Recognition of qualifications throughout Switzerland and internationally.
- Mobility into other parts of the higher education system.

VPET allows employers to recover the costs for the initial phase of education and training in the subsequent phases (Swiss Agency for Development and Cooperation [SDC], 2016, p. 10).[10]

We have already discussed BagoSphere, which is an interesting example of a company that is active in vocational education. Digital Divide Data (DDD) is another elea investment with a special focus on information technology (IT) skills. Unlike BagoSphere, which has activities in the Philippines only, DDD's operations are based on a global model. They service (mostly) international clients with a digital offering, and are interested in "sourcing with impact." Therefore, they are prepared to outsource work to young talented professionals at DDD subsidiaries in Laos, Cambodia, and Kenya. These young professionals, who are carefully selected from backgrounds of absolute poverty (e.g., those living in slums or rural areas), would otherwise have a very limited prospect of learning a trade, finding a job, and making a reasonable income. But thanks to DDD, they are trained in mastering the specific practical skills required to deliver on their tasks. For example, in 2017, DDD's Kenya operation became the first Amazon Web Services (AWS) partner in East Africa with the goal of training young people to master the deployment, management, and operations of cloud platforms. DDD, thus, plays a crucial role in developing a global market for IT talent. Equally important, these young talents receive training in general life skills in such areas as self-awareness and self-confidence, interpersonal behavior, communication skills, and personal ethics and values. They also learn how to develop ambitions, as well as how to set and pursue goals. With the income earned from such activities, these young professionals are in a position to provide livelihoods for themselves and their families, while having the opportunity to embark on a college education.

Amazi is another elea investment in this field. Based in South Africa, Amazi runs a chain of nail and beauty studios that is operated for women of color by women of color. Founder and CEO Divya Vasant observed that most offerings in the beauty market, with premium prices based on expensive global brands, only focus on the upper-class minority of the population. At the same time, recent developments in post-apartheid South Africa have led to the emergence of a low-to-middle-class client segment that also values beauty services and is willing to pay more than they do for the very basic services typically offered by home-based businesses that are often located in communities. Moreover, there is an abundant pool of talented, young women living in low-income communities who are deemed "unemployable" and have no access to the opportunities needed to gain a skill and earn an income. Taking this all into account, Amazi initiated a sophisticated recruiting, assessment, and training program to employ marginalized women (mostly single mothers) as beauty technicians, and to give them the opportunity to advance to more entrepreneurial roles, such as store manager, over time. The three-month intensive training program takes a holistic approach to prepare women to successfully join the formal world of work. Building self-confidence, developing personal abilities, and setting or executing their own personal ambitions and agendas are given as much attention as the technical beauty training they receive, so that their traumatic life stories do not hold these young women back.

In addition to its general investment criteria, elea is looking for the following business-model characteristics when considering investments within this theme:

- A demand-driven educational design based on a deep understanding of employment opportunities and requirements for success.
- Short programs of two to four months (rather than two to three years) that have very concrete, measurable skills development objectives that are directly linked to employment success.
- A state-of-the-art, interactive pedagogy that is often supported by technology.
- A substantial proportion of the curriculum is dedicated to life skills (such as personality building, behavioral development, self-efficacy experience, etc.) within the context of 21st century skills requirements and the future of work debate (www.cognizant.com).
- A special focus on the identification and selection of candidates based on a rigorous, holistic assessment of individual potential and willpower.
- Systematic help in post-program placement through a strong relationship with employers (e.g., long-term alumni community development).

Business models in this field typically have to find a careful balance between profitability and social impact. This is because targeting potential talent in poor rural or urban areas comes with a higher cost than focusing on urban middle classes that already bring a certain level of education and life skills.

4.2.3 Access to affordable, socially impactful goods and services (informal retail and last-mile distribution)

Across poor countries, consumers at the base of the pyramid lack access to affordable basic products and solutions that could dramatically improve their quality of life; for example, hygiene products, nutritional supplements, modern farm tools, mobile phones, or solar-based energy devices.

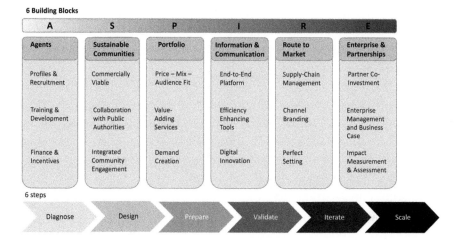

Figure 4.4 The ASPIRE framework for inclusive distribution.

Source: An adaptation based on Unilever

In India alone, this affects over 500 million people, mostly in rural areas, and puts significant pressure on them to migrate to big urban areas. Many business initiatives that have been inspired by this base-of-the-pyramid (BoP) thinking focus on lower-income segments of the new and fast-growing urban middle classes in many developing countries. One example is Jumia, based in Nigeria, which went public in 2019 and claims to be Africa's version of Amazon, targeting urban lower-to-middle-class customers rather than the base of the pyramid.

Global corporations typically have less interest in targeting BoP client segments at absolute poverty levels. One exception is Unilever. Together with the BoP Innovation Center (a Dutch non-profit organization), it launched the "ASPIRE" framework with a focus on absolute poverty as a component of its Sustainable Living Plan, a global corporate responsibility initiative (see Figure 4.4). As part of this plan, Project Shakti has trained over 72,000 female microentrepreneurs in India and has launched similar efforts in Bangladesh, Vietnam, Sri Lanka, and Egypt.[11] Many impact enterprises have also been focusing on how to service poor people in either urban slums or rural areas. In 2018, the World Bank Group published a very extensive review of over 300 impact enterprises (which were grouped into over 40 business models) that have developed market-based solutions for service delivery to poor people in various sectors and geographies (Tinsley & Agapitova, 2018).

So where are the challenges? Why don't we see a larger number of successfully scaled approaches for tackling this important aspect of absolute poverty? Based on our experience, we see four major barriers that need to be overcome:

1. **Consumer behavior and/or product fit**: Poor people have little money and no risk capacity, and they often lack knowledge about how products and services can enhance their quality of life. Products and services are also, sometimes, not designed to fit their specific needs. Entrepreneurs who are active in this area, therefore, face an ethical dilemma: liberal thinking promotes giving the consumer the maximum choice regarding her purchases, but what if these purchases increase rather than reduce poverty, as has occasionally happened? One example of such behavior is the aggressive sale of microloans to people who do not understand the very basics of credit; namely, that credit has a cost in the form of regular interest payments and has to be paid back at some stage.[12] Awareness campaigns would be one way to "nudge" and educate people on the effectiveness, efficiency, quality, and safety of certain products (e.g., in areas such as food, solar lamps, cooking stoves, hygiene articles, etc.). However, such awareness campaigns obviously increase the cost of marketing in market segments characterized by low margins, which often leads to either hybrid models, where campaigns are funded by philanthropic donations, or the cross-subsidization of some products by others.

2. **Difficult logistics at remote locations**: As soon as one leaves the few main roads around urban centers, the traffic in many poor countries becomes very difficult, particularly in Africa. Roads are often in poor condition and transport is slow. Furthermore, logistics companies are notoriously unreliable and corrupt, leading to leakage rates of transported goods at double-digit percentage rates. As a consequence, the cost of logistics is high, and the quality and time to market are poor.

3. **Small scale:** Poor households can only spend small amounts of money and, thus, can only afford to buy a limited number of goods. This limits the overall volumes that can be produced and puts pressure on margins while encouraging price increases. This suggests the need for creative ways to aggregate demand; for example, through agent networks, as was done by Copia (which is described in more detail a few pages further).

4. **Fragmented distribution structures and systems:** Traditionally, basic goods and services are sold and delivered through local traders and mom-and-pop shops, which are often highly fragmented distribution systems that lack professionalism and efficiency. Because of their local market position, particularly in rural areas, they often have pricing power that leads to stunning discrepancies in the cost of basic commodities (e.g., the prices for one kilogram of rice within 30 km of Nairobi can easily vary by 50% or more). Despite their shortcomings, these distribution systems are deeply entrenched in local structures and cannot easily be bypassed.

This important focus area of seeking to provide better access to affordable, life-enhancing goods and services as a means of fighting absolute poverty typically comes second to the focus area of agriculture in terms of its critical importance to the population and the number of people that it employs, as well as the income that it generates. At elea, we decided to follow two avenues to fight absolute poverty in this focus area, the first of which is to help improve individual mom-and-pop shops.

Small mom-and-pop shops are a typical feature of last-mile distribution to poor people. They often determine the day-to-day quality of life for millions by providing access to basic goods and services. They are, therefore, a crucial entrepreneurial cell with a huge social impact. In 2010, elea, together with FUNDES (a non-profit organization focused on microbusiness development in Latin America) launched an effort to improve the productivity, profitability, and impact of 800 mom-and-pop shops in La Paz, Bolivia; there are about 14,000 of these shops in total. These shops are mostly small and operate as "stand-alone" businesses; that is, they are not organized in cooperatives. Moreover, they are typically run by single mothers, with two to four children, who were never trained on how to run such a shop entrepreneurially and efficiently. Their weekly income for hard work over six to seven days is USD80–USD100.

Under the brand name "Mi Caserita," our joint initiative organized a tangible shop improvement effort for 800 shops, with dedicated coaches, each supporting 10 shopkeepers, over a period of five months. During this period, the shops were cleaned and better organized, with products grouped according to needs (e.g., hygiene articles were separated from breakfast products). The shopkeepers were trained to adopt a customer-oriented, entrepreneurial attitude (e.g., being friendly to customers encourages them to return, which leads to better income as a consequence); they introduced a daily recordkeeping booklet to keep track of daily revenue and costs; they met their fellow shopkeepers in the area and agreed on ways to collaborate (e.g., through joint purchasing); and they also met with their suppliers to encourage them to give them more marketing support. On average, half a year after this intervention, income went up by 30%, allowing an additional child to go to school. For a number of the shopkeepers, this initiative was truly life transforming in that they transitioned from mere "survival" mode to becoming passionate entrepreneurs with a perspective toward opportunities and a newly gained self-confidence to change things.

The second avenue chosen by elea to fight absolute poverty in this focus area is to identify and help grow innovative impact enterprises. We have already discussed Dharma Life quite extensively, but it is worthwhile mentioning it here as well, since it is a prime example of an impact enterprise at scale that provides access to impactful goods and services to people in remote areas. Through its hybrid structure and unique Dharma Life Entrepreneurs (DLE) network in India, it facilitates awareness campaigns that are funded by development organizations and corporations through philanthropic contributions. It also operates a distribution system that sells products and services and often facilitates access to credit.

Copia is another scalable, innovative impact enterprise. It serves poor people in rural Kenya with a catalog-based e-commerce approach. Customers can browse through a catalog of useful products at local Copia-agent sales points and place orders via a mobile application. Agents, who typically own a shop or a food stall, then pay Copia via a mobile payment system. Copia delivers goods within two to three days to agent locations where customers can pick them up without having to pay delivery charges. In addition to the agents' network, the other essential component of Copia's model is its logistics process: based on mobile-scanning technology, all ordered goods are traceable, and there is a logistics center that tracks the routes of the trucks and calls the driver in the case of unexpected stops at unusual places. Through this highly rationalized, controlled, technology-supported process, Copia has been able to massively reduce product leakage to a low-single-digit percentage (compared to often high-single-digit or even double-digit percentages in many parts of Africa). In 2017 and 2018, elea invested in two tranches of this promising growth opportunity for Kenya

– and potentially beyond. Furthermore, as a member of Copia's business-development committee, elea contributes its considerable last-mile retail expertise to discussions about new initiatives that have the potential to increase the company's impact and margins.

A similar approach is applied by another one of elea's investee companies, Essmart. This enterprise is building an efficient last-mile distribution channel in India that enables socially impactful goods, such as improved agricultural tools and energy-saving household devices, to reach and impact their intended end customers. Essmart partners directly with small, local mom-and-pop ("kirana") shops that are connected to a network and are supported by product promotions, sales, distribution, and after-sales service. This approach ensures that fairly priced, quality products are available directly at the places where people need them and where they already shop.

Some insights and lessons we have gained through our work with last-mile initiatives include:

- **Clarity about the customer segment and product mission is needed**: This is an area in impact enterprise where the temptation for "a drift in purpose" (i.e., trading off impact against financial returns) is huge. Addressing somewhat more affluent target customers or offering somewhat higher-margin products (with possibly negative consequences for one's quality of life, such as unhealthy food or dangerous electronic devices) is much easier and more profitable, but it eventually goes against the goal of fighting absolute poverty.
- **Digital solutions play a crucial role**: Be it the marketing and customer communication side, internal processes, or logistics, technology has a huge and growing influence on the effectiveness of business models. Together with FUNDES, elea launched an initiative called FUNDES Digital to leverage the decades-long expertise of FUNDES in this field, as well as some of our experience in working with mom-and-pop shops, by developing technological solutions, tools, and methods for them.
- **Understanding customer behavior is key to success:** Poor people have specific behaviors that may not be easily grasped by Western observers and often have deep roots in local cultures. This is particularly true with regard to hygiene and beauty products, as well as services. That is why investing into smart awareness campaigns is an

important element of impact-driven business development. It also calls for entrepreneurial creativity and innovation to adapt both products and distribution processes to local market conditions, thereby finding the right balance between affordable prices and aspirational qualities.

- **Transparency about the consequences of balancing impact and financial return is advisable:** Because of the specific customer behaviors of poor people and the challenging logistics of the regions where they live, there are clear choices to be made in balancing social impact and financial return goals when targeting absolute poverty levels versus lower-middle-income customer business models in this field. It is advisable to be transparent about these choices and how this balance will be achieved, either through hybrid models or by explicit cross-subsidization.[13]

4.2.4 Access to cash income for smallholder farmers from global agricultural value chains

An organization whose purpose is to fight absolute poverty with entrepreneurial means must address smallholder farmers, as they are an important group of people in the developing world who are often stricken by poverty. About two-thirds of the developing world's 3 billion rural people live in about 475 million small-farmer households, working on land plots smaller than two hectares.[14] Many of these households are living based on little more than mere subsistence farming. After feeding their own families and livestock, many of them are unable to produce a significant amount of surplus, which means that the income they earn from the sale of cash crops is far below elea's absolute poverty threshold of USD 3.00 per day. For example, farmers in Zimbabwe's lowlands make approximately USD 100 per annum in cash income. At the same time, farmers represent the prototype entrepreneurs. They were among the first in human history to make decisions about trading off short-term gains (through harvesting crops) for future returns from investments (through saving seeds).

It is a complex area that has been receiving substantial attention by development efforts in recent years and involves a broad spectrum of dimensions that range from national economic policies to evolving farming techniques, all the way up to national and international market structures and development characteristics. In line with elea's background, which is centered on access to globalization opportunities for under-privileged people, we have adopted a niche approach in this large area of alternative poverty-alleviation initiatives. This approach is focused on the (mostly) international commercialization opportunities for specialty agricultural products as a means of enhancing the cash income that small-holder farmers generate beyond that which they need to survive. We, thereby, help many farmers to overcome the typical obstacles that hinder them from selling their products to a larger client base. These mainly consist of insufficient product quality, lack of organization among indi-vidual farmers, insufficient understanding of marketing and sales require-ments, and limited business-management expertise.

As described earlier, Pakka was one of elea's first investments in this area. Pakka is a Swiss food company linked through a strategic coopera-tion with Fair Trade Alliance Kerala (India), a cooperative that covers approximately 5,000 smallholder farmers who produce organic cashew nuts. Pakka succeeded in building a sustainably profitable company that sells (among other products) premium cashew nuts through various chan-nels (both traditional and online) in selected European countries and, thereby, contributes to tangibly increased levels of cash income for these Indian farming families. elea was intensively engaged at the supervisory board level, and occasionally in highly operational matters, to help build Pakka from an early stage start-up to an operationally stable and success-ful impact enterprise.

Based on the experience and insights gained through this invest-ment, elea later made two investments in coffee businesses: Coffee Circle (already described earlier) and, more recently, Vega Coffee (www.vega-coffee.com). Vega Coffee sources specialty coffee from cooperatives in Nicaragua and Colombia and sells it to U.S. universities that are generally keen on expanding their offerings of organic products with acknowl-edged sustainability characteristics. A distinctive feature of Vega Coffee is that it has also trained farmers to roast the coffee beans on-site, thereby contributing to higher levels of local value added and, consequently, to higher cash incomes for smallholder coffee farmers.

Another elea investment is in Zimbabwe: with over two-thirds of the Zimbabwean population living on less than USD 1.25 per day, the lack of income opportunities that would allow Zimbabweans to lead a life beyond mere subsistence is striking. Two local social entrepreneurs set up B'Ayoba (www.bayoba.biz/) to provide a new source of income to remote rural farmers. B'Ayoba instructs rural inhabitants on how to collect fallen fruit from the local baobab trees, process the fruit into powder (and the seeds into oil), and sell the powder on global markets as a vitamin-filled food supplement. Baobab trees take around 30 years to produce fruit and only grow in rural areas, providing a unique opportunity for rural farmers to dominate a supply chain. Through collecting and delivering these fruits, farmers can increase their annual cash income by USD30–USD50 per annum.

Finally, elea has invested in Inka Moss, a company dedicated to the sustainable and ecological production of sphagnum moss, generating employment and income in the poor Andean communities of Peru at altitudes over 3,000 meters above sea level (www.inkamoss.com). Sphagnum moss is applied in horticulture because of its powerful characteristics as a high-performance moisture absorber, its antibacterial protection, and its heavy-metal absorption. This is a distinctive niche product that grows primarily in Chile, China, and New Zealand, in addition to Peru. The clients are large horticulture companies in Japan and parts of Europe (e.g., the Netherlands). elea's growth capital serves to realize opportunities for further expansion of the client base in order to broaden the social impact into additional communities.

As can be derived from these examples, elea looks for the following characteristics (beyond its general investment criteria) when considering investments in this theme:

- Attractive products at quality levels that are demanded by relevant, mostly international, markets.
- Market accessibility at profitable margins.
- Entrepreneurial organizations that effectively integrate and provide income to individual smallholder farming families.
- Solutions that ensure the availability of required working capital, which is often a big challenge for smallholder farmers, as financial institutions rarely grant credit on fair terms. More recently, peer-to-peer lending or crowdfunding concepts appear to be promising in this respect.

Businesses involved in agricultural value chains often benefit from investing in employee education. This is, however, expensive and puts them at a disadvantage when compared to similar activities in developed markets (where such education is often realized at the expense of governments). Hybrid models, whereby parts of an impact enterprise are funded through philanthropic donations that target specific educational efforts, are one solution for addressing this challenge.

4.2.5 Access to digital solutions for better livelihoods

The fourth investment theme refers to new technologies and digital solutions. On one hand, it is arguably the most impactful of all, as we have seen with Angaza. On the other hand, it is the one that is the least well defined in terms of the underlying theory of change due to its innovative character. It can include products, services, processes, platforms, and data that tend to overlap with the other three themes discussed: employable skills building programs often involve technological solutions for blended learning, informal retail and last-mile distribution models incorporate technological solutions, such as e-commerce and logistics tracking, and many global agricultural value-chain models require digital solutions for their supply and product collection, as well as their sales and distribution efforts.

Strengthening the financial inclusion of poor people is a large investment theme where digital solutions find effective application. One such investment that elea has made in this field is awamo (www.awamo.com). Only a small minority of the adult population in Sub-Saharan Africa is served by either a regulated or an unregulated credit bureau, which means that an estimated 400 million people lack access to credit. Existing financial institutions are highly immobile and rely on paper-based, non-transparent processes, thus creating multiple opportunities for fraudulent behavior. Additionally, many people do not have valid identity documents. The resulting financial services are inefficient and expensive and lead to stagnated economic growth.

To counter these problems, awamo established a digital mobile-banking platform and credit bureau that is designed especially for microfinance institutions (MFIs) and their clients in the unregulated market; their technology allows for increased security and less fraud. The company was set up in 2017, and its new technological solution has already been implemented among 350 MFIs, serving over 630,000 clients (as of the end of

2019). These clients are building a credit history that, in the medium-term, can positively impact their risk assessment and enable them to access finance at more affordable conditions. Negative credit histories, in turn, can help prevent these clients from becoming overindebted. awamo's vision is to create systemic change in the whole credit market, thereby meaningfully contributing to increased levels of financial inclusion. elea supports awamo with capital, management support, and access to its network. As an active member of their supervisory board, elea helps coach awamo's leadership team in managing its strategic growth and strengthening its organization at all levels.

Another example is iCow (www.icow.co.ke), a mobile application that provides smallholder farmers in Eastern Africa access to an extensive library of agricultural content for mobile-based learning over text messaging (i.e., SMS). Approximately 75% of people in Kenya make their living from farming. Although many countries, including Kenya, have a network of agricultural extension officers in place that should support the farming communities, access to information and know-how remains difficult. This is especially unfortunate as often a very little, but relevant, insight can lead to a significant improvement in the lives of families living from subsistence agriculture.

Su Kahumbu, the founder and a passionate organic farmer who is recognized as a pioneer in the agricultural sector, established iCow with the mission to inspire, enable, and support farmers across Africa. Having provided tips and advice to farmers through *The Organic Farmer* magazine, she conceptualized a scalable learning platform for smallholder farmers based on mobile-phone technology. One example is a gestation calendar with a sequence of over 100 messages, at 160 characters each, which is used during the nine months that a cow carries a calf. The goal of this calendar is to increase a farmer's income through increased productivity, improved livestock health, and reduced mortality. iCow has developed into a unique platform that provides genuine support to the whole ecosystem of smallholder farmers where it is available. The platform provides farmers with access to best practices and knowledge in livestock, crop production, farmer health, and soil fertility. It also connects them with experts and other vital stakeholders within their ecosystems. Since its launch, iCow has grown its customer base to more than 70,000 subscribers, many of whom have been receiving messages for several consecutive years.

4.3 Growth and scale

In all of its investments, elea looks for possibilities to scale up in order to maximize impact and support economic viability. Therefore, it is continuously seeking to identify leverage factors that can contribute to the accelerated growth of impact enterprises. In management and financial literature, the use of the term leverage is rather technical and describes the financial structure of a company regarding the proportion of debt to equity. It explains how the capital base of an enterprise can be expanded (i.e., leveraged) by accessing credit to complement equity, thus enlarging a company's balance sheet. However, in more general terms, and within the context of impact investing, leverage describes a mechanism by which a relatively small initial action results in a substantial, overproportional effect.

Impact-oriented enterprises typically use leverage to scale up their business activities. Given the positive influence of scale on both financial sustainability and impact, finding appropriate leverage mechanisms is of crucial importance to ensure the best use of scarce resources. In our experience, several different single leverage factors can be observed, such as organizational development, geographic extension, and technology deployment. These are not mutually exclusive but are rather combined in powerful business models.

4.3.1 Learnings from elea examples

Let us now take a look at a few examples of dominant leverage factors from elea's investment portfolio:

Organization: From 500 to 40,000 villages in India

Dharma Life's network has massively expanded its scale in recent years. When elea invested in 2014, it served approximately 500 villages. Today, its network of Dharma Life Entrepreneurs (DLEs) comprises about 16,000 DLEs, reaching approximately 40,000 villages and over 13 million people through its products and services and its awareness campaigns. Its leverage model builds on training and deploying DLEs to remote rural areas. In addition to market-based revenue from the sale of goods and services, its extensive reach at the base of the pyramid in India attracts philanthropic donations from private foundations, global corporations, and official aid agencies. One of their programs is called "Internet Saathi," through which Dharma Life (on behalf of Tata Trust and Google) has trained more than four million rural women on how to use smartphones and the internet. Also key to achieving leverage and scaling up a business is IT expertise, elea provided Dharma Life with a Swiss IT professional who advised on strategic IT questions, helped to implement a state-of-the-art enterprise-resource-planning and monitoring system, and built an internal development team to reduce dependence on external specialists. To further develop their IT systems, elea also introduced Dharma Life to Accenture Switzerland, which assists them in creating the right IT structures for their growing organization.

Geography: From La Paz to Nairobi

Based on the great success of the mom-and-pop shops program in La Paz (Bolivia) together with FUNDES, the idea was expanded in La Paz to the hairdressing sector, with similar positive results. As the method is generic and mom-and-pop shops exist in most poor countries, a similar project (the "Smart Dukas" program) was implemented in Nairobi, Kenya. The driving force for this project in Kenya was an international consulting project of MBA students at IMD that was commissioned and guided by elea. It analyzed the project in La Paz, identified other urban areas with similar retail distribution structures and characteristics, looked at possible local implementation partners, and came up with Nairobi as the location and TechnoServe as the local partner for carrying out the replication. After a highly successful transfer of methods from La Paz to Nairobi that yielded similarly attractive impact results, in 2019 elea decided to extend the program further with a special focus on creating business groups among shops and partnerships with large companies. Based on the successful pilot project with elea, TechnoServe was able to mobilize capital from other fund providers to expand the footprint of this effort in Nairobi and extend it to other cities in Kenya.

Technology: From 500 to 70,000 farmers

When elea first spotted iCow, it was serving approximately 500 farmers. Together with Accenture Switzerland, a strategic assessment was performed as a result of which the technology platform was massively upgraded. In addition, iCow entered a strategic alliance with Safaricom, the dominant telecommunications provider in Kenya, which helped to further expand iCow's reach. Over time, iCow's service was offered in Ethiopia and Tanzania as well. By the end of 2019, it served significantly more than 70,000 farmers. Su's dream is to cover one million cows with her program. Besides technology, an ecosystem approach is being pursued to achieve a larger scale and to strive for Africa-wide systemic change, leveraging partners such as the African Dairy Genetic Gain program. This program was initiated in 2015 and is funded by the Bill and Melinda Gates Foundation. Its main goal is to increase milk productivity in African dairy farming.

So what can we learn about leverage from these three examples? Leverage is the point where capital meets entrepreneurship. A necessary condition for an effective leverage model is entrepreneurial vision and ambition. In the case of Dharma Life and iCow, it was Gaurav Mehta's and Su Kahumbu's personal ambitions to make a difference by scaling up their businesses. In the case of mom-and-pop shops, it was elea's global scope that encouraged us to connect such distant areas as Bolivia in South America and Kenya in Eastern Africa, and to create an integrated leverage model. However, without capital, founder ambitions remain dreams without impact, because only capital can provide the necessary financial, technical, and human resources to make a leverage mechanism work in reality.

Technology is typically the most powerful single leverage factor that can help realize founder ambitions for scaling up a business. Take a look at elea's most impactful companies: mobile data and mobile money was essential in the case of Angaza, mobile phone and SMS communication proved instrumental in the case of iCow, and internet-based e-commerce was crucial for scaling up the Coffee Circle business, to name just three examples. That is why elea has emphasized IT skills from the outset, both from internal resources as well as via the strategic partnership with Accenture Switzerland.

That said, technology is typically not the only leverage factor, and it often works only when combined with others. The combination with organizational and talent development, in particular, can be extremely effective. Dharma Life leveraged its business model by focusing on recruiting and developing entrepreneurial talent with effective technological support in logistics, and this enabled the buildup of a network with a capacity to reach many millions of people. Dharma's combination of the commercially oriented components of its business model with more philanthropically oriented ones also helped it to scale up its business. While complicated from an organizational and leadership point of view, such combinations allow an impact enterprise to tap into different sources of capital and can be instrumental in helping them to scale up their business model in order to realize their full potential.

4.3.2 *Understanding leverage mechanisms*

A look at the oldest network of impact enterprises in Europe – and one of the most successful – may be useful for understanding how these combinations can work (bearing in mind elea's neutral stance on religions). Christian monasteries built massive organizations covering large parts of Europe in the 11th and 12th centuries (see Context Box 4.2). Thus, there are a number of relevant parallels between monasteries and impact enterprises that may inspire lessons to be learned. Both have the following characteristics:

1. Economic cross-subsidization between commercial and charitable activities to achieve economic independence.
2. Hybrid funding models that combined market revenue and charitable donations.
3. A strong focus on organization building, with decentralized, semi-autonomous cells and specialist management skills as the main instruments for sustained impact.
4. Organic development and an emphasis on leadership as a key means of leverage for scaling up.

CONTEXT BOX 4.2: MEDIEVAL MONASTERIES AS INITIAL MODELS FOR AN IMPACT ENTERPRISE

In the fourth to fifth centuries AD, a distinctive blend of Greek philosophy and Christian beliefs contributed over time to replace traditional hierarchies of antique Roman and Greek societies with ideas of individual conscience and will, of equitable individual liberty, and universal human rights. One of the expressions of this trend was the emerging and subsequent reforms of monasticism in Europe. Around 540 AD, Benedict of Nursia defined a rule that would provide a blueprint for Western monasticism during the following centuries. "Ora et labora" (pray and work) was one of its key statements. After the collapse of the Carolingian era, in 910 AD, the abbey of Cluny was founded with a view to reform monasticism toward stricter adherence to Benedict's rule and an ambition to create a network of monasteries:

> By the end of the tenth century, the Cluniac reform movement was sufficiently strong and confident to have hopes of reshaping the church and society at large. That strength and confidence turned on a new independence of liberty of the church ... Monastic communities were becoming harbingers of a new world. Within their confines, disciplined lives gave a dignity to labor, further dispelling the stigma of ancient slavery ... By the year 1000 AD, monasteries were becoming models rather than refuges. Monastic labor would soon be engaged in reclaiming and clearing enormous tracts of land in Europe, helping to create the agricultural landscape that survives even now. (Siedentop, 2013)

The Cistercian order, one of the offspring organizations of Cluny, reached such a scope and importance that it is seen as a forerunner of capitalism. Its monastic organization and its individual monasteries were in many ways a prototype of today's impact enterprises. Its priors and monks combined prayers with manual craftsmanship, thriving for spiritual and idealistic outcomes on one hand and material resources that would allow for economic independence on the other. Monastic economic structures followed – what we would today call a hybrid model: revenue was gained not only from selling products and services on markets but also from the charitable donations of nobles. There was substantial cross-subsidization between their agricultural and trading activities (e.g., crops, wine, and book production) and charitable goods and services (offering education to talented youths and shelter to destitute people).

The Carthusians, another monastic order during that time, divided their monasteries into an upper house (domus superior) and a lower house (domus inferior). The upper house was inhabited by monks who dedicated their lives to contemplation and intellectual work. The lower house belonged to lay brothers who labored on the land and tended the livestock. The lower house was the economic center of every Carthusian monastery.

Monasteries increasingly followed skills-based organizational principles. Already according to Benedict, the role of the cellarer was the most important lay leadership position at a monastery. He was responsible for the material well-being of the community and managed the economy, including the supervision of hired labor. Benedict's rule said: *"The ideal cellarer was prudent, of mature character, temperate, not a great eater, not proud, not headstrong, not rough-spoken, not lazy, not wasteful, but a God-fearing man who may be like a father to the whole community" (quoted in [Jamroziak, 2015, p. 57]).*

In the later middle ages, some Cistercian communities created differentiated administrative roles, such as the procurator, who represented abbots in legal and business matters, or the bursar, who supervised cash income. Specialized tools and methods were developed to support leaders: the Cistercians applied rational cost accounting and moved capital around from one venue to another. In 1495, the general chapter in Grande Chartreuse (the Carthusian mother house) demanded that every monastery submit an annual financial report, which was revised by a vicar, a procurator, and at least two monks.

The most critical leadership position was, of course, the abbot: the selection process and criteria for choosing abbots evolved and always included elements of bottom-up proposals by the monks and top-down confirmation by the responsible bishop. The qualities that monastic communities valued in their leaders was a combination of spiritual, moral, and practical skills, which is why these roles were so demanding that retirements and resignations were not unheard of.

The growth strategies pursued by monastic orders, such as the Cistercians who created a network of over 700 monasteries all over Europe, was essentially based on organic development. The key was leadership, in that successful monasteries sent promising leaders to other places with mandates to create offspring monasteries (see [Siedentop, 2013]; [Jamroziak, 2015]; [Mlinaric]).

Both the insights from elea examples as well as this historic excursion into the ancient world of Christian monasteries show that leverage models are complicated and driven by several different factors. Accordingly, it is advisable to understand the cause and effect relationships between such factors. We find the flywheel concept to be a helpful tool to guide and inspire such reflections. This concept was first published in Jim Collins's book *Good to Great* (Collins, 2001) and is based on the notion that innovations and changes rarely happen in one fell swoop. Rather, they occur through a process in which different components work together in a pro-cyclical way, like the relentless pushing of a giant, heavy flywheel that, turn upon turn, builds momentum until it reaches a point of breakthrough (see: www.jimcollins.com). In our experience, applying this concept in practice is particularly helpful for identifying the single success factors,

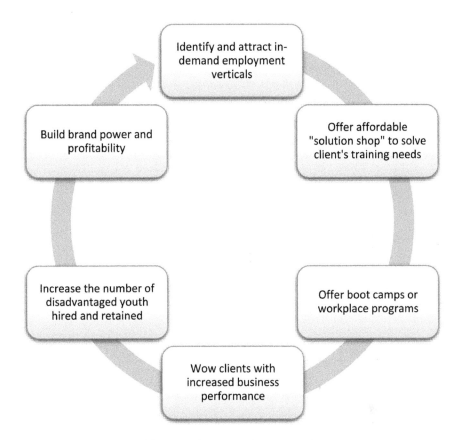

Figure 4.5 The flywheel framework (BagoSphere example).

Sources: www.jimcollins.com, elea

understanding the positive (and possibly negative) reinforcing relation-ships among them, and prioritizing a small number of those that really matter (i.e., where the focus should be placed). Such discussions not only clarify strategic directions but also support alignment on strategic per-spectives and priorities within the leadership team. (For an illustration with BagoSphere as an example, see Figure 4.5.)

Applying the flywheel concept may also trigger the possibly most pow-erful leverage factor of all; that is, managerial creativity. In his book *Leap*, IMD Professor Howard Yu researches why some companies survive for over a hundred years, and his conclusion is that such corporations were able to leap forward in their history by reinventing their businesses. He differentiates between puzzles, where more data is the key to a solution, and mysteries, where not even the question to be answered is clear (Yu, 2018). Looking back on some of our investments at elea, the real leverage, indeed, came from creative innovations. One example is Angaza, when the model was changed from a vertical strategy as a solar lamp manufacturer to a B2B strategy as a technology provider. Another example is Dharma Life, which undertook a bold shift from male to female DLEs, recognizing the increased leverage of women with families versus men.

4.4 Conclusions

4.4.1 Insights and takeaways

Finding the right investment focus is the task where the subtitle of this book – *A Learning Journey Toward Sustainable Impact* – fits best. What does "right" mean? It is about choosing themes and specific investments where there is a need and an opportunity for impact, while ensuring that these investments are suitable for the capacity, character, and capabilities of the investment organization in their quest to make a difference. One crucial insight across the four themes has been to establish a clear link to a big, relevant aspect of the fight against absolute poverty with entrepreneurial means, such as rural poverty or youth unemployment. Also, elea looks for underlying theories of change that are simple and "obviously plausible" to avoid having to consider complicated second- and third-order consequences. Finally, the focus is always on locally embedded initiatives rather than on "good ideas from the Western World that could help people in other parts of the world," as these are more likely to be successful.

The evolutionary path of finding the right themes and types of investment resembles a funnel more than a straight and speedy runway toward a clearly designated signpost. At elea, we started broadly: We invested in a business-plan competition and found out that this activity field is rather crowded. We engaged in companies as well as in development projects and learned that true entrepreneurial initiatives are much more sustainable and scalable. We invested in energy and water infrastructure and gained the insight that there are other types of organizations that are much better positioned than we are to succeed in such areas of engagement. Our ability to take our time to experiment and take risks allowed us to crystallize those focus areas and investment themes that we have described in this chapter.

Thanks to our institutional setup, we have been able to capitalize on the experiences we have had and the lessons we have learned throughout our journey. With our small professional team and high degree of continuity, we have always documented what we have learned, reflected on successes and failures, and adapted our approach. In doing so, we have maintained and updated an institutional memory that not only prevents us from making the same mistakes twice, it continuously nurtures our expertise and industry insights and gives us increasing levels of confidence to tackle ever more challenging investment propositions.

When deciding which investments are the right ones to invest in, elea strives to achieve leverage and scale, for the ultimate integration between entrepreneurship and capital is leverage. While an ambitious vision and an attractive theme based on a purposeful theory of change can go a long way to achieving impact and innovation, having the right leverage mechanism helps to maximize the use of capital. Here, the right leverage mechanism is typically a combination of factors that calls for entrepreneurial leadership skills in the areas of planning, organization, and execution, which is the topic dealt with in the next chapter of this book.

4.4.2 *Your point of view*

Learning objectives

After studying this chapter, you should be able to

1. differentiate between the "three stages of impact enterprise development," identify the phase in which elea invests, and explain the rationale behind this decision;
2. evaluate the practical implications of developing a theory of change for impact investment decisions;
3. describe the criteria used by elea to arrive at positive investment recommendations;
4. analyze and give examples of elea's investment themes and explain the rationale behind each theme to fight absolute poverty with entrepreneurial means; and
5. explain the importance of leverage when integrating entrepreneurship and capital, illustrate different leverage factors, and describe how they can be combined.

Reflection questions

1. If you are an entrepreneur, in which development phase is your enterprise? Would you contact a philanthropic impact investor such as elea for funding? Please use "the three stages of impact enterprise development" and justify.

2. If you are an entrepreneur, what is your theory of change? What is your investment theme and the narrative that explains the impact of your initiative? Explore potential alternative investment themes and evaluate them against each other. What is their specific purpose, and how do they relate to the "big societal challenges"? Why could they be attractive for both entrepreneurs and investors?

3. If you are an investor, put yourself in elea's shoes. Do you know any impact-oriented enterprises that you could recommend to elea for investment? Choose one and explain your rationale.

4. Think like an impact investor: would you recommend other investment theme(s) for elea to explore in its fight against absolute poverty with entrepreneurial means? If so, why?

5. After reading this chapter, what are the advantages and challenges of each of the four investment themes that elea has chosen? How do they compare in terms of attractiveness? Which theme would you favor, and why?

Right vs. right dilemma: Diversified vs. concentrated portfolio

Impact investments are risky. At the same time, understanding diverse investment themes, distinctive theories of change, and alternative business models is challenging. A portfolio of impact investments can be designed with two sets of guiding principles in mind. If the primary objective is to protect capital and minimize risk through diversification, a broad selection of investment opportunities along several independent risk factors should be pursued, such as by theme, geography, or type of business model. If the idea is to maximize impact and control risk by leveraging experience, insight, and expertise, then the portfolio construction should rather be based on a narrow choice of investment opportunities with concentrated bets on a certain theme in one geographical area, possibly combining business models that reinforce each other's impact within one ecosystem.

Put together two hypothetical portfolios of impact investments with alternative diversification and concentration parameters. Then debate the pros and cons of each portfolio type.

Notes

1. For similar frameworks, see (Petch, 2016); (Bhattacharyya, 2016).
2. Examples are: (Mentorphile, 2018); (Plano, 2013); (Martucci).[no year]
3. Organizations that we regularly meet that have similar approaches are Acumen (www.acumen.org), Mercy Corps Social Ventures (www.mercycorps.org), the Shell Foundation (www.shellfoundation.org) – however, only for grants, not for loans or equity, LGT Venture Philanthropy (www.lgtvp.com), and the Global Partnerships Social Venture Fund (www.globalpartnerships.org).
4. Balandina Jaquier sets venture philanthropy apart from impact investing in that the former neither requires nor expects a return of principal (Balandina Jaquier, 2011, p.20). With our three-stage model, we rather see impact investment opportunities as gradually evolving through philanthropic stages up to the achievement of systematic net financial returns.
5. (Bartlett & Ghoshal, 1994); (Gartenberg, Prat, & Serafeim, 2019); (Henderson & Van den Steen, 2015); (Muñoz, Cacciotti, & Cohen, 2017); (Quinn & Thakor, 2018); (Whiteley & Whiteley, 2006)
6. Digital Divide Data (DDD) is a U.S.-based social enterprise that recruits young, talented people from disadvantaged circumstances in Laos, Cambodia, and Kenya and provides them with IT training and IT work, so that they can develop professional skills and earn a living while pursuing a college degree.
7. Copia is one of the fastest growing enterprises in Kenya, offering basic and socially impactful goods to poor regions around urban centers.
8. Terminology can, sometimes, be confusing. In practice, there is no clearly accepted distinction between mission and purpose. In our daily work at elea, we use the terms purpose (why), vision (what), and values (how).
9. The Center for Theory of Change has an official website www.theoryofchange .org, which was created in 2002 and is itself a non-profit organization that was established to promote quality standards and best practice for the development and implementation of the Theory of Change. Its particular focus is on international development, sustainability, education, human rights, and social change. A free software tool to help develop a Theory of Change diagram is available on this website.

10. See also lessons from China's skills development efforts in Africa: (World Bank, 2018).
11. http://www.bopinc.org/updates/our-expertise-in-last-mile-distribution
12. For further examples, see also (Banerjee & Duflo, 2011), the "classic" book on this topic based on many years of empirical research about poverty by MIT's Poverty Action Lab.
13. See also the Shell Foundation's lessons learned in this field (Gomes & Shah, 2018). The Shell Foundation was the first significant external investor in Dharma Life. Their lessons in many ways parallel our own lessons, and we fully agree with their overall conclusions that, despite all the challenges, more social enterprise investments in this sector are both warranted and attractive.
14. For a comprehensive economic analysis of smallholder farming in nine developing countries, see (Food and Agriculture Organization of the United Nations [FAO], 2015).

References

Allman, K. A. (2015). *Impact Investment.* New Jersey: Wiley.

Balandina Jaquier, J. (2011). Guide to Impact Investing For Family Offices and High Net Worth Individuals: Managing Wealth for Impact and Profit.

Banerjee, A. V., & Duflo, E. (2011). *Poor Economics: A Radical Rethinking of the Way to Fight Global Poverty.* New York: Public Affairs.

Bartlett, C. A., & Ghoshal, S. (1994). Changing the Role of Top Management: Beyond Strategy to Purpose. *Harvard Business Review, 72(6),* 79–88.

Bhattacharyya, S. (2016, December 15). *The 5 Stages of Startup Development.* Your Story. Retrieved May 6, 2020, from https://yourstory.com/2016/12/five-stages-startup-development

Bundgaard, H., & Roy, J. (2014). *The Motivated Brain.* CreateSpace Independent Publishing Platform.

Collins, J. (2001). *Good to Great.* London: Random House.

Eisenstein, C. (2013). *The More Beautiful World Our Hearts Know Is Possible.* North Atlantic Books.

Food and Agriculture Organization of the United Nations (FAO) (2015). *The Economic Lives of Smallholder Farmers.* Rome: FAO.

Gartenberg, C., Prat, A., & Serafeim, G. (2019). Corporate Purpose and Financial Performance. *Organization Science, 30(1),* 1–234, C2.

Gomes, R., & Shah, M. (2018). *Last-Mile Solutions for Low-Income Customers.* Shell Foundation. Retrieved May 6, 2020, from https://shellfoundation.org/ app/uploads/2018/10/Shell-Foundation_Last-Mile-Distribution-Report.pdf

Henderson, R., & Van den Steen, E. (2015). Why Do Firms Have "Purpose"? The Firm's Role as a Carrier of Identity and Reputation. *American Economic Review, 105(5)*, 326–330.

Jamroziak, E. (2015). *The Cistercian Order in Medieval Europe: 1090-1500.* London: Routledge.

Martucci, B. (n.d.). *How to Win a Startup Pitch Competition - 12 Tips for Business Success.* Moneycrashers.com. Retrieved January 16, 2019, from https:// www.moneycrashers.com/startup-pitch-competition-guide/

McKenzie, D. (2015, August). Identifying and Spurring High-Growth Entrepreneurship: Experimental Evidence from a Business Plan Competition. *Policy Research Working Paper 7391. World Bank Group.*

Mentorphile. (2018, July 19). *The Pros and Cons of Business Plan Contests.* mentorphile.com. Retrieved January 19, 2019, from https://mentorphile .com/2017/07/19/the-pros-and-cons-of-business-plan-contests/

Mlinaric, J. (n.d.). The Economy of Cistercian and Carthusian Monasteries in Slovenia. Retrieved May 6, 2020, from http://www.eheritage.si/DDC/ DDC_007_006_SIHXTNDQJWVGGYJLRYUDXVTWCZPUIW.pdf

Muñoz, P., Cacciotti, G., & Cohen, B. (2017, October). The Double-Edged Sword of Purpose-Driven Behavior in Sustainable Venturing. *Journal of Business Venturing, 33(2)*, 149–178.

Petch, N. (2016, February 29). The Five Stages of Your Business Lifecycle: Which Phase Are You In? *Entrepreneur Middle East.* Retrieved May 6, 2020, from https://www.entrepreneur.com/article/271290

Plano, L. (2013, April 10). *Are Business Plan Competitions Worth Entering? Part 1: Pros & Cons.* Planoandsimple.com. Retrieved January 16, 2019, from https://www.planoandsimple.com/are-business-plan-competitions-worth-entering-part-1-pros-cons/

Quinn, R. E., & Thakor, A. V. (2018). Creating a Purpose-Driven Organization. *Harvard Business Review, 96(4)*, 78–85.

Schumpeter, J. A. (1976). *Capitalism, Socialism and Democracy.* London: Allen & Unwin.

Siedentop, L. (2013). *Inventing the Individual: The Origins of Western Liberalism.* Penguin.

Swiss Agency for Development and Cooperation (SDC) (2016). *Vocational Skills Development; Key to Employment and Income*. Bern: SDC.

TechnoServe. (2009). *Business Plan Competition Study 2009, a TechnoServe Practice Brief*. TechnoServe. Retrieved May 6, 2020, from https://www .technoserve.org/resources/business-plan-competition-study-2009- a-technoserve-practice-brief/

Thomas, D. F., Gudmundson, D., Turner, K., & Suhr, D. (2014). Business Plan Competitions and Their Impact on New Ventures' Business Models. *Journal of Strategic Innovation and Sustainability* Vol. 10(1), pp. 34–48. Retrieved October 14, 2019, from http://m.www.na-businesspress.com/ JSIS/DThomasWeb10-1.pdf

Tinsley, E., & Agapitova, N. (2018). *Reaching the Last Mile - Social Enterprise Business Models for Inclusive Development*. Washington: The World Bank.

Whiteley, A., & Whiteley, J. (2006, January). *Core Values and Organizational Change: Theory and Practice*. World Scientific Publishing Company.

Yu, H. (2018). *Leap - How to Thrive in a World Where Everything Can Be Copied*. New York: Hachette Book Group.

Amazi

Figure 1 Amazi beauty technicians serving customers in a store in Johannesburg (South Africa).

Source: AMAZI Beauty Pty Ltd

Angaza

Figure 1 Customer training on the use of Angaza powered solar lamps in rural Kenya.

Source: Angaza Design Inc.

Figure 2 Marketing campaign for pay-as-you-go solar lamps in Kenya.

Source: Angaza Design Inc.

Figure 3 Angaza founder Lesley Marincola receives the Skoll award 2018.

Source: Skoll Foundation

BagoSphere

Figure 1 BagoSphere founder Zhihan Lee.

Source: elea

Figure 2 BagoSphere's skills training in the Philippines.

Source: BagoSphere Pty Ltd.

B'Ayoba

Figure 1 Collecting baobab fruits in Zimbabwe.

Source: David Brazier

Baobab

Figure 1 A cracked baobab fruit with the powder-mantled seeds.

Source: David Brazier

Coffee Circle

Figure 1 Coffee Circle founder Martin Elwert with smallholder farmers in Ethiopia.

Source: Circle Products GmbH

Figure 2 Drying beans for Coffee Circle in Ethiopia.

Source: Circle Products GmbH

Digital Divide Data

Figure 1 Digital Divide Data's IT skills classroom in Nairobi (Kenya).

Source: Digital Divide Data

Dharma Life

Figure 1 Dharma Life founder Gaurav Mehta.

Source: Stefan Kappeler, elea

Figure 2 Dharma Life Entrepreneurs (DLEs) in a rural village in India.

Source: elea

Essmart

Figure 1 An Essmart partner shop in India.

Source: Adrian Ackeret, elea

iCow

Figure 1 A smallholder farmer in rural Kenya checking SMS messages from iCow.

Source: Barbara Minishi

Inka Moss

Figure 1 Farmer communities collect white sphagnum moss in the Peruvian Andes.

Source: Ana Elisa Sotelo

Figure 2 Drying white sphagnum moss in Inka Moss' facility in Jauja (Peru).

Source: Ana Elisa Sotelo

Smart Dukas

Figure 1 Smart Duka shop keeper in Nairobi (Kenya).

Source: TechnoServe Inc.

5

BUILDING AND LEADING AN IMPACT ENTERPRISE

Let us now switch perspectives. In the previous two chapters, we took the vantage point of a philanthropic impact investment organization when looking at impact enterprises. In this fifth chapter, we will adopt the point of view of a single impact enterprise. How should an impact-focused company set its aspirations and objectives? How should it be organized and run so that it can navigate through the inevitable ups and downs? What are helpful guidelines, methods, and tools to support the development and growth of such an enterprise, and how can an active investor best contribute?

It is at this very practical level where entrepreneurial talent, energy, and momentum combine with capital (both financial and non-financial) to achieve impact and innovation and to leverage the business to achieve growth. In most of its currently active investments in impact enterprises, elea works in close partnership with the leadership teams to support them in their impact value creation tasks, contribute experience and expertise, and act as a sounding board by reviewing their progress, challenging them in their views, and actively helping them to find practical solutions to problems.

At the core, designing, planning, building, and running an enterprise is about leadership and its essential tasks, which include defining a purpose and setting directions, building a team and organizing tasks, getting things done, and navigating through ups and downs. In addition to entrepreneurial qualities, carrying out such tasks requires leadership talent, skills, and relevant experience. These are, in our experience, the scarcest resources and the real bottlenecks to effectively integrating entrepreneurship and capital. To accomplish these tasks well typically calls for a combination of founder entrepreneurs and experienced professional executives.

Leadership is a field in which potentially huge synergies can be realized with the traditional corporate world. Many leadership practices are generic and can be applied to any organization, whether private or public, or in civil society. Therefore, an inclusive approach with bridge-building mechanisms can be helpful.[1] However, there are also traps to avoid: the transfer of methods and tools from the corporate world can easily overwhelm early stage, young enterprises that have a focus on impact, as they often lack relevant experience and are severely resource constrained. Translating and adjusting corporate practice to the specific circumstances of impact-oriented enterprises to make them relevant and useful should be one of the core strengths and capabilities of a philanthropic impact investor (as is the case at elea).

In the first section of this chapter, we will explore how visions, plans, and models can clarify purpose and direction as a first crucial step in building an impact enterprise. While a controversial field, it is our conviction at elea that visions, plans, and models are critical for making the case to deploy capital and for balancing ambitions and realism. Understanding the different components of impact value creation and how they relate to one another is a necessary foundation for designing roadmaps, establishing priorities, creating resource commitments, defining action plans, and ultimately, achieving positive results, both in terms of impact and financial returns.

That said, it is not necessarily an inspirational vision, a good plan, or a plausible model that will make or break an enterprise. Rather, as we will discuss in Section Two, it depends on whether one can build an effective leadership team and an organization that attracts talented people and encourages them to carry out the necessary tasks. Without such people who work together in alignment to progress on their journeys toward the stated goals, there is no impact. On this basis, the leadership team, together with their colleagues, must execute operational tasks on a daily basis with passion, energy, skill, and care to successfully navigate the inevitable ups and downs (Section Three). Most of the companies that fail do so because they are unable to properly manage daily operations. With this in mind, let us start with a discussion about vision, plans, and models, as they provide the platform for aligning teams and building organizations.

5.1 elea loves visions, plans, and models

On the basis of a defined purpose that articulates why it exists, which meaningful problem it is trying to solve, and with what underlying theory of change, an impact enterprise should design a future vision of how it could develop and what it could look like in, say, five years.[2] Only a convincing vision will enable the necessary alignment of the founding leadership team and their colleagues, and the mobilization of the required capital from its investors. What are the essential components of an enterprise-to-be that make a difference versus that which already exists? Which ones are the most innovative and distinctive? What would success look like? What are the risks and how could they be mitigated? At elea, when we engage in such a conversation with the founding leadership team to either develop a new or review an existing vision, we often structure the debate along the six different dimensions of a hexagon that comprises the following six elements: impact, offering, ambition, leverage, size, and organization, as well as the relationships between these (see Figure 5.1).

Based on our experience, such a structured and explorative, yet conclusive, dialogue is highly valuable. It allows for higher levels of specificity about impact and the market opportunity, as well as the balance between the two, often making synergies and tensions visible. It helps to clarify ambition levels (e.g., global versus local, broad versus focused) and to understand and prioritize leverage mechanisms. Furthermore, a look at the broadly estimated size of the envisaged enterprise and the resource requirements, such as the time needed to build it and procure other resources, often helps to calibrate a reasonable balance between entrepreneurial dreams and realistic feasibility. Once conclusions are reached and agreed to, short statements, possibly visualized along these six elements, can contribute to alignment of the team internally and the facilitation of dialogue with external stakeholders, such as clients and investors.

Visions can either be grand or modest, and they can either be expressed in the words of a dreamer or those of a technocrat. One of the most powerful articulations of visions that we have come across originated from a

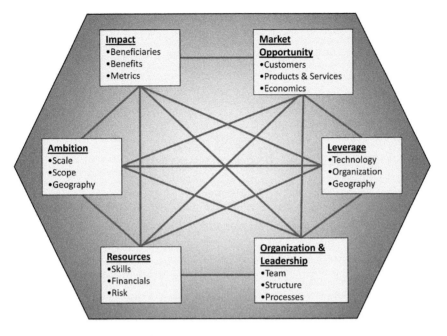

Figure 5.1 The elea vision hexagon.

Source: elea

blind person, Sabriye Tenberken, whom we met earlier in this book as the co-founder of Kanthari (a social entrepreneurship institute based in Kerala in Southern India). She developed and implemented an ambitious vision for herself, that of creating the first school for blind children in Tibet – a vision she realized together with her partner Paul Kronenberg. In doing so, she has inspired the kids in her school to articulate life dreams of their own, as she herself has done. For instance, one of them wanted to become a taxi driver. But since he is blind, he will never be able to drive a taxi. So he decided to become an entrepreneur that employs a taxi fleet instead.

With a reasonably specific and plausible, yet inspirational, vision statement as a starting point, more elaborate plans and models then provide the necessary grounding platform that allows for translating general goals and objectives into much more specific targets, roadmaps, priorities, and actions. Now, planning becomes the key to executing the vision. However, more often than not, entrepreneurs hate planning. They believe that the substantial effort required to work out a plan far outweighs its benefit.

They see it as a bureaucratic exercise that states the obvious and distracts them from what they perceive as the "real work" namely, to realize their vision – and they are concerned that the fast pace of enterprise development will have made any plan obsolete shortly after completion (see Context Box 5.1 for the evolution of planning and modeling over time).[3]

CONTEXT BOX 5.1: EVOLUTION OF PLANNING AND MODELING

One origin of systematic planning was communism. After World War I, the Soviet Union used central planning as one of the essential instruments to steer the economy and implement communism. The same was tried by Maoist China after World War II.

Business planning developed in the 1960s, as companies elaborated long-term plans based on statistics relating to environmental factors, market trends, and the assessments of a company's strengths and weaknesses. Back then, the future was seen as predictable, and therefore it made sense to establish long-term objectives and plan resources accordingly. This was usually done from a First World perspective and based on a fairly stable geopolitical setting under the Cold War conditions. It was inspired by an early example of scientific logistics planning when U.S. Defense Secretary Robert McNamara adopted this approach to support the U.S. armed forces in conducting the Vietnam War.

Planning has to be seen within the broader theme of the evolution of strategic thinking following World War II. In his book *The New Strategists* (from German: *Die neuen Strategen*), Günter Müller-Stewens, a former professor at the University of St. Gallen, describes how long-term planning as a key strategic instrument transformed into the development of business models (Müller-Stewens, 2019, p. 23 ff.). The turbulences of the 1970s, with the oil shock and consequent recession, challenged the systematic corporate planning methods that were introduced during the 1960s, as their ambition to set concrete long-term objectives was confronted with the reality of a future that seemed more and more volatile and difficult to predict. As a result, planning was complemented by the technique of building alternative scenarios in order to increase flexibility. In the 1980s and 1990s, the Shell Corporation pioneered scenario planning to reflect the ever-faster changing political and economic conditions.

In a 1994 Harvard Business Review article, Peter Drucker emphasized this thinking when he described the "theory of the business" as a set of assumptions about what a business will and won't do. He says that such assumptions are about markets and identifying customers and competitors, as well as their values and behaviors. They are also about technology and its dynamics, and about a company's strengths and weaknesses. In a way, a clear understanding of the assumptions is more important than the specific targets that result from them, as smart companies have to keep up with changing market conditions and will, therefore, have to constantly adapt the underlying assumptions (Drucker, 1994).

According to the standard description of the modern decision-making environment by the U.S. military, the world today is seen as "V.U.C.A." (Volatile, Uncertain, Complex, and Ambiguous). Charles-Edouard Bouée, the former leader of the global consulting firm Roland Berger, used this military concept as a starting point for an approach to business that he called "Light Footprint Management," where the goal is to maximize corporate agility and minimize heavy future resource commitments through capital-light business models and partnerships (Bouée, 2013).

Investors tend to see more use in a plan than entrepreneurs do. We nevertheless encourage our elea entrepreneurs to see its value for themselves as well, despite the effort it requires. At elea we love plans for several reasons: They help to clarify and debate the ambition level of either an entrepreneur or an entrepreneurial team. They encourage a higher quality thought process, which serves as the foundation of an enterprise development effort. They also provide a useful platform for a constructive dialogue about opportunities and risks, strategic directions, challenging (yet realistic) objectives, and the resources required, as well as about the actions, measures, and accountabilities needed to make things happen.[4] Finally, and very importantly, plans help to distinguish a "social enterprise" from a disguised charity. Brian Trelstad, a Partner at Bridges Ventures and former Chief Investment Officer at Acumen Fund, expresses this thought when he says,

I can often tell which 'social enterprise' is really a nonprofit in disguise when its business plan starts with a 'needs' section like a typical grant application might. These are often great social enterprises, but

[they] need philanthropic capital. When a business plan starts with a section on the 'opportunity,' that's when I sit up and ask if the team has the DNA for raising investment capital. (Byruck, 2015)

So we clearly side with Benjamin Franklin who is supposed to have said, "Failing to plan is planning to fail."

5.1.1 Choosing the right model

For specific recommendations on how to develop plans and models, we refer to a wide variety of practical guides available online.[5] While such guides are mostly applied to traditional business activities, many of the methods and templates are also valid for impact enterprises. Those guides that specifically refer to impact enterprises highlight the need to add reflections on social mission, theory of change, and impact measurement to the respective plans and models.[6] While the content, format, and style of plans and models do – and should – vary with the specific character of an impact enterprise and its leadership, some basic choices regarding the model of an impact enterprise keep recurring in the portfolio of elea companies. They represent answers to three important questions; namely:

- How is impact achieved?
- How will the enterprise make money?
- How will it grow?

Let's elaborate with a few examples.

Defining impact

Fighting absolute poverty with entrepreneurial means can either be addressed indirectly or directly and by targeting the demand side and/or the supply side of an impact enterprise. Indirect approaches are applied by models such as the one used by Angaza with its pay-as-you-go technology, which satisfies poor people's demand for socially impactful goods by facilitating the purchasing process. Last-mile distribution companies, such as Dharma Life, Copia, and Essmart, are examples of direct approaches that target the demand side as well to achieve impact. These enterprises strive to alleviate poverty by providing poor people access to impactful goods and services at fair prices. As in the case of Dharma Life, if many millions of people enjoy the use of solar lamps and their income-generation benefits, a better education, or just an improved quality of life, poverty is reduced and impact is achieved.

However, *demand*-driven impact models also raise critical issues that need to be satisfactorily addressed in a plan. What exactly are impactful goods and services? Do television sets lead to a positive impact? Are safer, but more expensive, induction stoves justifiable given the opportunity cost of an alternative use of the money? And who decides what is impactful or not, the customers or the company? These are complicated questions that deserve intense debates and which ultimately relate to very fundamental aspects of ethics; e.g., how to prioritize the individual liberty of consumers versus the higher thresholds of responsibility of the suppliers, who often have superior knowledge of the benefits or the damage potential of certain goods. Pragmatism and experience, rather than ideological debates, can help guide impact enterprises in making such important decisions. In the case of Dharma Life, we particularly liked the combination of selling goods and providing awareness and education as a suitable model. In addition to helping Dharma Life capture opportunities to sell hygiene products, a large global consumer goods company even funded a broad-based campaign on the health benefits of regular handwashing.

Direct approaches that use *supply*-driven impact models, particularly, refer to the opportunity to offer jobs to underprivileged people. Impact enterprises, such as BagoSphere or Digital Divide Data (DDD), pursue impact by recruiting, training, and facilitating employment to poor youth in rural areas, who normally do not have access to formal labor markets and their income-generation potential. Here, the link to fighting poverty is obvious, as new opportunities for poor people to earn income are created. The critical issues we are confronted with as we discuss this type of model with our impact entrepreneurs are more about how to increase impact and whether to put the emphasis on developing the attractiveness of job seekers or to strengthen employers in their approach to recruiting, integrating, and training underprivileged people versus those from the more middle-class talent segments.

In some models, impact is achieved on *both* the demand and supply sides. One example of this is the Amazi model, where unemployed women from low-income communities are identified for training and employment as beauty technicians, while their offering targets the emerging consumer who historically has not had access to the same quality and variety of self-care services as the high-income minority. A typical issue that needs to be addressed in such a case is which angle to prioritize: should the emphasis be on maximizing the training of the women or on generating demand for the services? An answer to such questions will have implications for the allocation of resources for investment.

Creating sustainable economics

A second category of issues and choices involving the models of impact enterprises refers to its economics and financial structure. In line with our positioning as a philanthropic impact investor, we strongly believe that impact enterprises have to become profitable – at some stage – in order to sustain their impact. But what does profitability mean exactly? In global value-chain models, such as Coffee Circle, Vega Coffee, Inka Moss, and B'Ayoba, the challenge is straightforward: the prices of the goods sold need to cover the full costs of production and distribution and should additionally allow for a surplus to compensate leadership and make necessary investments in equipment.

But what about Dharma Life, where part of the profit is achieved commercially by selling goods and services, but the other part comes from donations by either corporations or development organizations for specific awareness campaigns? Or consider BagoSphere, which has a hybrid model in which training courses are offered for a fee but students who cannot get credit from a microfinance institution may be funded by a philanthropic scholarship fund. Again, ideological debates about the quality of revenue derived from free, competitive markets versus philanthropic donations will not lead to satisfactory answers. The fact is that in many impact enterprises there are elements in their economic models that can be priced based on market mechanisms and others that cannot. Therefore, more often than not, impact enterprises achieve profitability through hybrid economic models where the profitable components subsidize the other components. Based on our experience in working with impact enterprises, it is important to establish transparency about the economic models used, because different types of revenue sources have different degrees of sustainability and need to be managed differently.

Developing a path for growth

Achieving scale is critical to maximize impact and often necessary to reach breakeven in financial terms. Thus, a continuous challenge that applies as equally to impact enterprises as to the more traditional corporate world is how to balance growth and profitability. This affects, in particular, those models where growth is driven by technology. For example, Angaza is attractively valued and was able to raise significant institutional funding due to the potential of its solutions and to its track record of having a fast development pace rather than because of its profitability. awamo had a similar choice to make – whether to emphasize the accelerated acquisition of new clients for its digital mobile-banking platform or to focus on capturing the profit potential of its existing clients.

The answers to the growth versus profitability challenge depend a lot on the chosen capital-raising strategy. Particularly in the technology space, many investors prefer sales growth over profitability, which means they do not mind if even the world's most valuable companies sometimes display annual losses in the billions of dollars, so long as they are investing and generating cash flows. What we find helpful in such cases is to distinguish "operational profitability" from the overall consolidated profits and losses (P&L). The former refers to the regular income and costs from current operations, while the latter includes investments for future growth. Such a distinction clarifies what new capital is used for and can help to prevent unsustainable structures where operational losses are permanently subsidized through the inflow of new capital.

5.1.2 *Process guidelines*

These examples should illustrate that the elaboration of convincing plans and models requires both good thinking and hard work. They need to be the result of an intense, iterative, content-driven learning and thought process that reflects a holistic understanding of the individual elements and key relationships between them. A superficial marketing story just to "sell" an idea to raise investor capital will not do. Moreover, plans and models, once developed, should be living documents that are regularly reviewed and adjusted based on new insights from (own or third party) successes and failures and from trends, changes, and disruptions in the relevant markets and broader contexts. That also means that plans should be materially revised when there is a clear need to revise them and not just because of an annual planning and budgeting calendar. Finally, plans and models have to be essentially created, owned, and further developed by the leadership team that is mandated to implement them; this comprehensive task cannot be delegated to advisors and specialists. However, internal or external experts can, and should, contribute in fields such as analytics and process. For instance, elea often supports the process by facilitating leadership workshops, contributing methods and instruments, and acting as a sounding board in challenging and improving the substance, form, and communication of plans and models.

Some additional process guidelines that we find useful are:

Differentiate between process and document: Plans and models create clarity about the content of a proposition by analyzing facts and answering critical issues. They also represent a platform for aligning ambitions and directions among the members of the leadership team and with external stakeholders. Importantly, the format and style of these documents should reflect whether they are being used for content development purposes or as a communication platform, for they will look different when used for an internal workshop versus, say, a presentation at an investor roadshow.

Favor "outside-in," not "inside-out": Impact enterprises are often deeply immersed in mastering their internal challenges and may, therefore, take too much of an inside-out perspective when planning and modeling their future. In our work with elea entrepreneurs, we encourage them to complement this view with an outside-in perspective in order to bring more objectivity into the debate. One good way that we can help them to achieve this is to systematically interview current and potential customers, or other types of stakeholders and experts, which allows for a sequence of analytics that derives internal resource requirements based on market needs rather than the other way around.

Be issue-oriented, not descriptive: Plans and models often suffer from too many descriptive parts and an insufficient focus on questions and controversial issues. Particularly at the beginning of a planning and modeling process, it is worthwhile spending substantial time on crystallizing the critical questions that need to be answered in order to arrive at a conclusion about the attractiveness and challenges of an opportunity. An activity description to "evaluate impact area Y" or "define customer segment Z" is substantially less powerful and thought-provoking than pointedly asking "what," "how," and "why" questions, such as: "How is impact in area Y created?", "How significant and sustainable is it?", "How does this support our purpose?", "What are the specific characteristics of customer segment Z as compared to others?", and "How can our offering meet their needs better than competitive offerings?" Such an approach not only clarifies expectations about directions but also allows for creativity in searching for answers.

Invest senior time upfront, not at the end: In line with the point above, involving leadership at the beginning of a planning and modeling process, rather than at the end, pays off. Through identifying the right questions early on, analytical efforts can be directed to the relevant areas and gaps of knowledge. It is often observed that leadership teams spend most of their time on reviewing plans and budgets for the next year at the end of the current year, when already 90% of the planning and budgeting work has been done. By contrast, focusing on critical issues and debating important directional alternatives at the beginning of a planning and budgeting cycle can lead to a more sustainable business model.

Because our strong convictions about the value of plans and models sometimes clash with the skepticism of our entrepreneurs, we make an effort to understand the barriers to modeling and planning in order to apply specific measures to overcome them. Does such skepticism stem from a lack of motivation in seeing the value of plans and models, or is it because the skills are missing and there is no capacity available? Motivational gaps can result from the fact that impact entrepreneurs often find their calling through an important life-changing event (i.e., a memorable "moment of truth") rather than through an analytical process of looking at market demand and impact opportunities and calculating revenue and earnings potential. Impact entrepreneurs often communicate exceedingly well and use their passion, charisma, and talent to convincingly tell their life's story to attract donors. However, they are often considerably less effective when giving a presentation to potential investors, as this requires them to focus on more analytical descriptions of impact and profit mechanisms, ambitions and targets, as well as on resource and organizational requirements. Encouraging impact entrepreneurs and their teams to recognize and appreciate the value of plans and models in such cases is often an important and highly valuable educational effort to crystallize the specific identity of an enterprise-to-be on a spectrum between a charitable organization, which has some entrepreneurial characteristics, and an impact enterprise, which has ambitious commercial goals in addition to its impact objectives.

If the skepticism of impact entrepreneurs stems from a lack of skills and/or capacity, ways should be explored as to how to bridge the gaps by simplifying planning and modeling tasks to those that are essential and by providing access to external resources, such as planning and modeling guidelines or expert networks. elea is in the process of strengthening the community among its elea entrepreneurs, which can be a valuable source for tapping into the experiences of peers.

At elea, we have learned much over the years about how to create, review, and adjust plans and models (see Practice Box 5.2 for some suggestions). This is an ongoing task that goes hand-in-hand with building the team and organizing the work necessary to execute plans and realize models, which is the focus of the next section.

PRACTICE BOX 5.2: SUGGESTIONS FOR VISIONING, PLANNING, AND MODELING

For Entrepreneurs

- Treat planning as a learning journey, not as writing a document.
- Invest a disproportionate time upfront to crystallize the right questions.
- Seek help from advisors, but don't delegate the thought process.
- Use methods and tools as means, not as ends; avoid emphasis of form over substance.
- Leverage the planning and modeling process for team building and alignment.

For Impact Investors

- Provide value-added challenges and advice (possibly through joint workshops).
- See your role as a complementary outside-in observer with higher levels of objectivity.
- Leverage your network of advisors and experts.
- Facilitate peer reviews.
- Avoid doing the modeling and planning work yourself.
- Define a small number of measurable and meaningful key performance indicators (financial and non-financial, impact-related).

5.2 Getting organized

An organization is a social unit of people that is structured and managed to meet a need or pursue collective goals.[7] An organization is also where the integration of entrepreneurship and capital becomes real in shaping people's daily work lives. It is, therefore, at the heart of the main theme of this book, as expressed in our formula for inclusive capitalism. Only organizations, ultimately, have the capacity to employ capital in a systematic, productive, and sustainable way, because they can create institutional independence from important individual personalities that are exposed to the vagaries and volatility of individual life journeys. Moreover, only organizations can systematically apply financial and non-financial leverage mechanisms.

Purpose, plans, and models may provide for highly attractive presentations and inspiring stories, yet it is, ultimately, the decisions, actions, and behaviors of organizations that bring an enterprise to life. Without an organization of people who do real work on a daily basis in an aligned and collaborative way, who take responsibility to get things done, who procure and manage resources, and who coordinate activities among themselves, all concepts about the future remain just inconsequential ideas without impact.

Building effective organizations is a highly challenging leadership task. This is true for all types of enterprises, but it applies even more so to impact enterprises. Within elea's philanthropic impact investment activities, the organizational dimension is essential. Already during a due diligence process, much effort goes into understanding the backgrounds, motivational drivers, and ambitions – as well as experiences, skills, general strengths, and shortcomings – of the key people that lead an enterprise. In this section, we will share our insights and lessons about how to address such challenges based on our work with elea entrepreneurs over the years. The starting point of any effective organization is putting together a team of like-minded people who commit to working together in the pursuit of a shared purpose and vision.

5.2.1 Building an effective team

The founding structure varies depending on the specific enterprise. In the case of Dharma Life, Gaurav Mehta was initially supported by his co-founders (classmates from his MBA class at London Business School) and then later became the sole leader. From the outset, Lesley Marincola of Angaza has been working together with her older brother, who has a PhD in Computer Science. He assumed the role of the Chief Technology Officer and has always respected her overall leadership mandate. Lesley has also been working with a third co-founder, whom she met through mutual Stanford connections, who assumed the role of COO. Coffee Circle was founded by three friends who met at a management consultancy. Zhihan Lee founded BagoSphere together with two university friends. This diversity of founding constellations based on sole founders or teams of family members or friends is typical, also for the broader portfolio of elea investments. Over the years, we could not identify one model that would be systematically more successful than another. However, we do hold a firm view that teams should, ultimately, be organized around the experiences and skills required by the impact enterprise-to-be rather than around the availability and volunteering motivation of family members and friends. The essential question is whether a team collectively has the passion, drive, and energy to transform purpose, vision, and plans into reality and whether it has the practical capabilities to get the job done.

While the requirements regarding the size and structure of the top team, with its specific roles and skills profiles, depend on the characteristics and strategies of an enterprise and will evolve over time, the role of a Chief Financial Officer (CFO) is critical in all investments. As impact enterprises pursue a dual mission that combines both impact and financial performance, financial abilities are essential and often underestimated by founding teams. Even once founding teams have come around to understanding and agreeing to the logic of having a qualified CFO, they are sometimes challenged to find one. Why? The role of the CFO has to meet a particularly high hurdle, both in terms of character and technical skills, which leads to demanding job profiles and a scarcity of suitable candidates. Integrity, reliability, and trust are essential qualities needed for this role. However, entrepreneurs often have a hard time extending trust beyond family and close personal friends. Furthermore, although having a brother or a good friend as a CFO in a core team may satisfy the requirements in terms of values and integrity, it raises other issues regarding professional qualifications and independent judgment. Identifying the right CFO is, thus, very challenging for an impact enterprise. An active investor, such as elea, can be particularly helpful as a sounding board and challenger in this regard (see Context Box 5.3).

CONTEXT BOX 5.3: WANTED – CFO

At an early stage of elea's development, we received a visit from a team of entrepreneurs who presented the investment case of an international impact company with business activities in India and Ghana based on specialty fair-trade and organic farm products. They knew a lot about retail customers and distribution characteristics, as well as about product management and certification methods, but financial transparency was lacking. We did not really understand the financial situation of this company. So, on the spot, we developed an overview of the current status with the help of a flip chart – one sheet for the assets and one for the liabilities.

Through this exercise, we concluded that the company was in severe financial distress and urgently needed fresh funds. We also recognized that – even though it was a small enterprise at an early stage – the challenges of managing its finances were considerable. There were some difficult legacy situations from different types of shareholders and creditors that weighed heavily on the balance sheet's liability side. Accounts needed to be consolidated across various legal entities in different jurisdictions. There were various types of complicated arrangements with business partners on the supply and distribution sides. The cash situation evolved in a very dynamic way, which required a timely monitoring of liquidity and tight management of working capital. Consequently, we made a positive investment decision conditional upon the hiring of a CFO who would have to be a member of the leadership team. (Fortunately, our professional network allowed us to quickly identify a suitable person with the right motivation and skills set. We were, thus, able to help the team meet the condition that we had established.)

Since then, this type of situation has repeated itself again and again. Impact entrepreneurs understandably nurture their ideas, passion, and ambition from the perspective of either a specific social problem to be solved or a specific solution to be applied. As their motivation is driven by the impact they want to achieve and not by the financial wealth created along the way, a systematic focus on financial issues and tasks is often lacking. At the same time, impact enterprises – as other ventures – frequently fail because they run out of money due to a lack of attention to funding and liquidity planning rather than due to bad strategies or unsuitable products. Such enterprises should, therefore, ensure early on that they have appropriate financial skills in order to maximize the probability of survival and success.

Not only the CFO but also all other members of the leadership team, who are identified due to the critical role they will have in the success of the enterprise, deserve a high level of scrutiny as they are appointed to their posts. Are their skills up to the task? What drives their motivation? How passionate are they, and how solid is their commitment to both social impact and financial success? Are they willing to dedicate a substantial portion of their life's energy to such a task over an extended period of time? Do they stand up to the founder and voice their own opinions? Is there alignment on aspirations and a shared agenda among the members of the core team? Do these people have a common foundation in terms of ethics and virtues? Can they effectively and efficiently work together? We encourage our elea entrepreneurs to make the necessary room for deep and honest reflection to find convincing answers to these important and often challenging questions.

5.2.2 *The power of partnership*

Once the team is initially configured, it should either implicitly – or, preferably, explicitly – agree to a set of principles that guides the attitudes and behaviors among individual team members. elea systematically applies six principles[8] that guide both internal collaboration as well as our relationships with investee companies, and we encourage our elea entrepreneurs to adopt similar principles with their respective teams. These principles are rooted in our framework of liberal ethics and reflect our conviction that a horizontal, trust-based alignment is superior to vertical patterns of hierarchical command and control in coping with the complexity of leadership when building an enterprise in today's global era. They include:

1. **Same agenda**: The success of the organization as a whole and a commitment to shared goals and principles must be given priority over particular divisional or functional ambitions, as well as the interests of individual team members.
2. **Involvement and engagement**: A partnership can only be effective if its members are involved and engaged. This means actively contributing views, ideas, and solutions to problems. It also means being transparent in articulating positions and changes of opinion. The basis of this principle is uncompromising integrity, discretion, and trust.

3. **Respect**: Each team member deserves the respect of other team members. Respect becomes evident when we listen to each other in order to understand each other's perspectives. It also calls for assuming good faith and best professional efforts when judging each other's views and actions. Respectful relationships require that conflicts between individuals be resolved openly and directly. Talking badly about colleagues behind their backs is disrespectful.

4. **Debate:** Important and controversial issues and decisions require intense, open debates within the team. Critical and sensitive arguments and opinions need to be articulated within the confines of human politeness, irrespective of hierarchies. Holding back one's opinion about important decisions is unacceptable. Equally unacceptable is extension of the debate beyond the team once a decision has been made (in other words, confidentiality is required).

5. **Mutual support**: Each member of the team has to view her colleagues as partners. A partner is somebody who wishes for and contributes to the success of his fellow partners. Support can range from verbal encouragement to active help in dealing with important business and personal issues.

6. **Contribution**: An effective partnership lives from the success achieved as a result of individual contributions. Contributions can vary in their nature and over extended periods of time. However, team members who cease to contribute over a longer period should lose their right to partnership.

The specific content and emphasis of such principles can, and should, vary depending on the character of an organization, the contextual circumstances, and the personal style of its leaders. Among our investee companies, we find both the team-oriented leadership approach as well as the more hierarchical one that is centered on a charismatic, strong, and decisive leader who finds it hard to build and lead a team of equals. While there is no one-size-fits-all approach to leadership in general, we encourage a process that actively uncovers and addresses the challenges of leading an enterprise in order to create self-awareness within the leadership team and to articulate principles that fit the very specific characters and styles of the people involved.

For such sensitive discussions, an impact investor like elea can contribute valuable input due to its positioning as an interested and involved party that does not have a specific organizational agenda. Therefore, elea is often asked to provide a balanced perspective that benefits from its intimate familiarity with the issues and yet brings a certain level of objectivity. Sole founders are often lonely in their role and tend to be grateful to have a sounding board for dealing with leadership challenges. This is particularly true when the problems at hand are complicated and involve different spheres, such as enterprise requirements, professional and personal ambitions and goals, family constellations, and deep, longstanding personal friendships.

Typical examples where elea was decisive in finding good solutions to leadership challenges were:

- Facilitating a dialogue between related founders (e.g., siblings or a married couple), where both skills and motivations diverged and differentiated roles within the enterprise had to be identified that reflected this diversity, while still helping to protect the integrity of their personal relations within the family.
- Resolving conflicts among founder friends whose career paths started to diverge and where solutions had to be found for how to either involve or compensate departing founders in a fair, face-saving way without damaging their personal friendship.
- Helping leadership constellations to evolve over time as enterprise requirements became more differentiated. One example are structures where the founding team consists of two founders who started out as equals, but over time, one becomes the CEO and the other develops into more of a supervisory (e.g., board level) and/or expert role.
- Convincing a sole founder to bring in and accept professional executives at an equal level (and with entrepreneurial incentives) to complement the founder in areas where he does not have particular strengths or experience but which are essential elements for the future success of an enterprise (e.g., deep industry or functional expertise).

5.2.3 *Process-oriented modus operandi*

With the core team in place and the principles on how to work together articulated and agreed on, an organization needs to establish a modus operandi that optimally supports these activities. The modus operandi (which is Latin for "way of executing") represents the sum of structures and processes that are carried out to achieve the objectives of an organization (see Context Box 5.4 for an overview of the role of organization and modus operandi in the corporate world).

CONTEXT BOX 5.4: THE ROLE OF ORGANIZATION AND MODUS OPERANDI

Conventional organizational literature was focused primarily on the structure of an enterprise. A handbook for "Managing the Modern Organization" from 1978 described this task as follows:

> Organization is concerned with the building, developing and maintaining of a structure of working relationships in order to accomplish the objectives of the enterprises. Organization means the determination and assignment of duties of people and also the establishment and the maintenance of authority relationships among these grouped activities. It is the structural framework within which the various efforts are coordinated and related to each other. (Haimann, 1978)

Whereas organizational charts describing the structure of an enterprise are still, by far, the most frequently used tools in this field, the increasing complexity and fast pace of change in our global era has broadly led to substituting structure for process. The perspective has shifted from looking at stable responsibilities and recurring tasks to looking at dynamic and adjustable sequences of single steps of activity. The term "process" is again derived from Latin: the verb "procedere" means "go forward." According to the dictionary definition, it is "a series of actions, motions, or occurrences." It also refers to a "method, mode, or operation whereby a result or effect is produced." Process today is often the principal organizational instrument for extending impact beyond individuals. Through clearly defined and institutionalized processes, organizations become less dependent on key individuals.

Based on their experience, global consulting firms analyzed the role of organization and modus operandi as two of the factors that contribute to the success of corporations. In the early 1980s, McKinsey & Company led an in-depth research effort on what makes companies excellent, and crystallized seven relevant factors (the famous "7-S model"), which

included strategy, structure, systems, skills, shared values, style, and
staff (Peters & Waterman, 1982). More recently, Bain & Company sur-
veyed 665 companies worldwide and found that six organizational characteristics are key to high performance (Mankins & Schwartz, 2016).
Accordingly, high-performing organizations are

- aligned with the company's strategy
- capable of executing strategy with the right talent, processes, and tools
- effective at making and executing critical decisions
- adaptable in the face of rapid change
- efficient in realizing the benefits of scale and scope
- engaged to go the extra mile

There are typically three different types of processes that constitute the
whole of an organization:

- **Operational processes**: They deliver the core elements of the
  value chain of a company. Some examples are processes that group
  all activities necessary to understand and respond to customer needs
  or processes that enable the management of a supply chain.
- **Support processes**: They enable and help to optimize the operational processes. Typical examples are human resources (e.g., recruiting, assigning, and developing people) or information technology
  (e.g., purchasing or developing and operating systems).
- **Leadership processes**: They support the leadership team in their
  activities to steer a company toward its ambitions and goals. Examples
  are planning, decision-making, and controlling activities.

All processes combined serve the purpose of moving and transforming
realities toward directions derived from the vision, plans, and models of
an organization. While often overlooked, processes also have an eminent
ethical component besides helping to achieve an organization's objectives
(in a somewhat technocratic fashion). If overly formalized and regulated,
they can actually reduce liberty and responsibility, as compliance with
formal rules replaces autonomous judgment and individual accountability. However, with smart design, they can encourage empowerment and
entrepreneurial initiative (i.e., the desire to engage) at all levels while

ensuring accountability and transparency. From our experience, impact enterprises have one important advantage versus traditional corporations in this regard: their strong sense of purpose encourages high levels of people engagement and creates an energized, inspirational culture. Since its inception, elea has never been asked to help motivate the people working in any one of its portfolio companies. Such levels of passion and enthusiasm are the source of envy of many established corporations.[9]

However, while impact enterprises often attract and excite great people, they are usually constrained in terms of organizational and process-design experience and expertise. This is due to the fact that there is very limited capacity available for creating and applying organizational methods and tools, and only very few, if any, of the team members have the necessary skills for such tasks. Often, these organizations are steered ad hoc, in more intuitive ways, with only a minimum of formalized procedures, limited transparency, and low degrees of standardization. Consequently, while lots of energy, initiative, and creativity do exist, very basic processes (such as sales and marketing planning, periodic management reporting on key performance indicators, standards for recruiting people, and criteria to evaluate new investments – to name just a few) are severely underdeveloped.

This is another area where an active investor like elea can help. It can provide support in convincing charismatic and creative entrepreneurs – who typically find structures, systems, and standards to be restraining and bureaucratic – to see the benefits of at least making some investments in such structures and procedures. For example, in one case, elea helped to institutionalize a monthly update call with board members and senior executive leaders based on a standard reporting format that combined both financial and impact-related key performance indicators. elea has also helped to leverage positive experiences from one organization to another by supporting judgment calls on the right balance between differentiation and simplicity, to avoid unnecessary complexity and bureaucracy.

According to our experience, the following guidelines have proven to be valuable:

- The structure and process architecture of an enterprise has to visibly reflect its plan and model. Consequently, a periodic review should take place to assess whether organizational resources are allocated to the areas of greatest impact and leverage of the enterprise's model, and the best people and teams should be assigned tasks that make a difference regarding both impact and financial success.

- Organizational tasks need to be defined in a way that is comprehensive enough to allow for the setting of clear accountability for results and outcomes (rather than for input and activity). A simple test is whether an enterprise can describe targets in the form of deliverables with three to five key performance indicators that are easily measurable.

- Accountability will only work if the individual in charge of a particular task has control over the most important resources necessary to deliver on that task. If internal, this means having authority over the people and teams involved. If external, it means having control over budgets and over the choice of partners and suppliers.

- Organizational tasks should be differentiating between regularly recurring processes (such as production and sales or annual budgeting and quarterly reporting) and one-off efforts to build or transform the enterprise (e.g., launching new products, evaluating an acquisition, and restructuring an activity). For the latter, project organizations that function as temporary task forces with project-related budgets should be introduced.

- Structures should be as flat as possible. New hierarchy levels have to meet a high threshold of value added, such as a different strategic layer (e.g., a regional versus a local geographic dimension or a new customer segment with different characteristics). The pure span of control considerations (i.e., the number of people reporting to somebody) is not a sufficient source of value added. For people with similar tasks (e.g., sales agents), a team of up to 15 individuals can report to one responsible sales executive.

- Recurring or one-off organizational tasks that embed rich knowledge in the form of learnings, technical know-how, and practical guidance (such as creating a new learning center or testing a new market opportunity) should be documented appropriately to allow a new team working on similar tasks in the future to build on the previously acquired insights and to avoid the repetition of mistakes.

(See also Practice Box 5.5 for some additional suggestions.)

PRACTICE BOX 5.5: SUGGESTIONS FOR ORGANIZATIONAL DEVELOPMENT

For Entrepreneurs

- Ensure that there are people with strong financial skills in your team.
- Dedicate enough time and thought to designing your team.
- Establish principles and rules of engagement for how you operate as a team.
- Create a process architecture to support organizational effectiveness and efficiency.
- Introduce and apply simple, yet relevant and effective, organizational instruments, methods, and tools (possibly with suitable external support).
- Seek out advisors to help on the people side of your organization.
- Regularly think through how your organization is likely to evolve over time.

For Impact Investors
- Make deep-dive personal interviews with founders a mandatory component of due diligence.
- Watch out for the need to change roles at the top; proactively provoke conversations on such topics.
- Encourage brutal honesty and transparency about personal agendas versus entrepreneurial needs.
- Share best-practice experience on people and leadership development among the entrepreneurs in your portfolio. Encourage peer-level mentoring and coaching.
- Help articulate job profiles for key positions in the leadership team.
- Support the drafting of principles and rules of engagement for core teams.

5.3 Navigating ups and downs

Design work on plans and models, teams, and organizations is a necessary foundation for the creation of an impact enterprise. However, the real test is how it successfully navigates day after day through the inevitable ups and downs during its build-out phase. In this respect, the leader and her team make the decisive difference. This raises questions such as: What is her agenda? How does she allocate her time and personal resources while keeping a healthy, balanced life? How are priorities defined? How are financial and other resources allocated and managed? Furthermore, in which areas and how can an active investor like elea help? These are some of the questions that will be discussed in this section.

5.3.1 *From self-awareness to effectiveness*

The starting point for the leader of an enterprise is to be self-aware. For this reason, at IMD, most leadership development programs start with raising levels of self-awareness. Telling life stories to others as a way of consciously reflecting on one's own development journey – with its highs and lows, its insights and learnings – and, consequently, gaining clarity on one's specific leadership profile, with its strengths and development needs, is one powerful technique for becoming more self-aware. People do not learn from acquiring experience but rather from reflecting on that experience. Other ways of increasing one's self-awareness include participation in commonly available surveys to achieve a more systematic insight about one's leadership profile and behavior versus others.[10] Is a person more extroverted or introverted; i.e., how easily does a person relate to people and things outside of herself as opposed to ideas and concepts within her mind? Does a person rely more on intuition and feelings or on facts and analysis when assessing a situation and making decisions? Is that person more directive in influencing others, or does she apply a more integrative style through building bridges and defining common goals? How opinionated and judgmental is that person versus listening to other views and developing new perspectives?

Finding the answers to such questions about oneself and, consequently, addressing the gaps identified are important tasks for any leader. Self-awareness is particularly important for impact leaders, as they face their specific challenges. Based on our experience, the entrepreneurs of impact enterprises exhibit a broad range of emotions, from feelings of overconfidence to those of insecurity. On one hand, they see themselves as major contributors to solving some of the world's greatest and most pressing problems. Seeing enterprises progress and receiving external recognition through awards and publicity motivates them and gives them a strong sense of achievement and satisfaction.

On the other hand, precisely because they internalize a special responsibility to make a positive difference in managing some of the world's most severe challenges, they can feel humbled and, sometimes, insecure. On top of this, they are confronted with the complex tasks facing every entrepreneur, such as reliably delivering products and services to customers; raising capital and nurturing investor relations; coaching, supporting, and controlling team members; managing multiple and diverse additional stakeholders (e.g., strategic partners, suppliers, diverse networks, and platforms); resolving tensions and conflicts in the leadership team across functions and personalities; and exploring new, innovative opportunities while coping with unforeseen external developments and shocks. And all of this happens in an environment with often unreliable infrastructure (e.g., electricity and communication breakdowns), issues related to personal safety, and limited mobility (e.g., unbearable traffic congestion and a lack of public transportation).

On top of all of those challenges, the lifestyles of entrepreneurs often leave little room for a satisfactory family life or time to cultivate friendships. A high degree of self-awareness as a first step to optimizing one's personal effectiveness is, therefore, a critical element of self-care in leading a healthy, balanced life. In a recent article, Professor Katherine Milligan, the former Director and Head of the Schwab Foundation for Social Entrepreneurship and the current Head of Gender and Diversity at Bamboo Capital Partners, referred to the risk of burnout by social entrepreneurs. Based on research that included in-depth interviews with 30 different social-change leaders, she emphasizes the importance of self-inquiry as a basis for shifting perceptions and behaviors for better self-leadership and the leadership of others (Milligan & Walker, 2020).[11]

This is, again, an area for potential contributions by an active investor. At elea, one-to-one mentoring between the leader of an impact enterprise and the responsible elea person happens frequently, and an ongoing, personal interaction between members of the two organizations is typically hugely valuable. Such regular dialogue can cover a wide array of topics that range from prioritizing operational tasks to testing new ideas, asking for input on difficult people issues, discussing relations with stakeholders, and providing advice on personal and family matters.

As a leader becomes more aware of his profile and skills set and gains more experience, he develops orientation and guidance on how to deploy his own personal resources and what can be delegated to others. A few practical recommendations include:

- Concentrate your time and energy on tasks and activities with the highest impact and the best fit with your specific personal strengths and skills set. The essential question to ask is whether your personal attendance really makes a difference. If you are more of an intro-verted person, spend your time on conceptual thinking and writing tasks, and let others represent you at internal and external social events. If you are an extrovert, identify somebody who can support you on intellectual tasks.

- Observe yourself and find out at which times you are most productive at which tasks.[12] Some people are creative in the office, while others have the best ideas during a walk outside or during leisure time on weekends. This depends on your very personal biorhythm and may even be geneti-cally influenced. Make an effort to shape your agenda accordingly.

- Plan ahead and define a small (maximum five) number of priority tasks and objectives for the weeks and months ahead. Proactively manage your agenda rather than let yourself be managed by other people. Plan time and energy for reflection. Set aside time for the unforeseen.

- From time to time, critically review your past agenda: Did you accomplish what you wanted? Could you have accomplished more with less input? Were there activities that you could have delegated?

- Be creative in mobilizing resources that help you to reduce your "To Do List" rather than adding to the number of issues you need to get resolved. Advisors are sometimes less than helpful in this respect, as they often have to prove their worth by raising new issues and contributing new ideas. As you delegate work, spend enough time upfront to clarify your expectations in order to avoid disappointment. Delegate responsibility for deliverables rather than just activities.

- Work hard on avoiding unnecessary distractions. Be disciplined in declining invitations to workshops and conferences that only flatter your ego but will not help you to advance your enterprise. Consider the full cost of long-haul trips (including sleep deprivation from jet lag and, consequently, reduced mental strength), and reflect on how you would justify the opportunity cost to your stakeholders.

- Be careful to protect a healthy balance in your life by dedicating sufficient time and energy to family, friends, and other, more personal, priorities. Even though as an impact entrepreneur you have chosen to invest a lot of personal energy into making the world a better place, you are not expected to shoulder the whole world's challenges, and you are entitled – as all humans are – to your portion of happiness.

5.3.2 Managing resources

While managing himself is the necessary foundation, the main task of a leader is, of course, to manage others. As most impact enterprises in elea's portfolio are knowledge companies; this means, primarily, managing the time and energy of employees and managing money. How can the time and human energy spent in an organization be optimized in the interest of its purpose and vision? Powerful, inspirational leaders who behave in a way that motivates, encourages, teaches, praises, supports, coaches, challenges, corrects, and – exceptionally – also sanctions team members are the most important component. Fortunately, impact entrepreneurs are often charismatic, people-oriented leaders who excel at this task.

In addition to being specific about expectations, targets, and objectives in terms of content (e.g., in the context of plans and budgets), it is advisable for leaders to describe the expected form and quality of a deliverable as well. Be it a proposal for a new market opportunity, a framework for financial controlling and reporting, a plan for a new offering, or a fundraising strategy, whether or not you as leader will be satisfied with the outcome largely depends on the resources needed and the amount of work put into the effort. It likewise depends on the qualifications, drive, and ambitions of the people mandated with the given task. The quality can vary by factors of two to three. Therefore, setting quality benchmarks upfront is an important tool for managing resources and getting things done.

Furthermore, sometimes form can nurture substance. For instance, writing a well-structured, conclusive three to four page memorandum instead of pulling together a presentation pack of 30–40 PowerPoint slides is much more demanding but can far outweigh its value and usefulness, as it requires much more effort to carefully think through the logic of a short paper with fully worded text. It is also important that leaders provide explicit feedback to colleagues about the quality of such papers, either by praising great examples or criticizing work that does not meet expectations, so that they can benefit from such exercises as a learning experience. A final essential element of managing resources is to hold individuals (or small teams of a maximum of three people) accountable for their respective tasks. Therefore, the minutes of leadership meetings should always include a list of decisions and action items with clear deadlines and accountabilities.

Productive meetings

In any organization – be it an impact enterprise, a private corporation, or a public sector entity – a large part of day-to-day activities happen in meetings. And yet, time and again, it is surprising, and somewhat disappointing, to see how many meetings take place that were not really needed, and how little thoughtfulness and creativity often goes into thinking through what a meeting should accomplish both in substance and in spirit. The leadership team of a company can make a huge difference in the effectiveness of time spent throughout the organization as they plan and conduct meetings themselves or help others to organize meetings. Those in charge of a particular task should first determine whether a meeting is needed at all to achieve a desired goal, and then, if so, clarify the expectations and define the agenda before scheduling the meeting. Only after this has been done should they determine who should participate. Furthermore, to be significantly more effective and more inclusive, once the meeting is scheduled, the proposed agenda and a list of expectations should be circulated to participants a few days in advance to allow them to provide input. Sending supporting documents out even at very short notice before the meeting may help to focus the mind of participants on the issues at hand while minimizing the time spent on a simple transfer of information.

Clearly articulating the objectives and behavior guidelines (in terms of how the meeting will be structured and how participants are expected to contribute) at the beginning of any meeting sets the tone and encourages participants to speak up. This can prevent people from either dozing off into the passive listening mode or becoming actively destructive. One recommendation based on our experience at elea is to differentiate between the specific discussion types required for each of the agenda items, being sure to leave room for contributions from each participant. As an example, four such discussion types can be distinguished:

1. **Pure updates and information exchanges:** These should be minimized, as they can be dealt with more efficiently in written form.

2. **Raising broader issues and framing discussions:** This is the most important – but also the most challenging – discussion type, and it is sadly often the most neglected one in many organizations. Its goal is to discuss issues that go beyond immediate, pressing business requirements; for example, new opportunities, organizational issues, or risks. The task of the leader is to ensure that the topic is prepared and positioned appropriately and that the right questions are posed. During the meeting, the leader must be more in a listening than in a talking mode to ensure that particularly contrasting points of view, as well as innovative ideas and non-conventional opinions, are brought to the fore. He should intervene when the discussion goes off on a tangent or when someone tries to manipulate the group for his own personal agenda, and he should help prevent the discussion from jumping too soon from the identification and analysis phase of an issue to defining and executing a solution.

3. **Decision-shaping discussions:** These are a different type of discussion in the sense that an issue in question is already well understood and a directional proposal has been made by a person or the team in charge. The objective is to challenge the choices proposed, contribute additional perspectives, and provide guidance on how to finalize decision-making. Here again, it is vital that critical voices are taken into account, so that those partners who have not yet had a chance to contribute their views will not feel discouraged from doing so. The role of the leader is to ensure that all relevant perspectives are brought into the debate before articulating his own views. If he does so prematurely, depending on his style, this may then discourage others from expressing their own opinions. Finally, at the end of the meeting, the leader should prioritize and synthesize the outcome and define the next steps.

4. **Decision-making discussions:** These are at the center of a large amount of academic management literature, yet in practice they often

tend to be the least interesting debates. This is due to the fact that, at this point, the homework has usually already been done, and the opinions have already been formed. Only rarely at this late stage are decisions fundamentally challenged. In this case, the task of the leader is to ensure that everybody stands behind the final decisions and supports them both internally and externally.

Fundraising and finance

In addition to managing the time and energy of the entrepreneurs and their teams, as well as of those working throughout the organization, another important resource that needs to be managed is, obviously, money. As these enterprises are typically not yet at a stage where they generate sufficient cash through their operations, they need capital for both bridging loss-making periods and making investments for future growth. Raising sufficient capital is, therefore, an important priority for any impact enterprise. Fundraising is both a strategic and an operational activity where the leadership team (especially the CEO and the CFO) need to be strongly involved. Strategically, fundraising determines the type and structure of future investor-stakeholders, with their specific economic interests and commitments as they evolve over time. Consequently, it influences how purpose and impact will be realized in the future and how the risk of drift will be managed. Along with the structure of the balance sheet (i.e., the mix between debt and equity), the degrees of freedom and the pace of future growth of the enterprise are significantly impacted. Moreover, depending on the chosen fundraising strategy, the influence of the founding entrepreneurs will become more or less diluted over time, which has significant implications for monitoring the business and leadership approach.

At the same time, fundraising is an important operational task that consumes a high level of quality time and energy and plays an important role in balancing the opportunities for success versus the risks of failure. Due to its critical importance, it is, thus, worth dedicating time and effort to developing and executing a well-thought-out approach. It is also an area where seeking help from a philanthropic impact investor like elea can be valuable. A first set of questions that the entrepreneurs must ask in determining an enterprise's approach to fundraising refers to the type of desired investors, with their specific pros and cons (including a thorough investor due diligence, which is often lacking). Is there a deep-pocketed, passionate family member or friend in sight who sympathizes with the cause and will be a patient investor? The challenge posed by such investors is that they may bring emotional factors into investor relationships that can be hard to control, particularly in times of distress. So what are the trade-offs of choosing more commercially minded investors, such as venture capitalists or institutional impact investors, as compared to more philanthropically oriented foundations? The former may contribute more professional investment expertise and be tougher on financial performance while being less sensitive to a drift in purpose. The latter may be more patient but also more onerous in terms of impact reporting requirements and slower at decision-making, particularly in critical times.

Then there are questions related to the type of capital desired; e.g., how to mix debt and equity and what role to give to grants. Patient debt may be easier to raise in early stages of development, but it also loads the balance sheet with liabilities that can limit flexibility later on. Working capital is crucial, particularly in agricultural value-chain investments, but it is difficult to access and often very expensive. Equity, on the other hand, dilutes the founders' ownership and may cause a drift in purpose or lead to complicated shareholding structures later on. Grants and donations allow for continued balance-sheet flexibility but may give undue influence to donors and could dilute the character of an impact enterprise in the direction of a charity organization. These are all questions that must be answered taking into consideration multiple perspectives; i.e., those of the founders and the existing outside investors, as well as those of future investors that may either be outside (institutions or private individuals) or inside (future leaders).

Finally, there is the question of quantity and timing. Fundraising is very demanding on the capacity of the leadership team and, therefore, represents a huge opportunity cost. Limiting fundraising to short periods of time while pursuing the ambitious goal of securing a few large investors can reduce this opportunity cost. However, it also raises issues regarding dependence on a small number of investors. On the other hand, permanent fundraising with a higher number of smaller investors represents a constant drag on time and energy, yet it provides for more diversification and a continuous, often productive dialogue with investors.

As can be seen from this initial list of strategic and operational questions, fundraising is a complicated topic. The enterprises with the most convincing fundraising approaches that we have come across in our work with elea companies regularly do the following:

- They systematically broaden their expertise of available funding approaches and their network of potential capital providers, often by actively searching for advice and knowledge from their current external investors.
- They proactively design a long-term desirable shareholder structure with a view to potential exit scenarios. Often, this includes a small number of active, diverse, yet complementary shareholders with strong alignment in terms of both social impact and commercial interests.
- They tap into the potential for grants and patient debt to keep the liability profile of the balance sheet lean. They mobilize matching grants from those development finance institutions with fast decision-making processes and less onerous reporting duties.
- They find ways to concentrate ownership and control with the founding group as long as possible, through the employment of a mix of convertibles and different classes of shares (including preferred shares).
- They are creative in mobilizing working capital through the design of their model. Peer-to-peer lending for financing agricultural production can be an attractive source of sustainable and inexpensive working capital.
- They carefully plan their fundraising cycles depending on important milestones in their enterprise development story (e.g., after reaching impressive profitability, growth, or innovation indicators).

Choosing high-quality investors and a well-thought-out approach in the field of fundraising can determine the success or failure of an impact enterprise and is, therefore, in the highest interest of both entrepreneurs and investors.[13] It is one more reason why it is so crucially important to have a qualified CFO on board who thoroughly plans cash flows and considers contingency measures – always with a glass-half-empty approach – to be prepared for adverse scenarios.

5.3.3 Handling crises

Helping entrepreneurs to navigate through crises is a regular elea task. As Ben Horowitz writes in his book, *The Hard Thing about Hard Things – Building a Business When There Are No Easy Answers*, virtually all of the great founder entrepreneurs he has met as an investor in the technology start-up sector in Silicon Valley have gone through what he calls "the struggle" (see Context Box 5.6 for some excerpts of this description). This coincides with our experience: before the current pandemic, around one-third of elea's investments were exposed to at least one more-or-less dramatic crisis situation during their period as an active elea investment.

CONTEXT BOX 5.6: THE STRUGGLE

- Is when you wonder why you started the company in the first place.
- Is when your employees think you are lying and you think they may be right.
- Is when food loses its taste.
- Is when you don't believe you should be CEO of your company. The struggle is when you know that you are in over your head and you know that you cannot be replaced.
- Is when you want the pain to stop. The struggle is unhappiness.
- Is when you go on vacation to feel better and you feel worse.
- Is when you are surrounded by people and you are all alone.
- Is the land of broken promises and crushed dreams.
- Is a cold sweat.
- Is not failure, but it causes failure. (Excerpts from [Horowitz, 2014, p. 61])

As we are writing these lines, all elea investments are more or less in crisis mode due to the Global Covid-19 Crisis. Issues that were already identified before the crisis have now become even more urgent. Thus, addressing them can often no longer be postponed. Furthermore, in those cases where trust between elea and the entrepreneurs was not already actively built during "normal times" to sustain the deep and challenging dialogue needed in times of crisis, it turns out to be very difficult to build it now under stressful conditions.

While at the time of writing these lines there was not yet an end in sight to the current global health crisis, some general observations can already be made with high confidence. The type of support and services that an organization like elea can offer has never been in higher demand than now. All entrepreneurs are in need of a trusted investor and partner who is committed to helping them survive and find their way back to sustainable impact and a financial performance track. Their specific needs range from advice (through the sharing of experiences with others), practical solutions to problems, access to important contacts, and quick, non-bureaucratic emergency funding up to – more often than not – someone who is available to empathetically listen to all of the professional and personal concerns affecting them. The role that elea plays varies. Sometimes, it is to push entrepreneurs to come up with a realistic worst case scenario, which is challenging for some glass-half-full entrepreneurs. It can also be to see opportunities and suggest offensive measures – besides the necessary defensive actions needed to protect the core. What is already clear is that, while not all companies may survive in their current form, many will come out strengthened, having learned many relevant lessons from this unprecedented experience.

More generally, at elea, we distinguish between two types of crises, "people crises" and "things crises." In reality, situations can include both types, and one type can turn into the other type, but it is valuable to distinguish them, as they need to be handled differently. Examples of people crises are a breakdown of confidence within the founding and leadership team or with a key outside investor. At one of our impact enterprises, two founders who agreed in principle on a transition of CEO responsibility from one founder to another were not able to openly address all the issues surrounding this transition due to emotional hurdles. Consequently, the company was paralyzed for months and missed important deadlines. In another example, elea had agreed on a clear plan forward with an investee company and later found out via internet that this company had agreed on a plan with another outside investor that was in direct conflict with the plan elea had developed with them. What makes people crises so difficult is that they go deep into character traits, personality structures, ethics, and values and, thus, cannot be easily fixed. There is no way around long, deep dialogue between the parties involved to deal with these people crises, which may eventually be supported by a neutral mediator to arrive at an agreed diagnostic of the situation as a basis for developing viable solutions. More often than not, incompatible personalities have to separate from each other. Then, the task is to maximize fairness and minimize damage as the separation terms are discussed and agreed upon.

Things crises are different, while not necessarily easier to resolve. They often result from overconfidence in revenue generation and/or capital raising, relative to cost development. Several of our impact enterprises, particularly in the area of global agricultural value chains, went through such a growth, liquidity, and restructuring crisis. Such crises follow similar patterns; for example, when initial success on the revenue front encourages the buildup of substantial resources and excess capacity – sometimes to handle expected future production and sales volumes, sometimes to build up additional products and services. At some stage, when revenue growth slows for whatever reason, these resources remain underutilized and must be financed. So a gap opens between revenue and cost that can rapidly turn into a liquidity crisis with existential threats to the very survival of a company. The answer inevitably lies in cutting costs, which is particularly hard for impact enterprises with a growth DNA, and proves to be especially challenging for impact entrepreneurs with high ethical sensitivity, as they have to lay off colleagues whom they had struggled to recruit not long before then.

The source of such crises can either be homegrown, resulting from specific behaviors and actions of the entrepreneurs and their teams, or it can come from unexpected external events that are beyond the influence and control of the people in charge. As an example of the latter, BagoSphere was existentially threatened by a sudden new requirement for a license to operate (a regulatory change that was totally unexpected) that put the company almost out of business. It took many months of intensive, and exhausting, crisis management for BagoSphere to get back on track by successfully applying for this license while procuring the survival of the company in the meantime. Another example of such an externally provoked crisis was Dharma Life's shocking experience as India demonetized its currency in November 2016 (see Context Box 5.7).

CONTEXT BOX 5.7: MANAGING A CRISIS IN INDIA

On November 8, 2016, India's prime minister announced that all banknotes of 500 and 1,000, Indian rupees would not be valid anymore on the following day. They could either be maintained by opening a bank account or by exchanging the notes into newly created bank notes. The stated objective was to fight corruption and accelerate financial inclusion. Unfortunately, the banking system's capacity to handle such a shock was far overestimated, such that many people, particularly among the poorest Indians living in rural India, saw their savings threatened.

Dharma Life had just celebrated an extraordinary month, particularly because the revenues from the Diwali festivities had reached a record level of USD 530,000. The month following the prime minister's announcement, revenue fell by 94%, to USD 32,000. Dharma's customers simply lacked the cash to continue buying Dharma's products. It took six months for revenue to reach pre-crisis levels. Dharma was hit at two levels: First, the Dharma Life Entrepreneurs (DLEs) could not service the credits with Dharma Life for holding stocks of goods locally. Second, Dharma Life quickly ran out of liquidity to continue purchasing and paying salaries to staff. Gaurav impressively acknowledged immediately that this was a potentially life threatening crisis. However, he could also convincingly argue that, while it would take several months to fix this, it was not a permanent threat to Dharma's model.

He and his team extended the credit terms to the DLEs, and he declared a state of emergency regarding liquidity management (e.g., by delaying salary payments). Based on timely cash planning, he convinced the board to consider a temporary bridge-financing facility. elea committed a loan of USD 300,000 within just a few days and then helped convince another major sponsoring foundation to commit USD 500,000 within days (without the usual time for in-depth financial analysis and key performance indicators). Fortunately, the crisis could be overcome after 9 to 12 months without lasting damage. Key to this success was a reliable cash management system, as well as a founder-CEO who immediately recognized the sense of urgency without falling into panic mode and who had a close, trust-based relationship with his investors, who were represented in the board. This facilitated positive decisions within days, not within months as is typical for at least some more traditional foundations.

What can an external investor like elea contribute in such situations, and what are some of our lessons and insights from such experiences? An important, and crucial, role is to bring the entrepreneurs and their teams to acknowledge a development as a crisis with potentially fatal consequences. The semi–objective, outside position of an active investor sometimes helps them to see realities in a clearer, more sober way, whereas company insiders may be more resemblant of a frog in a water tank whose water temperature is constantly increasing. Acknowledging a crisis involves instilling both a sense of urgency and the need to transition into crisis mode by reprioritizing plans and resources while at the same time inspiring confidence that the crisis is manageable.

elea has the benefit of a professional team that has experienced several types of crises and can, therefore, offer specific advice on what to do and how to set priorities in such a situation. With regard to people crises, elea can (and sometimes does) act as a neutral mediator to resolve tensions within the leadership team. Depending on who the other external investors are, elea can also facilitate a dialogue between the entrepreneurial team (which may be shocked and tempted to panic) and other external investors, with their specific characteristics and interests (e.g., a venture capitalist who may be calculating when to write it off or a charitable foundation that may not see the urgency of making certain decisions). As the India example shows, an investor like elea can provide very tangible assistance as well, such as helping to put together an emergency bridge-financing package.

As a philanthropic impact investor with patient philanthropic capital providers, elea has the privilege of taking sides with the company as long as possible. We strictly observe the old banker's saying not to "throw good money after bad." Bad in this context means either unviable companies and/or unethical people. Yet we are often working alongside the entrepreneurs to save the company while other external investors are already concentrating on minimizing exit costs. We also work hard to be fair in situations where we have decided to exit. In the example mentioned above, where we were not told the truth regarding an alternative investor arrangement with a conflicting plan, our exit decision was firm. We cannot compromise on a lack of confidence, since it is in stark contrast with two of our highest virtues; namely integrity and partnership. However, we conducted an on-site workshop on partnership values to articulate our ethical stance, and we delegated (and funded) a team member on-site for a few months to help with the transition.

5.3.4 *Developing people*

While being challenged day after day by pressing operational duties already in normal times and more so in crisis situations, entrepreneurs, together with their teams, have to somehow set aside capacity to create the foundation for the future of the company. The most important task in this respect is people development. A systematic approach to performance measurement and management is an important basis for identifying and leveraging ambitions and potential in people. Yet, realistically, impact enterprises at the early stage in their development will neither have the capacity nor the expertise to introduce and apply very sophisticated performance measurement systems and tools. It is also an area where overengineering in the corporate world has become quite common, with the consequence that some high-profile companies, such as Accenture, Facebook, Microsoft, and Goldman Sachs, have replaced formal, structured performance reviews with informal, yet more frequent, feedback mechanisms.[14]

However, some simple, yet effective, performance management methods are essential for the future of a company. First, there has to be transparency at the leadership team level of an organization about the best performers and/or those with the highest potential: Who are the ones who carry the current operations? Which ones have substantial potential to grow? Who are the fast-trackers among the most recently hired team members? How happy are they? What are the risks of them leaving? What can be done to keep them passionate about their roles and to open up attractive opportunities for them in the future? Assigning leadership team members as mentors for high-potential individuals can be a good way to keep close track of their positive development strategies, to ensure inclusion and visibility (e.g., through share ownership), and to pick up on early signs of dissatisfaction and flight risk.

At the other side of the performance spectrum, those with performance issues have to be analyzed taking into account the nature of the issues at hand. Is it a lack of motivation or a lack of skills that leads to unsatisfactory performance? In the case of a lack of motivation, the task of the leader is to find out why this is. Does it have to do with job circumstances, or is it related to external factors outside the job (e.g., a family conflict, health problem, financial distress, etc.). A good understanding of the issues involved allows for an assessment of whether something can be done about it, and if so, what. If the performance issue is related to a lack of skills, the best approach is to help a person to develop these skills, either through direct coaching and feedback or through a more formalized, possibly external, skills development program. A simple matrix can help categorize different approaches depending on the type of performance issues identified (see Figure 5.2).

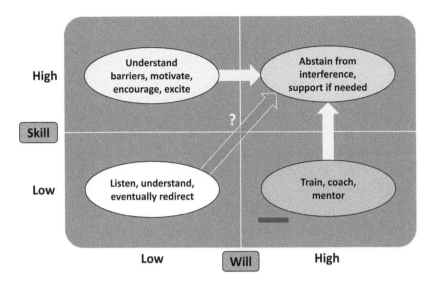

Figure 5.2 The skill/will matrix for people leadership.

Source: An adaptation based on www.stellarleader.com

With regard to the desired characteristics of a tool used for gathering performance information and carrying out performance review discussions, in line with our partnership principles, we prefer a two-way dialogue on mutual expectations, goals, achievements, and disappointments over a top-down, one-way, hierarchical appraisal. It should start with a self-evaluation given that, in our complex world, nobody usually knows better how a task was performed than the one in charge of that task. For highly critical positions, the views of peers, subordinates, and eventually even clients, must be considered, in addition to the opinions of superiors. A system that differentiates between a relative performance evaluation vis-à-vis peers (usually suitable for the fair allocation of financial rewards) and an absolute assessment of contributions and capabilities (as measured against a development path) is superior to a mono-dimensional, judgmental, vertical performance feedback from a boss to his subordinate. It should likewise include a mandatory feedback loop where the superior receives (hopefully) open, honest, and constructive feedback from the person being evaluated.

As an organization evolves over time, the crucial leadership roles will change and develop. Being flexible and open to change and at least trying to regularly think ahead about alternative scenarios will help the leadership team to maintain the initiative and can, at least to some extent, mitigate the consequences of unexpected departures by important people. Changes in roles within the organizational structure are natural and, while often painful, they are frequently a key to success, as they allow younger talent to flourish and realize their potential. The most important lesson we have learned at elea, based on several experiences of this type, is to confront such situations as early as possible and with brutal honesty and transparency. Natural temptations to delay such delicate conversations should be actively resisted. If conducted at an early stage of a foreseeable change, conversations can be more constructive and lead to creative solutions as opposed to requiring urgently needed emergency measures without much room to maneuver. Such an early and open dialogue provides flexibility and may be more digestible for the people involved.

What is true at the top is also valid for other members of an organization. The earlier and more systematically that people-development options are explored, the more likely a leader will further advance her professional profile. The best elea entrepreneurs spend a considerable amount of time and thought on such questions of people and leadership development. The opportunity – and the need – for proactive people development as the organizations of impact enterprises evolve was also one of the driving forces for elea's decision to work with IMD through the elea Center for Social Innovation. We wanted to create platforms for exchanging best practice experiences in this field and for skills building, both on the job as well as through more formal executive education programs. A clear commitment to people development within the vision and value statement of an impact enterprise will help to signal the crucial importance of this part of the leadership arena. Outstanding skills in the area of recognizing and leveraging the huge and diverse potential in talented people are, in some ways, at the heart of combining entrepreneurship and capital. This is because capital is only worth as much as there are people with a set of skills to make good use of it.

At elea, we keep close contact with our investees during normal times, and even closer contact during crises. Based on our experience in navigating through ups and downs, we have summarized some of our insights from these frequent interactions for the benefit of both entrepreneurs and investors (see Practice Boxes 5.8 and 5.9).

PRACTICE BOX 5.8: SUGGESTIONS FOR ENTREPRENEURS IN NAVIGATING THROUGH UPS AND DOWNS

During Normal Times

- Spend your personal time and energy on where you have the greatest impact and the best fit with your strengths and skills.
- Understand your own biorhythm and plan activities accordingly.
- Lead by asking questions, not by giving commands.
- Invest enough time upfront when tasks and project mandates are specified.
- Tailor your leadership style to the needs and skills of your team. Focus on helping those who are willing and have the potential. Do not micromanage those who are capable. Do not waste energy on those who are unwilling and unable.

In Times of Crisis

- Concentrate on resolving the crisis, not on "feel good measures."
- Regularly communicate what you know, what you do not know, and what you are working on.
- Seek out help, but keep control of the main activities. Free yourself up from tasks that can be delegated.
- In the interest of sustainable impact, be tough on the substance (the "what") but soft on the ways (the "how").
- Leverage your team. Do not bypass it.

PRACTICE BOX 5.9: SUGGESTIONS FOR INVESTORS IN NAVIGATING THROUGH UPS AND DOWNS

During Normal Times

- Stay in close contact; build a trusted relationship with the entrepreneur.
- Be helpful on request, but avoid leadership distraction and operational interference.
- Make your network available to facilitate access to relevant sources of expertise and contacts.
- Contribute to strategic thinking beyond day-to-day tasks.
- Build personal relationships with other investors.

In Times of Crisis
- Be available to empathetically listen.
- Help entrepreneurs to define the core of their business, as this is what needs to be protected through the crisis.
- Push thinking on realistic worst-case scenarios; encourage a glass-half-empty perspective to support survival.
- Provide emergency funding if needed without becoming the lender of last resort, and only do so for otherwise viable business models.
- Advocate for emergency funding with other investors if needed.

5.4 Conclusions

5.4.1 Insights and takeaways

We have covered a lot of ground across many themes in this chapter: from analyzing and planning to organizing and getting things done; from ambitious purpose and vision statements for improving the world to practical daily matters, such as how to plan and run a meeting; from dealing with things crises to dealing with people crises; and from shaping matters within one's leadership influence to reacting to outside events and developments beyond one's control. The leadership tasks that are necessary to develop an enterprise at this stage are overwhelming and will bring any leadership team to their limits in terms of capacity, skills, and energy. Thus, in addition to the sheer complexity of these tasks, there is a constant race against time and a continuous change of context. This means that not only the leadership capacity is stretched, but there are also enormous demands on openness and flexibility to deal with, and there is a need to adjust to new circumstances.

Yet, there are no shortcuts available, for resources are always constrained and there is no capacity for luxury solutions or overengineering. Priorities will always only include the must-haves and almost never the nice-to-haves. There may be some possibilities to leverage the capacity of entrepreneurs with additional experienced executives, but in general, there are clear limits to delegation. And still, we pointed to several opportunities where an active investor like elea can be helpful in providing advice, methodological support, and practical assistance. Our experience shows that such a contribution can be valuable under three conditions: it should resolve an existing, relevant, and important problem rather than add to the list of challenges and open issues (which tends to be very long anyway); it should not in any way dilute individual executive responsibilities; and it should be provided by professionals who have the relevant skills and experience (which is why we put so much emphasis on professional development at elea).

5.4.2 *Your point of view*

Learning objectives

After studying this chapter, you should be able to

1. identify the key elements for building and leading a sustainable impact enterprise and articulate how they relate to each other;
2. define a vision for an impact-focused company (using the elea hexagon method) and highlight the most critical interdependencies between the different components;
3. evaluate alternative models for impact enterprises, taking into account their impact mechanisms, their economic characteristics, and their growth patterns;
4. describe the main factors for success in building an effective leadership team at the top;
5. explain the essential elements of a process-oriented method toward building an effective and efficient impact enterprise;
6. differentiate best practices for normal times versus times of crisis; and
7. summarize how an active philanthropic impact investment organization like elea can contribute to building and leading an impact enterprise.

Reflection questions

1. Based on your knowledge of impact-oriented enterprises, how would you rank the key building blocks for a successful organization in terms of their importance and challenges?
2. Put yourself in the role of an impact entrepreneur. How would you answer the following questions based on the example of an impact company that you are familiar with:
   a. How does the vision combine impact objectives and business opportunities? Are there tensions or trade-offs between the two? How can they be resolved?

    b. How do you define success? What are different elements, and how would you rank them?

    c. What do you consider to be the greatest challenges in building and leading such an enterprise? How would you tackle them?

    d. Where are the greatest risks? How can they be mitigated?

3. Where do you stand on the planning debate? What are the pros and cons of having plans? Do you see value in planning? Why? Do you share elea's perspective about the importance of plans?

4. How do you organize a leadership team? How do you choose its members and why? What is your role, and what are theirs? Explain the rationale.

5. In your experience, what are effective, yet simple, instruments to assess people's performance, and how do you develop people toward realizing their potential? Describe good and bad examples from your areas of familiarity.

6. How do you envision the contribution of an active investor to your enterprise? What types of leadership styles foster/hinder collaboration? In which areas should an investor contribute, in which not, and why?

7. In your experience, what are some of the main reasons why enterprises fail? How can the risk of failure be mitigated? What are your most important insights and lessons from managing crises?

8. Evaluate yourself in light of this chapter's recommendations for becoming a self-aware and effective leader. What are your strengths? How could you develop yourself in terms of your weaknesses?

Right vs. right dilemma: Choice vs. nudging at the base of the pyramid

What are the responsibilities of impact enterprises and investors vis-à-vis the consumers at the base of the pyramid? Paraphrasing President J. F. Kennedy in 1962: Do poor people have the right to safety, the right to be listened to, the right to choose, and the right to be informed? Where does the duty of entrepreneurs and investors to protect such rights end, and where does the freedom of poor people start? Should impact entrepreneurs and investors have a view about which products and services are "best" for poor people, and should they influence their purchasing decisions? Or should they just offer those products and services that are in highest demand and make the most economic sense? Is such pure pragmatism ethically acceptable even though poor people may purchase goods and services that make them poorer and/or damage their health? Or do ethics rather demand that entrepreneurs and investors take a stance on which goods and services are best suited to improving the livelihoods of poor people and then "nudge" their behaviors in this direction; e.g., through awareness and education campaigns?

Debate the pros and cons of each stance.

Notes

1. This is one of the core messages of *Inclusive Leadership*, a book written by one of the co-authors, see (Wuffli, 2016). Several ideas and examples in this part build on Part Four of *Inclusive Leadership*.

2. In our experience, 5 years is a useful time horizon; it is sufficiently far away to allow imagination to flow, and yet it is still within the range of a foreseeable future. Three years is often too short to be able to assess the results of strategic choices and resource deployment, and 10 years is too far away to encourage clear commitments.

3. According to an article by Manvi Sharma published in *Business Management Ideas*, there are nine major barriers to planning/management; namely, (1) dynamic and complex environments, (2) reluctance to establish goals, (3) resistance to change, (4) constraints, (5) time and expense, (6) psychological difficulties, (7) technical problems, (8) misunderstanding, and (9) the lack of an appropriate "planning climate" (Sharma).

4. In this regard, we concur with the introductory statement in a handbook developed by McKinsey & Company (2007) that states the benefits of venture business planning as follows:

    - It forces the founders to systematically think through their ideas, creating the necessary momentum.
    - It uncovers gaps in knowledge and indicates how to close them in an efficient and structured way.
    - It encourages decision-making and focus.
    - It serves as a communication instrument between all stakeholders.
    - It provides an overview of required resources and indicates resource constraints.
    - It helps prepare and test for stress situations.

5. Examples of guides on how to write business plans or develop business models are (e.g., *What Is a Business Model?* [Ovans, 2015]; *Business Plans: A Step-by-Step Guide* [Entrepreneur, n.d.]; *7 Steps to a Perfectly Written Business Plan* [Rampton, 2019]). A frequently used template to articulate and visualize business models is the "Business Model Canvas," which was created based on the input of 470 practitioners from 45 countries (Osterwalder & Pigneur, 2010) to present a simple framework for visualizing business-plan and model components.

6. For example, see (propel nonprofits, n.d.); (MaRS, n.d.); (Byruck, 2015); (Aps, 2016). See also a study that analyzes the differences in the business models of business versus social enterprises based on two case examples (Rahmani Qastharin & Liu, 2014).

7. http://businessdictionary.com/definition/organization.html

8. These principles originate from the turbulent time when your co-author became Group CEO of UBS in 2001 in the midst of a major governance and confidence crisis. The challenge then was to build a team among diverse personalities with a commitment to a shared agenda bound to achieving success for UBS. See (Wuffli, 2016) for more details.

9. Swiss pharmaceutical company Novartis is an example of this: it adopted 10 principles to guide the organizational behavior of its people (copied from [Raitner, 2019]), having been inspired by a highly provocative book entitled *Unboss* (Botter & Kolind, 2012). These principles mirror behaviors that we observe in elea enterprises on a daily basis. They include:

    1. Focusing on purpose rather than profit
    2. Dissolving the old hierarchy and encouraging everyone to work together
    3. Transforming your business into an unlimited social network
    4. Becoming a great place to work and attracting the best people
    5. Stepping aside and letting your co-workers take the lead
    6. Turning customers into partners and advocates for your cause
    7. Getting rid of rigid pay scales and bonus schemes, as well as selfish employees who care about such things
    8. Involving people outside of your company – also in research and development
    9. Tolerating mistakes and talking openly about them
    10. Strengthening dialogue throughout the organization through the use of social media

10. For example, the Myers-Briggs Type Indicator, MBTI (www.myersbriggs.org), or Organizational Culture Inventory, OCI (www.humansynergistics.com).

11. Burnout among social entrepreneurs is a true issue. Social Impact Award's (SIA) academic partner, the Vienna University of Economics and Business and its Social Entrepreneurship Center, conducted a survey among SIA alumni that included questions about personal well-being. Outcomes show that social entrepreneurs are challenged: more than 40% were exposed to some level of burnout, and 5% might have experienced severe burnout (see [Pignet, 2015]; [Cacciotti, 2019]).

12. It took one of the co-authors many years to find out which tasks should ideally be done during which times of the day, which days of the week, and which seasons of the year and how to organize the agenda accordingly. What he learned was that his effectiveness varies not by a few percentage points but by factors of two to three, depending upon which time/day/ season is chosen. For instance, writing a speech on a quiet morning at 7 a.m. can be done in an hour's time. The same task would take three hours on any busy afternoon toward the end of the week and would still not reach the quality of the early morning draft.

13. See also Horowitz (2014) for useful and practical advice in the critical field of fundraising. It provides the perspective of the co-founder of one of the leading Silicon Valley venture-capital firms (Andreessen Horowitz) and is based on many years of experience as a serial start-up entrepreneur.

14. See (Reflektive, 2018); (Cappelli & Tavis, 2016).

References

Aps, J. (2016). A Business Planning Guide to Developing a Social Enterprise. *Social Entrepreneurship Support Network of the Baltic Region*. Retrieved May 7, 2020, from http://www.socialenterprisebsr.net/2016/04/a-business-planning-guide-to-developing-a-social-enterprise/

Botter, J., & Kolind, L. (2012). *Unboss*. Jyllands-Postens Forlag.

Bouée, C.-E. (2013). *Light Footprint Management: Leadership in Times of Change*. Bloomsbury.

Byruck, M.. (2015). Business Plans and Planning for Social Enterprises and Nonprofits. *socialgoodguides.com*. Retrieved May 7, 2020, from http://www.socialgoodguides.com/business-plans-and-planning-for-social-enterprises-and-nonprofits-guide/)

Cacciotti, G.. (2019, February 20). Why Social Entrepreneurs Are So Susceptible to Burnout. *Thomson Reuters Foundation News*. Retrieved May 8, 2020, from https://news.trust.org/item/20190220111328-g7kid/

Cappelli, P., & Tavis, A.. (2016, October). The Performance Management Revolution. *Harvard Business Review*. Retrieved May 8, 2020, from https://hbr.org/2016/10/the-performance-management-revolution

Drucker, P. F.. (1994, September–October). The Theory of the Business. *Harvard Business Review*. Retrieved October 14, 2019, from https://hbr.org/1994/09/the-theory-of-the-business

Entrepreneur. (n.d.). Business Plans: A Step-by-Step Guide. *Entrepreneur*. Retrieved May 7, 2020, from https://www.entrepreneur.com/article/247574

Haimann, T. (1978). *Managing the Modern Organization.*

Horowitz, B. (2014). *The Hard Thing About Hard Things – Building a Business When There Are No Easy Answers.* New York: HarperCollins.

Mankins, M., & Schwartz, D. (2016)., February 9). *Building Your Own High-Performance Organization.* Bain.

MaRS. (n.d.). *Business Plans for Social Enterprises (SE) and Social Businesses.* Retrieved May 7, 2020, from https://learn.marsdd.com/article/business-plans-for-social-enterprises-se-and-social-businesses/

McKinsey & Company (2007, 4th. Edition). *Planen, Gründen, Wachsen – Mit dem professionellen Businessplan zum Erfolg.* Heidelberg: Redline Wirtschaft.

Milligan, K., & Walker, J. C.. (2020, April 8). Self-Inquiry for Social Change Leaders. *Stanford Social Innovation Review*.

Müller-Stewens, G. (2019). *Die Neuen Strategen–Gestalter Der Unternehmenszukunft.* Stuttgart: Schäffer-Poeschel Verlag.

Osterwalder, A., & Pigneur, Y. (2010). *Business Model Generation.* Hoboken, NJ: John Wiley & Sons.

Ovans, A.. (2015, January 23). What Is a Business Model? *Harvard Business Review*. Retrieved May 7, 2020, from https://hbr.org/2015/01/what-is-a-business-model

Peters, T., & Waterman, R. (1982). *In Search of Excellence.* New York: Harper & Row.

Pignet, S.. (2015, November 9). Social Entrepreneurs Burnout. *Creators for Good*. Retrieved May 8, 2020, from https://www.creatorsforgood.com/2015/11/09/social-entrepreneurs-burnout/

propel nonprofits. (n.d.). *Social Enterprise Business Plan.* Retrieved May 7, 2020, from https://www.propelnonprofits.org/resources/social-enterprise-business-plan/

Rahmani Qastharin, A., & Liu, D. (2014). *Business Model Differences Between Business and Social Enterprise*. Stockholm: KTH Royal Institute of Technology.

Raitner, M.. (2019, July 18). Unboss Instead of Egomaniacs. *Führung erfahren*. Retrieved May 27 from https://fuehrung-erfahren.de/en/2019/07/unboss-instead-of-egomaniacs/

Rampton, J.. (2019, February 19). 7 Steps to a Perfectly Written Business Plan. *Entrepreneur*. Retrieved May 7, 2020, from https://www.entrepreneur.com/article/281416

Reflektive. (2018, May 8). These Five Companies Are Trailblazing Performance Management. *Reflektive*. Retrieved May 8, 2020, from https://www.reflektive.com/blog/companies-trailblazing-pm/

Sharma, M.. (n.d.). 9 Major Barriers to Planning/Management. *Business Management Ideas*. Retrieved May 7, 2020, from https://www.businessmanagementideas.com/planning/9-major-barriers-to-planning-management/7505

Wuffli, P. A. (2016). *Inclusive Leadership: A Framework for the Global Era*. New York, London et al: Springer.

6

SUSTAINING IMPACT AND INNOVATION

How can impact and innovation be sustained? Effective governance mechanisms, particularly supervisory boards, are important levers in this regard. This area is challenging and often does not receive the attention that it deserves, but it is instrumental for ensuring a close integration between entrepreneurship and capital and keeping the perspectives and objectives of investors, entrepreneurs, and other stakeholders aligned, thereby avoiding a drift in purpose. However, alignment on impact objectives is only possible when impact is being systematically measured and managed. Although this is a frequent topic at impact investing conferences, clear, globally accepted standards that would allow for comparing alternative methods in terms of their scope, relevance, effectiveness, and quality have not yet emerged. The Operating Principles for Impact Management, which were launched in 2019 by the International Finance Corporation (IFC) in consultation with key stakeholders from industry, are a promising step in this direction. Ultimately, organizations across private, public, and civil-society sectors will have to effectively collaborate in order to mobilize the resources and build the capacity required to establish new ecosystems with a more aligned inclusive capitalism.

6.1 Effective governance and supervisory boards

Whenever elea approves investments in impact enterprises, the approach to governance and the role and composition of the supervisory board (hereafter simply referred to as "the board") are important topics for discussion. Is there a governance model beyond the entrepreneurs based on which supervisory functions are separate from executive tasks? If not, is this planned, at what stage, and how will it be done? If yes, is the board in a position to add value by providing advice and guidance and by challenging decisions and contributing risk-mitigating checks and balances? Or is the role of the board minimized to monitoring legal compliance and watching out for risks? Is there an agreed board agenda, and how relevant is it to the success of a company? Do board members have the relevant skills and experience, and do they spend sufficient time and energy with the company to be able to add value? How involved are they, and in what matters can and should they be involved? How are individual board members selected, and what are the guiding thoughts behind the composition of the overall board?

Based on the answers to these and other questions, elea then decides whether it should appoint someone to the board as its representative, and if so, whom. For equity or equity-linked investments, elea typically asks for board seats and considers this to be an important part of impact value creation. Accordingly, working toward effective governance and board structures is an important, yet challenging, task for elea colleagues. elea board representatives typically attend six to eight board-related meetings per year, with many specific interactions between meetings.

6.1.1 Board basics

What can we learn from governance and board experience in traditional corporations and civil-society organizations regarding best practice? Academic literature and the experience of one of the co-authors with several boards of large and small, profit and nonprofit organizations suggest several principles and recommendations to get the basics right and to ensure appropriate board leadership. In this section, we will thus summarize our understanding of "best practice" along the dimensions of a board's mandate, role, and composition, as well as its structure, modus operandi, logistics, and leadership.[1]

Mandate, role, and composition

- The board is the highest authority of an enterprise. It should oversee strategy, organization, and leadership, and it should ensure compliance with the law and appropriate control of risks. It should inspire, support, and challenge the executives in charge of overall management, and it should be accountable to its owners, and eventually other stakeholders, for success and failure. Human dynamics is as important as formal procedures.

- The board should include a selected number of independent personalities that are sufficiently involved and familiar with the company and strong enough to challenge the entrepreneurs on important issues.

- Depending on the size and complexity of an enterprise, the board should have a large enough number of members to ensure a certain level of diversity and to allow for some specialization within committees, yet it should be small enough to permit cohesion and a spirit of partnership. In our experience, seven to twelve members is a reasonable range, and they should have experience and skills that are relevant for the success of a company. The board should also be diverse in terms of backgrounds, skills, and personalities. "Subjective diversity," such as personality, character, ambition, and style, is as important as "objective diversity," such as relevant experience, gender, nationality, and age.

- Besides diversity, a board must have a set of shared objectives, values, and principles regarding the culture and direction of an enterprise. There should also be a good chemistry between board members to allow for constructive dialogue at high-quality levels.

- Board additions should be driven by a specific need for incremental qualities, not by the availability of an interested candidate. The process should start with a profile of desired characteristics in terms of perspectives, skills, experiences, and personality traits to ensure that each board member makes a difference in his contribution. Board members must have the capacity to familiarize themselves with the industry and the company, and they must make a commitment to serve at least five to seven years.

Structure, modus operandi, and logistics

- As an enterprise increases in size, the board should be supported by specialist committees that have a written mandate. There should be a good balance between striving for efficiency and maintaining the board's holistic accountability to the company's owners and other stakeholders. Financial results and impact performance, as well as plans and budgets, should always be discussed by the entire board.

- The board should regularly meet, both physically and by telephone/ video conference, and meetings should follow an agenda that reflects the leadership priorities of the company. Members of the leadership team of the enterprise should be present during parts of the board meeting, and they should have the opportunity to express their assessment of the "state of affairs," their concerns, and their requests for support by the board. Each board meeting should consist of an active, open, and honest Q&A session between the board and the executives to encourage a sense of responsibility on the part of the executives vis-à-vis the board with regard to the results of the company. Each board meeting should also have a private session without executives attending.

- The board meetings need to be well prepared and have a well-thought-out agenda. For complicated matters, particularly for issues requiring a decision, agenda items must be supported by concise documents distributed in advance of the meeting, so that all board members have an opportunity to come to the meeting prepared. Furthermore, most of the meeting should be in the form of a dialogue; listening to lengthy slide presentations is usually not time well spent for board members.

- There should be a person who acts as the board secretary to ensure proper meeting logistics, organize timely circulation of the agenda and supporting documentation, take the minutes, and organize a timely follow-up. Minutes should be circulated among board members (and eventually executives) within a reasonable time after the meeting, when the discussions are still present in the minds of the attendants.

Leadership

- A board must have a chairperson. The chairperson's specific role, focus, and priorities depend on the needs of a company and its governance. These should be agreed among the board members and with the executives to clarify mutual expectations. These requirements shape the desired profile and characteristics of the chairperson who, while seeing herself as a leader, should be committed to strong partnership values. Having been a CEO before helps, both in terms of experience and credibility, among board peers and executives.

- The chairperson leads the board, organizes the dialogue with both owners and other stakeholders, and, with the executives, ensures high-quality and timely decision-making, and is available for and capable of handling crises. Her tasks include: leading meetings, assigning account-abilities to the board and its committees, and, with the executives, identifying the issues that a board faces and orchestrating a process for prioritizing and addressing them. Then, acting as a bridge-builder, she should ensure the broad-based participation of board members and a constructive dialogue between insiders and outsiders, with executives as well as with mission-critical stakeholders. And finally, as an effective coach to the executives, a chairperson should give and accept feedback and nurture a mutually respectful, trusting partnership.

- Effective board meetings are at the core of good governance. The chairperson must take time to prepare the agenda, think through the sequence (from the more entrepreneurial and strategic to the more reg-ulatory and statutory items), and allocate time respectively. She should then ensure the appropriate format, content, and quality of supporting documentation. Executives are often tempted to reuse the same docu-mentation as the one used for executive management, even though the scope and objective of board discussions are distinctive and require a different set of information. Short, concise memos are preferable to lengthy PowerPoint presentations. Moreover, there should be a limit on the amount of information distributed. Board packs exceeding 1,000 pages that are distributed only three to four weekdays before a meeting may create an impression of industrious diligence but hardly contribute to focused and effective debates.

- As the chairperson conducts the meeting, complicated decision-finding processes need to be carefully staged. The style of discus-sion should thus match the desired outcome under each agenda item. A chairperson needs a high degree of flexibility and adjustability to adopt such a multi-style-meeting management approach. However, it is essential to leverage the diverse personality types and skills of individual board members present at the meeting. The chairperson should also decide on which executives, other members of manage-ment, or outside experts should be invited to the meeting, being sure to strike a balance between the inclusiveness and conclusiveness of discussions. Furthermore, the meeting should be planned and conducted with the goal of achieving desired outcomes and minimizing disruptive surprises. After the meeting, the chairperson must review the minutes and ensure follow-up on decisions and action items.

• The board should meet regularly without executives to discuss management performance, delicate and confidential matters, and also board-internal issues, such as its own constitution (e.g., board roles and committees), its effectiveness, its modus operandi, and the quality of its teamwork. The chairperson needs to reflect on how such sensitive issues can be discussed in a productive manner. For example, starting a board meeting with a dinner for specific leadership-related or strategically oriented topics, where a more flexible time allocation is possible and the setting is more informal, can be very valuable.

6.1.2 Governance for impact enterprises

The last 30–40 years have seen a dramatic evolution in governance at many organizations worldwide toward new and unprecedented levels of professionalism and quality. Currently, we can distinguish between three basic governance concepts. First, there is the traditional "western-style" corporate approach to governance that is primarily seen in large and medium-sized, publicly listed companies and is, to a significant and growing extent, shaped by ever more detailed regulations and codes of conduct. Boards run according to this model are typically rather large (10–15 members) and follow ever stricter guidelines regarding diversity. According to many regulations or codes of conduct, the majority of board members should be independent, whereby the criteria for determining independence are far from clear and do not follow global standards. In light of the various crises over the last 20–30 years, which were to some extent due to insufficient governance, the focus of this approach is often on compliance and risk control to protect the downside rather than on entrepreneurial ambitions and opportunities that reflect the upside opportunities of corporate activity.

Privately held companies (e.g., those held by private-equity companies or families) provide an alternative model that is centered on entrepreneurial ownership and value creation. According to this model, boards are smaller, and the criteria for their composition prioritize competence, relevant experience, and industry expertise, as well as a dedication of substantial time rather than formal diversity and independence. A central element of this approach is to attract, excite, and retain passionate, capable, and experienced business leaders as board members who design and deliver on entrepreneurial initiatives in strong alignment with executive management (see Context Box 6.1 on the debate of entrepreneurship versus correctness in governance).

CONTEXT BOX 6.1: ENTREPRENEURSHIP VERSUS CORRECTNESS IN GOVERNANCE

Steffen Meister, the Chairman of global private-markets investment firm Partners Group, published a book in 2018 entitled *"The rise of 'Governance Correctness': How public markets have lost entrepreneurial ground to private equity"* (Meister & Palkhiwala, 2018). In this book, Meister goes back to one of the beginnings of capitalism, when the original joint-stock company, the East India Company (EIC), was founded in 1600 by a royal charter from Queen Elizabeth I. It was a response to the difficulty of separating ownership from control that resulted from London merchants financing trading ships that were far away, sailing in the Asia-Pacific region. The EIC's governance framework gave investors a voice in the management of the company, while financing ships that would cross oceans and building an infrastructure to trade with distant lands. With the industrial revolution in the 19th century, the limited liability corporation was created to form a basis for attracting all the substantial capital required for mass production. It was also a starting point for an increasing rift between the shareholders of a company and their management. With the development of stock exchanges early in the 20th century and the institutionalization of savings through pension funds, life insurance companies, and mutual funds – which accelerated after World War II – corporations grew more and more distant from shareholders. The term "corporate governance" entered common usage in the 1970s as a response to the increasingly absolute power of the CEO, particularly in American corporations.

Meister argues that boards increasingly focused on compliance to control their members' individual liability as opposed to helping companies realize their entrepreneurial potential. This was largely a result of the development of codes and detailed regulations following the Asian crisis, the burst of the dot-com bubble, and the major governance failures around the turn of the century. An example, is the Sarbanes Oxley Act which was issued in 2002 by the U.S. Congress to enforce comprehensive internal control systems throughout the corporate world for companies with U.S. ties. He coins the term "Governance Correctness" to describe the phenomenon of boards focusing on formal procedures and control, and he uses the example of obsession with independence to show how dysfunctional this form of governance has become (Meister & Palkhiwala, 2018, p. 16 ff.).

Meister asserts that private-markets investment companies as enterprise owners are providing an effective alternative governance model that goes back to the roots of capitalism. Companies owned through private equity typically have smaller boards with clearer mandates, individual skills profiles, a more intense assignment, and close financial alignment to management in order to achieve value-creation objectives (Meister & Palkhiwala, 2018, p. 45 ff.).

And finally, a third governance concept (which is of lesser importance for the reflections in this book) includes those governance principles that apply to organizations that fulfill both an economic and a political role. Examples include enterprises owned by sovereign wealth funds that follow political and economic thinking and are often instrumentalized for national policy agendas beyond striving for economic effectiveness.

Amidst this field of tension and competition between different approaches to governance and boards, impact enterprises are called to position themselves to sustain both long-term impact creation and economic viability.[2] Thus, early-stage impact enterprises are in a very different situation regarding governance. Typically, the entrepreneurs who are governing, controlling, and leading these enterprises are mostly helped by a select number of advisors from a broad and diverse circle that can include friends and family, angel investors, experienced entrepreneurs, and executives, as well as other experts. At this stage, the board is usually seen as one of many formalities that are necessary to create a legal entity that complies with the law and where costs are minimized. Only over time may some of the advisors be asked to become board members, and, consequently, the board starts to assume a more active governance role in guiding, advising, and challenging the team in charge of execution.

The governance of impact enterprises typically has specific characteristics that are different from those of traditional corporations. They often attract very high-profile industry leaders as advisors or board members whose main experience centers around much larger and more complex enterprises. Although these leaders can make extremely valuable contributions, their presence on the board can also lead to significant expectation gaps, with the potential for mutual disappointment. Consequently, the level of diversity is more pronounced, as boards typically combine current or former business executives as well as impact representatives (such as elea colleagues) and can cover a range of ages between people in their early thirties up to those in their late seventies or even eighties. Board members usually serve on an honorary, non-paid basis, as impact enterprises at this stage cannot afford to pay them market-level compensation. This leads to highly varying degrees of dedication in terms of time and effort, ranging from a few hours per year up to a few days per month. With all of this diversity, however, we encourage our elea entrepreneurs to clearly define the roles and expectations of board members (being sure to show how distinct they are from other, less committed advisory roles) and not to compromise on "passion for the purpose" and "empathy for the team" in terms of choosing current or potential board members.

As impact enterprises are still small, with only very limited balance sheets, their focus is naturally more on the "what," the "how," and the "why" of building an enterprise rather than on protecting what exists (e.g., by reviewing and auditing existing financial assets). In addition, the board will naturally watch out for the many possible risks that can threaten a company's existence at this early stage, which range from issues such as a problematic strategic and competitive positioning to tensions and conflicts within the leadership team, the insufficient handling of operational tasks or bad financial structures, and a lack of cash-flow planning. As impact enterprises often operate in poor countries with underdeveloped public institutions and unstable political constellations, boards constantly have to consider unexpected developments that are out of their control and could substantially challenge the success of a company. So, in short, the boards of early stage impact enterprises are often even more challenged than those of traditional corporations: they have to cope with many diverse, important, board-relevant decisions while being confronted with sometimes inexperienced and young executive teams, and they dispose of only very scarce resources.

As a consequence, the boards of impact enterprises pick and choose from both of the first two governance approaches described above and have to concentrate their focus on those areas where they can make a difference. In our experience at elea, there are four ways to facilitate this. First, the board has to be regularly informed about relevant trends and developments, both within the company and externally, as well as on the important decisions and priorities of executive management. By insisting on a systematic and structured rhythm of information flow along defined financial and impact-oriented key performance indicators, surprises are avoided. Moreover, a framework that guides the executive team toward a disciplined management process for informed operational decision-making and priority setting should also be established.

Second, the board should proactively make its expertise and experience available in a flexible manner, for phone calls at the right time between the right individuals on specific, relevant topics can be as valuable as formal board meetings. Rather than insisting on a demanding, regular meeting schedule for all board members – which may discourage those high caliber, but very busy, ones from engaging – a flexible approach with a minimum of mandatory meetings and additional mechanisms, such as committees, task forces, and occasional ad-hoc conference calls, may be more effective.

Third, the board should concentrate on those areas where it can make a difference and complement the executive team in its tasks, rather than spending time second-guessing operational decisions. In the areas where it can make a difference, it should not shy away from also getting operationally involved and working directly together with the leadership team. Typical examples are evolving leadership structures (e.g., coaching or changing a CEO or CFO), medium-term strategic direction setting (e.g., balancing impact goals and financial objectives), investor relations, fundraising initiatives (e.g., defining sources and types of new capital), and financial management (e.g., balance-sheet structure and cash planning).

Finally, the board is often most useful in times of crises. In such situations, its role is to recognize and help the executive team acknowledge and accept a crisis. Then, the board has to support the executive team with a good balance between a sense of urgency and constructive, calm optimism as the organization enters into crisis mode, with a focus on thinking through all of the consequences and taking the necessary measures. Often, the board also has to provide specific support in such situations (e.g., organizing bridge financing among shareholders and other capital providers). Earlier investments into the establishment of strong personal relationships among board members can prove immensely valuable when a crisis hits an enterprise.

In summary, ensuring effective governance and board work at an impact enterprise is challenging and requires substantial effort and investment. A philanthropic impact investor, like elea, can play a valuable role in helping to create a workable approach at early development stages and in organizing and facilitating board work going forward. Thereby, its specific task is to keep the company's purpose and impact aligned along its development journey while supporting economic success. Often somewhat underappreciated and underprioritized by entrepreneurs, effective governance and supervisory boards are a crucial mechanism for institutionalizing an enterprise and realizing its sustained impact and innovation potential. This obviously requires clarity on what is meant by impact and how it is measured and managed, which will be the theme of the next section.

6.2 Measuring and managing impact

Through the work we engage in with our impact entrepreneurs, we often get a firsthand glimpse at the very specific impact that they have as we visit their operations on-site in the field. We have chosen a few of those examples here. The following stories are about some of the beneficiaries of impact enterprises within the elea portfolio that have already been mentioned.

6.2.1 elea impact stories

Margarita (54) is a mother of eight children and a grandmother of six grandchildren. She lives in Pusacpampa, a small community of approximately 20 smallholder farmer families situated 3,340 meters above sea level in the Andean region of Junin in Peru. The livelihoods in this community come primarily from growing and selling potatoes and several other types of vegetables, as well as from holding a few sheep. Annual average cash income per family is estimated to be around USD800–USD1,000. Margarita belongs to a group of (mostly) women across 40 communities in this region that collects "white moss" (a.k.a. sphagnum moss), a wild plant with special characteristics that makes it particularly valuable to wrap premium flowers, such as orchids. Inka Moss buys the white moss from these collectors, processes it in a factory (cleaning, drying, separating qualities, and packaging), and then ships it to its clients across the world. Per collected bag of white moss of approximately 15–20kg in gross weight, Margarita receives about USD 2.50. In 2019, she collected 140 bags and used the resulting cash income of USD 350 to buy uniforms, books, and food to facilitate the school attendance of her grandchildren. Going forward, this incremental income will continue to improve the quality of Margarita's life and that of her family.

Yessena (in her early 40s) is the mother of two daughters and a smallholder coffee farmer in Rosas, a small town near Popayan in Colombia. Colombia is the world's third-largest coffee exporter after Brazil and Vietnam, and it is well known for the quality of its highland coffee. She owns 2,500 small coffee trees, which each yield a pound of coffee annually. The price per pound for regular green (i.e., unroasted) coffee beans is between USD 0.50 and USD 1.00, which leads to an annual cash income of around USD 2,000. Two years ago, she was discovered by Vega Coffee and trained as a coffee specialist to produce higher quality coffee and learn how to roast. Today, together with six peer coffee farmers in the region, she runs Vega Coffee's local roasting factory (with the support of CAFICAUCA, a regional coffee cooperative) for one week a month, and she produces high-quality specialty coffee at a 70%–100% price premium over regular qualities. This shift to higher quality coffee and local roasting (versus shipping green coffee abroad) has permitted her to triple her annual income to approximately USD 6,000. In addition, she is seen as a pioneer and role model in the region and has encouraged and inspired many other (mostly female) coffee growers to upgrade their coffee quality as well. Vega buys roasted specialty coffee from a community of 800 farmers in this region and sells it to U.S. universities with organic and fair-trade labels. Its approach to roasting coffee on-site has, so far, remained unique in Colombia.

Gideon (32) is the father of three children and lives in the village of Ziwa Sirikwa, which is situated in the midwestern part of Kenya's Great Rift Valley. He is a smallholder farmer who produces both crops and livestock on his five-acre piece of land. Prior to becoming a customer of iCow, Gideon faced several challenges in farming. The greatest of these were how to identify, prevent, and control diseases and how to choose livestock feeds. Gideon became a farmer because this was what was done in his region, but he never received any formal education in farming.

Initially, he started with one cow and one calf as well as two chickens. He struggled to grow his poultry flock, because he regularly lost chickens due to disease. His annual cash income at the time was approximately USD800–USD900, with significant volatility. In 2017, Gideon subscribed to iCow for lessons on how to improve his poultry and dairy farming. Over time, these lessons became his agricultural reference material. Besides providing valuable specific insights and recommendations, they changed his perception toward farming. He increasingly saw it as a business, an entrepreneurial activity that could be continuously improved and made successful based on know-how gained from experience and on decisions made with relevant information. The health of his cows has since improved, and the mortality of his poultry has been reduced, thanks to better and more diverse food planted on his farm and effective vaccinations. He now has three cows and 20 chickens, and he has become more productive in growing maize and other crops. As a result of this increased productivity, he has been able to reach an annual cash income of up to USD2,000–USD2,500. This has allowed him to pay down his debt and prepay the school fees of approximately USD 350 per annum for his three children. Previously, he sometimes missed paying installments for school fees and, consequently, his children were sent home.

Sopheap (37) grew up in a family of four in the Battambang Province of Cambodia. Her mother worked as a teacher at a public school, and her father was a mechanic in a local factory. Surrounded by public servants in her family and neighborhood, she had to make a decision about her career and was told that being a teacher was the best and most secure job – with retirement benefits from the state. After graduating from high school, she passed the state placement exam and was accepted into a two-year program to become a certified primary teacher. She spent her free time learning English and computer skills, even teaching English to small children for practice. In 2003, Digital Divide Data (DDD) launched a new branch in Battambang, after having been operational for three years in Phnom Penh. Sopheap was accepted as an associate and was promoted a year later to lead a team of 10 people. Over time, she became the general manager of DDD's Battambang office, leading over 150 people. At this time, she decided to pursue her master's degree in international management at U.S. Portland State University with the help of a scholarship and a student loan provided by DDD. After graduation in 2013, she returned to DDD to serve in a number of different leadership roles, and in 2016 she became a member of DDD's executive team. In 2019, she was responsible for over 1,300 employees across Asia and Africa. Through her experiences at DDD, Sopheap grew into a confident and thoughtful leader who is capable of making tough decisions, and most importantly, she fulfilled her dream of studying at university. She now has the chance to mentor and coach other young people so that they can grow in their careers and learn from her experiences.

Another example from DDD is **Damaris** (who is in her mid-twenties). She was born in Western Kenya and raised by her aunt from the age of four, when her mother passed away. Her aunt was a primary school teacher who made sure that Damaris received a proper education, even though she couldn't always afford the school fees. Upon graduating from high school, Damaris qualified for university but could not afford the tuition. She, therefore, stayed home and helped her aunt on the farm by selling vegetables and fresh fruit juice at the market. The proceeds just covered their daily expenses. Two years later, Damaris heard about DDD and applied for a job. She had to travel eight hours from the countryside into the city for the interview. It was her first time in the city and her first job interview. Damaris was nervous and excited by the prospect of working and continuing her education. She was surprised that a company was willing to provide her not only employment but also schooling. DDD offered Damaris a job, and within a week she started training and working there. After an initial introduction, she started as an associate, transcribing handwritten documents in different languages. This job brought her a regular and stable monthly income of approximately USD 100. After a year, she earned a DDD scholarship and enrolled at Kenyatta University to study for a Bachelor of Science degree in Information Technology. Upon completing her studies, she will have a good chance to earn a market salary that allows her to make her own choices in life, either pursuing a career as a professional or raising a family.

An example from Amazi is **Tsholo** (23) who grew up in a township in the area of Johannesburg, South Africa. The overall lack of job prospects, particularly the lack of access for poor black people to high-quality and affordable education, drove her to severe depression, which led to multiple suicide attempts. With help from a friend, Tsholo was introduced to the Amazi Academy and was accepted as a student in 2019. The goal of the Amazi Academy is to nurture untapped talent, but the core of its purpose is to help women in need to get back on their feet and find a purpose in life. As Tsholo puts it, "I am breathing. I did not know that I needed to learn how to breathe. Through the workshops at Amazi, I have accepted my depression, but I have also learned that I do not need to become the emotion."

Another example from South Africa is **Ncebakazi** (29). She had a difficult upbringing, with death and violence as constant companions in her life. Nceba lost her father at a young age and was forced to drop out of school because her mother could not afford to pay the school fees. In her teens, her partner (also the father of her child) departed and left her as a young single mother. Soon after that, a tragic accident took the life of her sister's child, for which Nceba largely blames herself. As a coping mechanism, and given the need to escape her reality, Nceba found herself in unhealthy and abusive relationships. When she first came into contact with Amazi at age 25, she was working as a security guard at a leading retailer and was struggling to survive. She describes her journey with Amazi as a miracle that saved her. Working on a daily basis through deep, uncomfortable conversations with her Amazi life coach, she learned how to overcome her past and to change certain things that she did not like about herself. As a consequence, she gained more self-confidence and was able to become a nail technician and then advance to store leader. Now, she is being groomed for the role of Quality Controller at Amazi. As she relates, "I had no sense of purpose before Amazi. I was an angry woman. I look at our Amazi mission statement and realize that it's not just words; my life is a real testament of Amazi's mission."

And finally, here are two examples from BagoSphere: **Lisa Tiña** (25) grew up as the sixth of eight children in the Negros province of the Philippines, in a rural village near the city of Bacolod. Lisa's father worked as a farmer who could barely make ends meet, while her mother stayed at home to look after the large family. Regularly, Lisa could not bring enough food to school to eat lunch. When she graduated from high school, she was distressed by her family's economic situation and decided to look for work to support her family. She took on different menial jobs immediately after high school, earning on average PHP 2,000 (USD 45) per month. She eventually followed her employer from Bacolod to Manila but was not able to find a more promising opportunity. After two years, she heard about BagoSphere's training program to become a call-center agent, which promised to offer a salary of several times her previous income. She thus decided to go back to Negros.

Lisa performed well in BagoSphere's application process: BagoSphere saw her as a very shy girl with potential, particularly in learning how to converse in English – skills that she was not able to see in herself. However, when Lisa heard about the tuition fee of PHP 18,000 (USD 400) that she would need to pay back after finding a job, she was afraid and decided not to continue. She worried about what she would do if she could not pass and find a call-center job and if her parents would ultimately have to pay this large amount. After much encouragement, Lisa took the risk and enrolled. She found the training to be very hard and demanding but also a life-changing experience that taught her communication and life skills, from budgeting to how to make friends. She gained a confidence in herself that she had never felt before. After several application attempts, she was offered a job in a major Business Process Outsourcing (BPO) company in Bacolod City, with a monthly salary of over PHP 10,000 (USD 225). She has been working in the call-center industry for several years now, taking on roles with more and more responsibility, while remaining engaged within BagoSphere's alumni community to help the next generation of students unlock their potential. She married in December 2019 and now plans to start her own family.

Jarold Galamiton (23) grew up in Tigbauan, close to Iloilo City in the Philippines, as the middle child of five. His father died when he was seven years old, and his mother supported their family through a small store that she managed. Jarold was studying for a bachelor's degree in Marine Engineering in Iloilo City in the central Philippines when he had a severe road accident. The accident resulted in the amputation of his left leg and caused him to lose his self-confidence. In spite of urgent financial needs, he did not even look for a job because of his low self-esteem. He thought, "What would the future bring with only one leg?" He eventually learned about BagoSphere's newly established training center in Iloilo. Free of cost, thanks to a scholarship, Jarold applied for the one-month call-center training program. One week after graduating from the course, he was offered a job with one of BagoSphere's BPO partner companies in Iloilo. From someone without career prospects who had previously mainly relied on his family, Jarold is now earning PHP

10,000 (USD 225) every month, and he has gained back his self-esteem. Recently, he got a job at the Prosthetic Center that provided him with his prosthetic leg, so that he can now inspire other people in similar circumstances.

6.2.2 Impact measurement methods

Listening to these, and many more, stories from individual elea beneficiaries touches hearts and minds. It illustrates absolute poverty in its many dimensions, and at the same time it provides tremendous satisfaction to see how entrepreneurial solutions can make a real and sustainable difference. It also demonstrates the limits of a systematic and analytical approach to impact measurement and management. How can such very individual, complex, and multifaceted examples be aggregated into analytical indicators that permit a comparison of alternative impact models and the setting, as well as controlling, of impact objectives?

Around the time when elea was created in 2006, the number of available impact measurement tools was starting to grow, and scholars were starting to systematically categorize those that are publicly available (Maas & Liket, 2011; Clark, Rosenzweig, Long, & Olsen, 2004) (see Context Box 6.2 for an overview of impact measurement methods). In the meantime, the field has further proliferated into many more and different methods, some publicly available and some proprietary[3], and it has become virtually impossible to find and agree on a common standard for specific methods.

CONTEXT BOX 6.2: IMPACT MEASUREMENT METHODS

Maas & Liket, 2011 developed a systematic classification method and researched 30 quantitative social impact measurement methods. elea analyzed these methods and looked in depth at five that seemed to fit the purpose; namely, to be helpful for screening, evaluating, and reporting initiatives with a focus on impact rather than process effectiveness. These five are briefly described hereafter:

1. **Balanced Scorecard:** This method was initially developed for regular business organizations to measure important non-financial key

performance indicators (Kaplan & Norton, 1992). In 2003, Kaplan et al. created the Public Value Scorecard for non-profits, an adaptation of the Balance Scorecard (Kaplan & Moore, 2003). This scorecard for non-profit organizations differs from the for-profit version in three ways. First, financial performance is understood as a means to an end (i.e., a broader societal purpose) rather than an end in itself in the form of financial value creation. Second, the adapted scorecard focuses not just on the clients who pay for the service, or the customers who benefit from the organization's operations, but also takes third-party payers and other stakeholders of the non-profit enterprise into account. Third, other institutions active in a particular industry are not seen as competitors but as co-producers and partners with the shared goal of trying to solve a given problem.

2. **The Bottom of the Pyramid (BoP) Impact Assessment Framework:** This instrument was developed by Ted London (London, 2009). Its goal is to understand who at the bottom of the pyramid is impacted by an investment in a social enterprise and how they are affected. Therefore, it examines the positive and negative impact of investment activities on the following constituencies: sellers (local distributors or producers), buyers (local consumers or agents), and communities and looks at potential changes in economics, capabilities, and relationships for these three groups.

3. **The Measuring Impact Framework (MIF):** This methodology was developed in 2008 by the World Business Council for Sustainable Development (WBCSD) and aims at helping corporations to understand their contribution to society (World Business Council for Sustainable Development, 2008). The MIF consists of a structured approach with four very generalized steps that need to be appropriately tailored to the business and its operating context in order to produce meaningful results.

4. **The Participatory Impact Assessment (PIA):** This method was developed in 2008 by the Feinstein International Center of Tufts University (Catley, Burns, Abebe, & Suji, 2008). According to Catley et al. (2008), the PIA is not only a tool to capture what impact has been created but also to understand why it has occurred. However, the methodology does not provide detailed steps on how to measure social impact but is rather a description of an approach that needs to be adapted to different contexts.

5. **The Social Impact Assessment (SIA):** This traditional approach has its roots in the U.S. National Environmental Policy Act (NEPA) of 1969 and has been adapted to a more democratic, participatory, and constructivist understanding since then (Vanclay, 2006; Burdge, 1987). In 1980, the International Association for Impact Assessment was created with the intent to bring together all those who were responsible for and had to figure out how to conduct impact assessments that would meet the NEPA requirements (www.iaia.org). Typical elements of such impact assessment models include: the participation of stakeholders, the establishment of baseline conditions, the scoping of important issues, the prediction of likely outcomes and the community's likely responses, the development of mitigation strategies, and the implementation of monitoring schemes (see, for example: [Burdge, 1990]; [Rickson, Western, & Burdge, 1990]; [Interorganizational Committee on Guidelines and Principles for Social Impact Assessment, 1994]; [Becker, 2001]).

As there remains a desire to have at least some level of common understanding in approaching the challenging task of impact measurement, a number of impact investment firms (among them LeapFrog, with Dr. Andrew Kuper as a significant driver), in coordination with the International Finance Corporation (IFC), have agreed to nine Operating Principles for Impact Management (www.impactprinciples.org) (see Figure 6.1). As of April 2020, there were 94 signatories worldwide who had made a commitment to adhere to these principles.[4]

6.2.3 elea's impact measurement method (eIMM)

In very general terms, two approaches to impact measurement can be distinguished. One group of methods looks at individual investments with substantial depth to understand how an investment addresses a problem, how it realizes a theory of change, and how it leads to an output, an outcome, and, at the end, to impact. Such analyses tend to be very thorough and can help an entrepreneur to steer his impact enterprise in accordance with the desired impact objectives. However, the main disadvantage of this approach – besides the considerable effort and costs involved – is its lack of comparability with other types of impact companies and initiatives.

INVESTING FOR IMPACT: OPERATING PRINCIPLES FOR IMPACT MANAGEMENT

Strategic Intent	Origination & Structuring	Portfolio Management	Impact at Exit

1. Define strategic impact objective(s), consistent with the investment strategy. 2. Manage strategic impact on a portfolio basis.	3. Establish the Manager's contribution to the achievement of impact. 4. Assess the expected impact of each investment, based on a systematic approach.	6. Monitor the progress of each investment in achieving impact against expectations and respond appropriately.	7. Conduct exits considering the effect on sustained impact. 8. Review, document, and improve decisions and processes based on the achievement of impact and lessons learned.

5. Assess, address, monitor, and manage potential negative impacts of each investment.

Independent Verification

9. Publicly disclose alignment with the principles and provide regular independent verification of the alignment.

Figure 6.1 Operating principles for impact management.

Source: International Finance Corporation (IFC), World Bank Group. www.impact-principles.org

An alternative approach follows a more standardized set of indicators that are seen as relevant for measuring the impact of one investment in comparison to others. While this approach lacks sufficient specificity and depth to be of use for the entrepreneur as a controlling instrument, it is valuable for comparing impact objectives and results across different investments, thereby supporting rational capital allocation decisions and the ongoing controlling and benchmarking of impact results along the development journey of an enterprise.

From the outset, elea has made a commitment to systematically measure and manage its impact. As an active investment manager, the second approach supports our core tasks; namely, to select and then continuously monitor our investments as rationally as possible in order to optimize the use of our scarce capital and knowledge base. In 2009, shortly after becoming operational, we developed the elea Impact Measurement Methodology (eIMM) as a proprietary method for systematically measuring and managing our impact (see Figure 6.2). In 2011, eIMM was

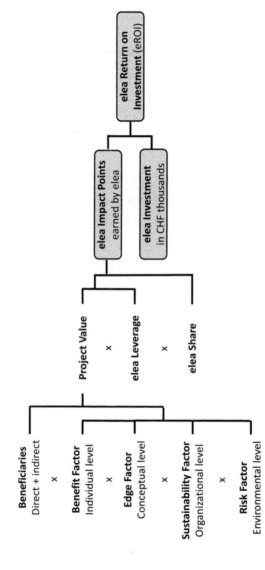

Figure 6.2 The elea impact measurement methodology (eIMM).

Source: elea

considered to be sufficiently robust to warrant an external audit, which has been carried out since then by BDO AG, Switzerland, a company of the international BDO audit firm network. elea was pleased that BDO acknowledged that its impact measurement method is in line with the International Standard on Assurance Engagements (ISAE 3000), being the first philanthropic impact investment organization in German-speaking Europe to receive such an endorsement from BDO.

As we set out to develop eIMM, we pursued the following objectives:

1. Establish a common language when talking about the success of our engagements.
2. Support rational capital allocation when deciding on new investments.
3. Set impact-related medium-term goals and control their achievement.
4. Communicate expected and achieved impact to our philanthropic investors' circle in the context of our regular reporting, and help investors internalize the idea of impact.

Along the development process, we were guided by the following principles:

- **Comparability before specificity**: While we were ready to share and discuss our impact projections with our elea entrepreneurs, it was never the intention that they could use this method to steer their enterprise.
- **Simplicity**: The method had to be simple enough to allow for meaningful results without unduly diluting the efforts of our small team from its core task of finding, evaluating, and supporting impactful investments.
- **Easy data access**: The required factual and judgment-derived data should be easy to obtain and to document in a standardized and consistent way, enabling validation through external audit.
- **Consistency over time:** Our model should be generic and robust enough to allow for consistent measurement over 7 to 10 years, avoiding recalibration and restatements.

Within this framework, we then started to systematically measure our investment proposals by creating our own new artificial currency; namely "impact points." Impact points are calculated with an algorithm that multiplies the (elea-independent) value of an investment with the estimated leverage that our organization brings in terms of contributions of expertise, advice, and guidance.

The investment value is derived from the core metric "lives touched (direct + indirect)" multiplied by four different factors; namely, benefit, edge, sustainability, and risk. Each of these factors has a series of subcriteria that are described in an internal handbook and are regularly reviewed by the team (and by BDO during the annual audit). For every new investment proposal brought to the attention of the board of trustees, a detailed impact analysis with specific medium-term impact objectives is mandatory. We also produce an annual impact report, the PIPR (philanthropic investment performance report), which includes a master document that covers all elea investments and a customized version for each member of our investors' circle that covers his specific portfolio of investments. This reporting is the result of a formal session held by an internal rating committee that follows clear procedures on deciding changes in single risk factors. The protocol for this session is also audited by BDO. The PIPR contains a portfolio impact performance review as well as investment-specific information regarding qualitative developments and changes in individual impact factors. It has a very similar format to the annual performance reviews of private-equity funds (see Figure 6.3 for a sample excerpt from the elea investment performance and impact report).

What did we learn from applying eIMM over more than a decade, and what are the limitations of such an approach? Overall, the systematic use of this method has clearly enhanced the rationality, effectiveness, and professionality of elea's investment decision-making. It has crystallized a focus on higher impact investment opportunities during sourcing and due diligence, and it has allowed for plausible impact-related comparisons between alternative proposals. It has also permitted a differentiated assessment of the progress achieved after investment, as all impact factors are regularly discussed. As we now have aggregated data across a number of investments over a decade, we are starting to see overall trends that help in the internal management of our resources.

This method has not only provided great insights into allocating philanthropic capital and setting and controlling impact-related medium-term goals, it has provided great insights into what works and what does not as well, thereby providing important lessons on how to evolve elea's strategy and organization further. In addition, it has boosted elea's credibility in its regular communication with external philanthropic investors, given that such a formalized (and externally audited) impact reporting

elea Philanthropic Investment Performance Report

Illustrative example

Portfolio overview

Investment structure

40% Equity
40% Grants
20% Loans

Sectoral allocation

40% Global agricultural value chains
33% Digital solutions
27% Employable skills building

Regional allocation

36% Africa
29% Asia
35% Latin America

Investment report

Assets	Launch year	Investment (CHF)		elea Impact Points		eROI	Management attention
		2018	Total to date	Stake	2018	Total to date	
Active projects								
Project 1	2016	70'000	280'000	33.0%	+1'835	4'200	15.00	
Project 2	2015	180'000	340'000	30.0%	+2'124	6'492	19.09	
Project 3	2017	25'000	125'000	12.5%	+3'204	5'920	47.36	
Total		**275'000**	**745'000**		**+7'163**	**16'612**	**22.30**	

Figure 6.3 Excerpts from a sample elea impact report.

Source: elea

is still very rare. Several members of elea's investors' circle like the elea Impact Measurement Methodology so much that they consider the realization of impact points from their philanthropic investments as a personal achievement and, as a consequence, are personally committed to achieving impact points. In a sense, they "own" the impact points generated.

At the same time, such a method has its limitations. It only works with a straightforward purpose and a plausible theory of change, as it does not foresee a complicated analysis of the secondary and tertiary positive and negative consequences and side effects of an investment. Also, this model does not yet represent a comprehensive formula, whereby the single factors and relationships among them follow empirically tested algorithms. Over time, in 5 to 10 years, with a few hundred investments observed, such algorithms may evolve and eventually become sufficiently robust to support a liquid, secondary "market of impact" (possibly based on blockchain technology).

Also, such a method cannot be applied mechanically. It requires some level of judgment, and it is particularly useful as a complement to other instruments, such as on-site visits and company-specific analyses. Certainly, it will never replace the need for close and frequent personal interactions between investors and entrepreneurs. Yet, despite these limitations, it has been our experience that such an attempt to analytically measure impact in addition to applying other instruments, as well as intuitive and emotional decision factors, can make a huge positive difference.

6.2.4 elea's impact

Having discussed the method that elea uses to measure the impact of single investments in its portfolio, the question arises as to how elea views the impact it has achieved during its learning journey of close to 15 years so far. An attempt to make such an assessment has many dimensions, some of which are open to quantitative analysis, while others require qualitative judgments. An assessment of elea's impact should consider achievements at the level of the individual investments in its portfolio in addition to its overall performance as an investment organization.

Since 2008 up to the second quarter of 2020, elea has made 40 investments in entrepreneurial initiatives that pursued the objective of fighting absolute poverty with entrepreneurial means. Those 40 investments were realized together with 34 different partner organizations. One-third of those were project-oriented organizations on behalf of public-sector or private

Number of investments = 40

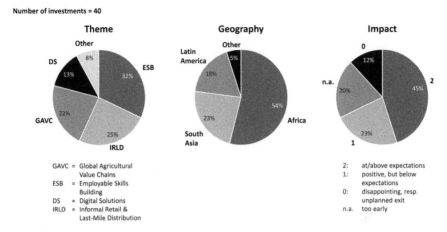

Figure 6.4 The elea investment portfolio (2008–Q2 2020).

Source: elea

sponsors[5], and two-thirds were companies focused on directly achieving impact through business activities. Regarding the impact achieved according to eIMM, we can say that 45% of the 40 investments realized an impact at or above expectations, and 23% realized an impact that was positive but below expectations. Of the group, 12% were disappointing and/or had to be exited early, whereas for the remaining 20%, which are more recent, it is still too early to say. Of 19 active investments in companies, 12 have good potential for a profitable exit, 4 within one to two years and the others within three to five years. For the 7 remaining active investments, it is too early to say (see Figure 6.4 for an overview of elea's 40 impact investments to date).

What do these numbers tell us about the performance of the overall portfolio? As there are no clear external benchmarks, and as elea's investment approach has been evolving over time, this question is hard to answer. A convincing response would have to include an assessment of whether alternative uses of resources in the field of fighting absolute poverty or in other impact areas would have yielded better results. Rather than going out on a speculative tangent with hypothetical answers, we limit our evaluation to the four following, high-conviction statements:

1. Through its partners, elea has achieved substantial, measurable positive social impact that cumulatively benefits more than 10 million people. (The reach is much larger when taking the total impact of these projects and companies within their communities and value

chains into account.) The consistent application of the eIMM at the level of 40 single investments over more than 10 years provides valuable insight on where and how impact was realized.

2. As a result of continuously and systematically reflecting and improving its approach throughout this learning journey, elea is a more effective and impactful investor today than it was in its initial stage. As an example, investments undertaken between 2010 and 2012 into employable skills building were much less impactful than subsequent investments into this theme. An important confirmation of our initial assumption was that the most sustainable impact typically results from local entrepreneurs finding creative solutions to relevant local problems. Importing seemingly good ideas from somewhere and finding someone locally to bring them to life rarely works.

3. Over and over again, elea has experienced that philanthropic impact investing is a marathon and not a sprint and that there are no easy shortcuts. It takes a huge amount of patience to help companies develop and grow from an early post–start-up stage so that they can reach the scale and stability that make them attractive for impact funds, which have both impact goals and financial return targets. While initially considering 4 to 7 years from the first investment to profitable exit, it seems to take 7 to 10 years instead. These journeys are typically not linear but rather follow up-and-down cycles (and sometimes sideways deviations). External shocks are the rule, not the exception. Their path resembles what former Google executive Ann Mei Chang explains in her recent book *Lean Impact*: rather than developing perfect plans followed by sophisticated execution, she recommends a process of continuous testing and iterative adjustments to allow for "learning while learning" (Chang, 2019, p. 15ff.).

4. Over the course of its learning journey, elea has increasingly appreciated the enormous value of close personal interaction with its entrepreneurs in the spirit of partnership. With growing experience and knowledge within elea's team, this (non-financial) contribution to impact value creation increasingly matches the contribution from the financial capital invested in terms of its importance. These include efforts in areas such as strategy and organizational development, leadership coaching and governance, sales and distribution, financial management and fundraising, and – more often than not – crisis management.

What can be said about how elea is doing as an organization? We regularly assess elea's performance and impact in addition to the impact achieved with its portfolio of investments. One important performance dimension is the evolving size and quality of its investors' circle, while another is the attractiveness of elea as an employer of talent, as well as its working atmosphere and culture. And finally, we look at the development of our global charisma as a knowledgeable, innovative, and influential organization.

Both the growing momentum of impact investing, in addition to a reasonably good track record and increasing experience internally, have proven to be highly beneficial to elea in recent years and will, hopefully, endure through the enormous challenges posed by the current Global Covid-19 Crisis. A recently introduced key performance indicator that regularly measures the "life span" of elea (which is, in essence, calculated by dividing average capital by annual operating cost) points to a robust foundation for continued positive development over the next 7 to 10 years. This gives elea the necessary confidence for further expansion and for strengthening its global profile as an impact-oriented and innovative organization.

We also recognize the limitations of elea's operating model, as it has no operational leverage. Its flywheel turns by virtue of achieving sustainable impact with its investment portfolio. This, in turn, encourages philanthropic investors to contribute their capital, which allows elea to fund its professional staff, thereby nurturing its capacity to support existing investments and to search for further attractive ones. This flywheel is linear and not exponential. Both searching for and supporting investments, as well as building and strengthening relationships with philanthropic investors, is dependent on the intensity and quality of the efforts of its people. Hence, the scalability of elea as an organization is limited. This relates to an argument we will make in the next section of this chapter; namely, that sustainable impact ultimately transcends single organizations.

6.3 Beyond single organizations – toward aligned ecosystems of inclusive capitalism

The term "ecosystem" refers to earth science and means "the living things in an area and the way they affect each other and the environment." Adapted to economics and other social activities, it relates to a group of businesses or other social entities that affect each other and work well together. In recent years, awareness about the potential benefits of aligned ecosystems in the area of entrepreneurship and impact capital has risen significantly, and consequently, a series of platforms have emerged to facilitate the building of targeted ecosystems through active networking.[6] This trend emphasizes bridge-building rather than raising walls and marks a positive contrast to fragmented silo thinking, which is too often found in our complex global era.

This development is in line with, possibly, the most actionable of the UN Sustainable Development Goals, SDG 17, which aspires to achieve "sustainable development through global partnerships." It is meant to bind all other development goals together and addresses five crucially important areas for global collaboration; namely, finance, capacity building, systemic issues, technology, and trade. To support its realization, SDG 17 calls for the private sector to play a special role. In other words, it advocates that private companies and businesses, in addition to private philanthropy, should work together among themselves, as well as with other civil society and governmental entities.

6.3.1 Learnings from elea's cross-organizational partnerships

Since the creation of elea, we have embraced this concept of leveraging the power of ecosystems through partnership across organizations and sectors. One of the most successful initiatives to date in this regard has been a strategic partnership with Accenture AG, the Swiss subsidiary of the global professional services company Accenture Plc. In 2012, Accenture AG chose to become a member of elea's Philanthropic Investors' Circle with an engagement that included both a financial and an in-kind component. The latter consists of the Swiss subsidiary's commitment to an Accenture-wide social responsibility program under the umbrella theme "Skills to Succeed." Through this in-kind support, elea can access Accenture's pool of consultants and engage them in assignments with its portfolio companies. This ranges from strategy workshops and financial modeling to IT consulting and even the development of specific applications. Since the launch of this agreement, Accenture has been essential in helping to define the iCow strategy and to migrate the iCow application in Kenya to a scalable state-of-the-art platform running on the cloud. For Dharma Life, Accenture provided project management resources and advised and oversaw a complex upgrade of Dharma Life's SAP-based enterprise system.

Corporate partnerships like the one elea has with Accenture provide multiple win–win opportunities: It accelerates the impact realization of an enterprise through access to resources at a level that it could otherwise not afford, thereby complementing elea's contribution of resources and expertise. For global corporations like Accenture, it allows for the effective and credible positioning of their commitment to solving global societal challenges and enables their executives to significantly enhance their inclusive leadership qualities. Last but not least, it also provides a model for an ecosystem whereby the collaboration between a single impact enterprise and a global corporation, which is facilitated by an investment management organization, can create impact and innovation that far exceeds the sum of its parts.[7]

Another example of an ecosystem created through strategic alliances is elea's partnership with Partners Group Impact Investments (PGII). Unlike elea's philanthropic investment approach, with its focus on fighting absolute poverty and its selection of early stage companies and convertible or equity investments, PGII operates in a broader field of impact opportunities and looks at opportunities with a larger investment size and a higher level of maturity and operational stability. Potentially, PGII provides an ideal exit opportunity for elea's investments as they reach higher levels of growth and maturity. At the same time, PGII has an interest in supporting elea's sourcing and screening capacity and, thus, makes philanthropic donations to elea that nurture elea's pipeline and facilitate co-investments.

Additional examples include partnerships with public-sector development-finance organizations. The mom-and-pop-shop program in Bolivia benefited from a matching grant of the Inter-American Development Bank. B'Ayoba, Essmart, and awamo received an investment from DEG (Deutsche Entwicklungsgesellschaft, a subunit of German KfW, Kreditanstalt für Wiederaufbau), which matched other external investors' contributions (including the one from elea). These examples, again, illustrate how resources and competences can be pooled across single organizations to accelerate and boost impact and innovation.

However, we still observe that many people working in public-sector development aid agencies perceive business as a foe rather than a friend. They are deeply suspicious of market mechanisms as solutions for societal problems. The description of SDG 17 by MDG (UN Millennium Development Goals) Monitor, an information platform created by several UN departments (among them the UN Development Program [UNDP] and the UN Children's Fund [UNICEF]) and funded by Google and Cisco, is revealing in this respect. They say that private-sector support is only encouraged provided that "it does not pursue narrow-minded agendas." It sees the "lack of profit" of civil-society organizations and their roots in the local communities as a reason for local people to have greater trust in them (www.mdgmonitor.org). In these circles, it is often argued that critical goods and services (e.g., medication and health devices) should be given to poor people for free without recognizing the negative unintended consequences (e.g., a lack of incentives for healthcare companies to engage).

Similarly, on the other side of the coin, corporate leaders often see business organizations and business approaches as the only way to solve today's massive challenges. They behave in line with the "law of the instrument," which was founded by psychologist Abraham Maslow in 1966. He said, "I suppose it is tempting, if the only tool you have is a hammer, to treat everything as if it were a nail."[8] According to this view, only business corporations have the resources, expertise, organizational capacity, and leadership that it takes to make substantive progress in this area, because, in their minds, they are the ones with the right tools for getting the job done. Here the MDG Monitor rightly warns that private companies should avoid taking over functions traditionally done by civil society, such as disaster relief.

Then there are a number of NGOs that are deeply suspicious of both public-sector development aid agencies and business corporations. These organizations have usually gained massive power through their capacity to mobilize public opinion via social media, but without proper legitimacy, governance, and control of such power. Nonetheless, they sometimes consider themselves to be morally above both the public-sector and private corporations and justified in nurturing a claim to "the absolute truth." In our view, such polarizing attitudes are not constructive, often stem from ideological lenses, and do not do justice to the complexity and scale of the challenges that we face today.

The granting of the 2019 Nobel Prize in social sciences to three economists that empirically analyzed poverty and asked "what works" rather than "what ideology is superior" is an encouraging sign toward an ecosystem thinking that is shaped by openness, pragmatism, learning, partnership behavior, and evolutionary development – an attitude that we strongly favor at elea. We often find such pragmatism in elea investments. Dharma Life, as an example, saw its purpose early on as building an ecosystem for rural development in India that goes far beyond Dharma Life as a single organization. That is why the founder was actively looking for partnerships with global corporations and international development-finance organizations. BagoSphere also continuously explores partnerships with universities and private-sector corporations. And, finally, DDD sees itself as an ecosystem contributor, partnering with NGOs to identify and recruit talent from slums and with corporations to purchase their services and guide their skills development (e.g., by enabling underprivileged youth to acquire certifications from Amazon Web Services). Moreover, several impact enterprise initiatives, which elea has only recently invested in, see new market-based ecosystems as solutions to severe societal problems that result from profound system failures. Some examples are:

1. **FUNDES' "Eco-tienda" Program in Latin America**: In a similar effort as elea's mom-and-pop shop initiative in La Paz, Bolivia, a decade ago, this recent program (which covers Colombia, Peru, and Bolivia in Latin America) facilitates direct collaboration between small retail shops and local producers of healthy organic food. It allows these shops to serve younger customers who are increasingly sensitive to food quality under ecological and fair conditions while providing local eco-farmers with direct distribution channels so that they can avoid expensive "middle-men" structures.

2. **Leap Skills (**www.leapskills.in**) and Virohan (**www.virohan.com**)**: Both of these recent elea investments address a broken labor market in India. Approximately 80% of the students who completed studies at a state college in third-tier cities do not find jobs, although many fast-growing companies complain about not being able to recruit the right type of human resources. Leapskills gained relevant expertise from intensely collaborating with state-college presidents to enable last-year college students to successfully achieve employment through a targeted blended-learning process. Leapskills now works with private corporations to help them professionalize their recruiting, induction, and training processes. For its part, Virohan

is building a network of schools to carefully recruit and train non-medical hospital personnel for the fast-growing healthcare sector.

3. **iGrow** (www.igrow.asia): This is another recent elea investment in Indonesia that provides a solution to the broken market for working capital in agriculture by offering peer-to-peer lending opportunities to middle-class savers who are seeking fair financial returns, while allowing smallholder farmers access to working capital at affordable terms.

All of these examples of partnering across organizations, and sometimes across societal sectors, within specific ecosystems share a few common characteristics:

• They are entrepreneurial initiatives that approach the problem they are trying to solve from a systemic perspective that transcends the boundaries of single organizations and often involves private companies, public-sector organizations, regulators, and other actors.

• They are shaped and driven by inclusive leaders (often those who have worked in both business and civil-society organizations) who seek collaboration with other entities based on an "ecosystem" mindset; i.e., one in which distinctive organizations with complementary capabilities work together to achieve massive and sustainable impact. This is based on a virtue of humbleness and recognition of the fact that the scope of many societal challenges far exceeds the capacity of a single organization.

• While they typically share a healthy dose of skepticism vis-à-vis state bureaucracy, they are guided by pragmatism rather than ideology, and they work together with regulators toward workable solutions to practical problems.

• They respect professional competence and specialist expertise within their own organizations as well as in those with whom they partner. They acknowledge the complexity of multi-stakeholder partnerships and the need for well-thought-out communication, decision-making, and execution mechanisms.

Apart from a mindset of openness, innovation, and pragmatism, all of these factors boil down to the application of knowledge, experience, and skills – in short, having the capacity to make ecosystems and cross-organizational collaboration work.

6.3.2 Strengthening global partnerships
through capacity building

When analyzing how the MDG Monitor describes SDG 17, it is striking that there are very concrete recommendations on finance, while the advice regarding private-sector support and capacity building remains vague. This focus on finance rather than other contributions, such as capacity building, is possibly a reflection of traditional development thinking, which says that a lack of financial resources is the greatest bottleneck to achieving impact. However, in line with the overall theme of this book, we view the integration of financial resources with entrepreneurial capacity as essential for achieving efficiency and success. For governmental entities, this integration could lead to the enhancement of professional capabilities and skills, such as digitally supported, non-bureaucratic approval and regulatory processes and a citizen-friendly service culture.

Peter Maurer, the President of the International Committee of the Red Cross (ICRC) and former Swiss Ambassador to the UN, brought this thinking to the point when he wrote an article that promoted the need to improve the effectiveness of humanitarian aid at the global level. He suggested, among other levers, an improved concentration of insights, capabilities, and resources within those organizations that are best equipped to contribute to overcoming the massive challenges of the many humanitarian crises of our times. He also stated that no sector should act in an isolated fashion, but rather that nation states, international organizations (such as the ICRC), local and global civil-society actors, as well as private business organizations should collaborate in order to achieve comprehensive, sustainable solutions (Maurer, 2019).

This raises the question of the principal distinction between the roles of actors from the private sector and those from the public sector. elea is an example of an entrepreneurial, private-sector approach to impact investing. It distinguishes itself by an investment process that is based on measuring impact, its roots in liberal ethics, and its skeptical attitude toward state intervention. However, while we are liberals, we are not libertarians, which means we are not in the camp that bashes states and international organizations. We believe that the challenge of erasing absolute poverty is so enormous that it is crucially important to include public-sector entities within an ecosystem in which distinctive actors reinforce each other's strengths rather than focus on dysfunctional, polarizing turf debates. That said, we are likewise convinced that the strengths of states are different from those of private entrepreneurs. The best states are excellent at delivering corruption-free, convenient, and non-bureaucratic services to their citizens. They build and maintain modern infrastructure to boost their attractiveness for business, and they provide safety and enforce the rule of law equally for of all their citizens. Switzerland, Singapore, Estonia, and Botswana provide some examples of excellence in these areas.

At the same time, there is very little evidence that states are good entrepreneurs or that they are capable of developing sustainably successful, innovative, and competitive global enterprises. Wouldn't it, therefore, make sense for states to concentrate on what they are (at least potentially) very good at, as opposed to competing with the private sector in providing entrepreneurial market solutions? Our liberal ethics framework also calls for differentiated responsibility thresholds, depending on the levels of liberty and capability. In this respect, what is true for individuals is true for countries and regions too: those individuals and countries with wealth and capabilities should assume particular responsibility for improving the world. Not surprisingly, corrupt and ineffective, or even failed, states are often the root cause for persisting barriers in the fight against poverty. Professor Andreas Wimmer, a Swiss professor who teaches at Columbia University in New York, demonstrates this in his book *Nation Building – Why some Countries Come Together While Others Fall Apart*. He says that Botswana became a successful nation because it delivered valuable goods and services to its citizens, whereas failed states, such as Somalia, breed instability and terrorism (Wimmer, 2018).

If done well, global agenda setting can help create awareness about global challenges and broadly mobilize forces toward finding effective solutions. The UN Millennium Development Goals (MDG), the predecessor of today's SDGs, have already demonstrated how a globally coordinated approach toward a shared agenda can be quite effective, and the same holds true for the SDGs. One of the primary success drivers of both was that, while supported and agreed to by national leaders, the goals have been developed in a broad-based global dialogue with society (both civil-society organizations and private-sector leaders) rather than by governments alone.

We believe in an approach that encourages the building of ecosystems across sectors and leads to a more inclusive capitalism that addresses societal challenges and builds on entrepreneurship and capital to achieve impact and innovation guided by the following principles:

- The acknowledgment of diversity as a source of strength rather than of tensions and conflict.
- The encouragement of active partnerships among different types of organizations on the basis of their distinctive roles, competences, resources, and accountabilities.
- The creation of transparency and minimal governance standards about the purpose, impact, vision, and ethical principles of such organizations.
- Promotion of the development and dissemination of empirically tested, impact-oriented, practical knowledge on workable versus non-workable solutions.
- Adoption of a mindset of pragmatism rather than ideologies.
- Encouragement of rational, fact-based and relevant global dialogue about meaningful solutions to serious societal problems.

As several of these points involve accumulating knowledge and expertise, the role of academic institutions in driving impact and innovation should not be underestimated. They can provide important contributions by creating and disseminating knowledge and experience about cross-sector perspectives, which institutions are best at doing what, and which types of partnerships can be successful and why. They can also bring diverse people together to work on specific, complicated problems, thereby developing mutual knowledge, respect, and trust.

6.4 Conclusions

6.4.1 Insights and takeaways

Chapter Six started with a perspective on governance and supervisory boards at the level of an individual impact enterprise and ended with a call for strengthening global partnerships through capacity building. With that, we have closed the circle of the book – going from the great global challenges that societies are facing, to the very practical suggestions about how to integrate entrepreneurship and capital at the level of investment management and impact organizations, and back. What are some of the insights and takeaways of this last part?

First, the role of governance and supervisory boards should not be underestimated. While these are complicated topics in many ways that often do not seem to match all of the pressing priority items on the agenda of a dynamic post-start-up to early growth company, they are important in terms of sustainability and the long-term health of an organization, and they can be decisive in times of crises. In addition, it is important to think hard at the outset about what should be achieved with measuring impact. An approach and method should be chosen that is aligned to these objectives. Even simplified methods can easily cause substantial effort and management distraction, and there is clearly a temptation of doing "l'art pour l'art." Continuous checks on the balance between the practical benefits derived from using a method versus the cost of development and regular implementation (including the opportunity cost incurred) is necessary. Finally, the power of ecosystems is huge: they are typically challenging to bring to life, as they call for the management of many diverse organizational relationships, but they can provide real leverage by turning diversity into strength and innovation.

6.4.2 Your point of view

Learning objectives

After studying this chapter, you should be able to

1. identify and discuss best practices for impact enterprise governance models and supervisory board characteristics;
2. develop key impact indicators to be used by impact enterprises considering the examples of individual beneficiaries;
3. evaluate the relevance and applicability of elea's Impact Measurement Method (eIMM) for both impact investment organizations and impact enterprises;
4. define ecosystems that generate win–win opportunities for partnerships across organizations or sectors and give examples; and
5. recognize the powerful influence of integrating financial resources with enterprise-building efforts on the efficiency and success of impact enterprises.

Reflection questions

1. In your experience, are there other significant levers for achieving sustainable impact and innovation besides the three identified in this chapter? If so, which ones? Why?
2. Based on your knowledge of both traditional corporations and impact enterprises, what are the differences in governance principles and practices between them? What can traditional corporations learn from impact enterprises in this respect, and vice versa?
3. Describe your experience with supervisory boards. What were good versus less good examples? In which areas do you see the most discrepancies between reality and best practice? Make suggestions about how the "best practice" list could be modified or complemented.
4. How do you keep the perspectives and goals of entrepreneurs and investors aligned to minimize the risks of a drift in purpose? Have you ever been in a position where you had to dissent in a board meeting and stand up for your convictions vis-à-vis other board members? Elaborate.
5. Have you applied impact measurement methods (as an impact investor or an entrepreneur)? What were their characteristics, and how can they be compared with the elea method in terms of relevance, effectiveness, and efficiency? Would you include other criteria? Which ones, and why?
6. Put yourself in the position of either an impact investor or an impact entrepreneur. Have you come across ecosystems that have provided systemic solutions to structural problems? If so, then describe. What lessons could be learned?
7. What experience have you had in building collaboration between private, public, and/or civil-society partners? Describe your key insights.

Right vs. right dilemma: Breadth vs. depth in impact measurement

An essential feature of impact investing is impact measurement, with the aim of understanding both financial and social returns. However, impact measurement is complex and costly in practice, and there is great variation in approach and rigor. This carries a risk for the emerging field of impact investing: if a certain level of rigor in impact measurement is not established across the industry, the label "impact investing" runs the risk of becoming diluted and used merely as a marketing tool for commercial investors.

Investment organizations have to make choices between broad-based methods that allow for comparability across different enterprises and in-depth analyses that provide highly specific insights. Both approaches are valuable. A broad scope helps in deciding resource allocation across a portfolio of investments but has clear limitations in understanding the effectiveness of single strategies. An in-depth focus leads to greater insights about whether a theory of change actually works in practice (e.g., when it includes randomized control trials) but is typically not helpful in comparing the impact across different types of strategies and models.

Debate the opportunity costs of these choices by elaborating on the pros and cons.

Notes

1. See e.g., (Price, 2018); (Guyan, 2019); (Wong, 2011).
2. For the specific characteristics of governance in a social enterprise, see: (World Economic Forum, 2012).
3. For a comprehensive overview, see (Hofer, 2017). Interesting practitioner examples of standards or single methods include Acumen Strategic Management System and Acumen Scorecard Framework (http://www .acumensms.com); the Global Impact Investing Network (GIIN) Impact Reporting and Investment Standards (IRIS) (http://iris.thegiin.org); the Social Entrepreneurship Initiative & Foundation (SEIF) (http://www .social-impact.ch); Bamboo Capital Partners Impact Report (www .bamboocp.com) PYMWYMIC Impact Report (www.pymwymic.com). LeapFrog uses a proprietary measurement system called FIIRM (financial, impact, innovation, risk management).
4. In July 2020 elea became a signatory to these principles as well.
5. In an initial stage of elea's development, a significant part of its investments were in projects. These were temporary efforts carried out by employed project leaders to achieve certain objectives within our impact themes. The intention behind these engagements – besides enabling impact – was to gain experience and learn from both successes and failures in order to evolve toward a more distinctive and entrepreneurial investment focus.

The major insights gained during this phase included a confirmation of our initial view; namely, that entrepreneurial companies are a more effective and sustainable way of achieving impact and innovation in our field. We also learned that it is almost impossible to transform a project funded by public development aid and/or by private charitable giving into a sustainable, market-oriented entrepreneurial activity. As a consequence, and in line with our initial intentions, we increased the proportion of investments in impact enterprises within our portfolio.

6. Examples include the WEF Young Global Leader program (www.weforum .org), the Aspen Network of Development Entrepreneurs (ANDE) (www .andeglobal.org), the Unreasonable Group (www.unreasonablegroup.com), and the Global Opportunity Collaboration network (www.ocimpact.com).

7. An organization that builds on collaboration between global corporations and local initiatives is the Earthworm Foundation (www.earthworm.org). Earthworm works with diverse partners to make value chains an engine of prosperity for communities and ecosystems.

8. (McRaney, 2012)

References

Becker, H. A. (2001, January 16). Social Impact Assessment. *European Journal of Operational Research, 128*(2), 311–321.

Burdge, R. J. (1987). The Social Impact Assessment Model and the Planning Process. *Environmental Impact Assessment Review, 7*(2), 141–150.

Burdge, R. J. (1990)., March-June). The Benefits of Social Impact Assessment in Third World Development. *Environmental Impact Assessment Review, 10*(1-2), 123–134.

Catley, A., Burns, J., Abebe, D., & Suji, O. (2008). *Participatory Impact Assessment – A Guide for Practitioners.* Medford: Tufts University - Feinstein International Center.

Chang, A. M. (2019). *Lean Impact – How to Innovate for Radically Greater Social Good.* Hoboken NJ: Wiley.

Clark, C., Rosenzweig, W., Long, D., & Olsen, S.. (2004). *Double Bottom Line Project Report: Assessing Social Impact in Double Bottom Line Ventures – Methods Catalog.* The Rockefeller Foundation. Retrieved May 20, 2020, from https://centers.fuqua.duke.edu/case/wp-content/uploads/sites/7/2015/02/ Report_Clark_DoubleBottomLineProjectReport_2004.pdf

Guyan, A. J. (2019, March 22). Best Practices for Boards and Individual Directors. *The National Law Review.*

Hofer, E. (2017). *Analysis of the Current State of Impact Measurement Practices in Impact Investing.* St. Gallen: University of St. Gallen (Master Thesis).

Interorganizational Committee on Guidelines and Principles for Social Impact Assessment. (1994). *Guidelines and Principles for Social Impact Assessment.* U.S. Department of Commerce; NOAA; National Marine Fisheries Service.

Kaplan, R. S., & Moore, M. H. (2003). The Public Value Scorecard: A Rejoinder and an Alternative to "Strategic Performance Measurement and Management in Non-Profit Organizations". In *The Hauser Center for Nonprofit Organizations.* Harvard University: The Kennedy School of Government.

Kaplan, R. S., & Norton, D. P. (1992, January-February). The Balanced Scorecard - Measures That Drive Performance. *Harvard Business Review*, pp. 71–79.

London, T. (2009, May). Making Better Investments at the Base of the Pyramid. *Harvard Business Review*, pp. 106–113.

Maas, K., & Liket, K. (2011). Social Impact Measurement: Classification of Methods. In R. Burritt, S. Schaltegger, M. Bennett, T. Pohjola, & M. Csutora, *Environmental Management Accounting and Supply Chain Management* (pp. 171–202). Dordrecht: Springer Netherlands. doi:10.1007/978-94-007-1390-1_8

Maurer, P.. (2019, February 16). Wie wir für die kommenden Krisen gewappnet sein können – IKRK-Präsident Peter Maurer über die Zukunft der humanitären Nothilfe. Retrieved May 11, 2020, from https://www.nzz.ch/meinung/humanitaere-arbeit-am-scheideweg-ld.1453952

McRaney, D.. (2012, March 27). Maslow's Hammer: Are we Entering a New Phase in Anthropology? *Psychology Today.* Retrieved May 11, 2020, from https://www.psychologytoday.com/us/blog/you-are-not-so-smart/201203/maslows-hammer

Meister, S., & Palkhiwala, R. (2018). *The Rise of 'Governance Correctness': How Public Markets Have Lost Entrepreneurial Ground to Private Equity.* Baar Zug – Switzerland: Partnersgroup.

Price, N. J. (2018, September 17). Board Governance Best Practices. *Diligent.com.*

Rickson, R. E., Western, J. S., & Burdge, R. J. (1990)., March–June). Social Impact Assessment: Knowledge and Development. *Environmental Impact Assessment Review, 10(1–2)*, 1–10.

Vanclay, F. (2006, January). Principles for Social Impact Assessment: A Critical Comparison Between the International and U.S. Documents. *Environmental Impact Assessment Review, 26(1)*, 3–14. doi: 10.1016/j.eiar.2005.05.002

Wimmer, A. (2018). *Nation Building – Why Some Countries Come Together While Others Fall Apart.* Princeton University Press.

Wong, S. C. (2011). *Boards: When Best Practice Isn't Enough. McKinsey.*

World Business Council for Sustainable Development. (2008, April 29). *Measuring Impact Framework Methodology: Understanding the Business Contribution to Society.* WBCSD; IFC. Retrieved May 11, 2020, from https://www.wbcsd.org/Programs/People/Social-Impact/Resources/Understanding-the-business-contribution-to-society

World Economic Forum (2012). *The Governance of Social Enterprises: Managing Your Organization for Success.* Geneva: World Economic Forum.

OVERALL CONCLUSIONS AND OUTLOOK: IMPACT ORIENTATION FOR INCLUSIVE CAPITALISM

elea has faced many challenges and risks along its journey to date, which has required much patience and, in particular, hard work. Based on our experience, there is no silver bullet. Even those experiences that, with the benefit of hindsight, turned out to be less than successful have provided many valuable lessons. The tagline to elea's brand says: "Impact through Entrepreneurship." Indeed, over and over again, we have confirmed our initial assumption that the entrepreneurs make the difference: their role is crucial in terms of designing, building, and leading impact-oriented enterprises. Yet we have also learned that an active impact investment organization such as elea can contribute substantially and in several ways to the success of aspiring impact enterprises. It starts with effective processes for choosing promising investment themes and applying rigorous methods in evaluating and selecting individual investment opportunities that have a good potential for sustainable impact. Then it is about closely collaborating with the entrepreneurs in a spirit of partnership to provide them support in important and critical areas that make a difference to impact value creation. This requires drive and energy, professional skills, and dedicated capacity within a clear framework of ethical guidance.

Sustained momentum

Throughout this journey, it has been gratifying to observe how the trends of impact entrepreneurship and impact investing have been gaining enormous momentum over the last decade, particularly in recent years. We have seen it along all three essential dimensions of elea's work (i.e., sourcing impact investments, finding philanthropic investors, and building a professional team). At the beginning, it was a lot more difficult than it is today to find suitable investment opportunities that fit the criteria of our philanthropic impact investing approach. Furthermore, when elea was created, it was quite an uphill battle trying to convince wealthy individuals, companies, and foundations to make investments in a philanthropic way into companies striving to create both profit and impact. Articulating this middle ground of philanthropic investing, which is not charitable giving but significantly differs from regular business investments, was not at all easy. While it still needs explaining, investor interest and engagement for this type of investing have clearly increased. Philanthropic organizations are also more willing today than in the past to consider investing at earlier stages of an impact-enterprise development process, given the recognition that there is a need for philanthropic investing at these earlier stages.

Finally, we have observed a tremendous growth in demand for employment in this area, from both young, talented people as well as seasoned professionals who want to open a new chapter in their careers as they search for more meaningful purpose. This has reached a point where we see elea effectively competing in the talent market with established global leaders in the fields of consulting, finance, and other professional services. All of these trends are a reflection of the inherent power of capitalism, with its encouragement of entrepreneurial initiative, innovation, market-based solutions, and competitive strategies in addressing the world's greatest challenges.

While there are indications of some "bubble-building" in impact investing, we consider this trend to be structural and long term. As the world's global challenges become more widely acknowledged and receive more sense of urgency and higher levels of attention, looking for ways in which an inclusive, impact-oriented capitalism can meaningfully contribute to dealing with them is becoming more and more widespread across geographies and sectors. This will hopefully also include an acknowledgment of tensions between different global challenges (e.g., fighting poverty and addressing climate change) as well as a search for pragmatic, constructive, and integrative solutions. Impact investing is here to stay. It is not a temporary fad.

From discount to premium

The sustained momentum of these trends is underlined by the fact that impact entrepreneurship and impact investing are stepping out of their niche and becoming mainstream, alongside the growing field of sustainable finance, on the basis of increasingly meaningful ESG criteria. These trends are thus converging more and more with the broader corporate world. For example, in 2019, the topic of the annual CEO Roundtable at IMD was about putting meaningful purpose at the center of strategy. Furthermore, for the first time, the Executive MBA program at IMD (for corporate executives aged 35–50 years old with 15–20 years of professional experience) included a discovery expedition that was organized by the elea Center for Social Innovation at IMD to Lima, Peru. The participants attending this part of the program worked for an entire week to understand impact investing in a Peruvian context. This included interviewing impact entrepreneurs and working on a detailed elea case study that allowed them to elaborate and pitch their own impact investment recommendations. The students demonstrated a tremendous curiosity and passion, and they showed a visible sense of urgency to add this type of perspective and expertise to their leadership skills profile.

And yet important hurdles remain. It is still hard to raise impact capital, and it is often unclear what impact exactly is and how it can be measured. Moreover, it is even harder to identify promising impact enterprises with a visible pathway to profitable growth. There is not (yet) a secondary market for impact that indicates how societies value impact in financial terms. However, if there were one, many impact initiatives would most probably trade at a discount rather than a premium. In addition, professionals working in the impact sector are still expected to accept lower compensation for the benefit of being able to pursue meaningful purpose in their careers. It may take another one or two decades for society to incentivize and reward efforts in this field, not only rhetorically but also with hard currency.

Hopefully, after a couple more decades on this journey, the corporate and impact worlds will have converged, to a large extent, and will share some common characteristics of inclusive capitalism as follows:

- A broad-based, generally accepted, and integrated impact orientation underpinned by impact reporting standards alongside financial performance reports for enterprises that indicate in what areas and how an enterprise serves societal needs and solves its problems

- A large universe of investment opportunities that allows investors to put together specialized portfolios that distinguish between impact fields in addition to the traditional distinctions related to industries and geographies
- A comprehensive body of academic research and practitioner insights into what it takes to successfully address great societal challenges and a broad-based acknowledgment that an inclusive approach to capitalism is a significant part of the solution rather than a problem
- A global marketplace with a liquid secondary market for impact companies and a sophisticated set of impact indicators that are not only measured but also traded in the form of blockchain-based tokens with impact assessments encrypted in smart contracts
- A significant number of impactful and innovative companies that trade at similar premia and multiples as today's most successful ventures in areas such as artificial intelligence, robotics, financial technology, or biotech.

If this book can further nurture and accelerate a momentum that leads toward this kind of a vision based on a more inclusive capitalism, then its objective will have been more than accomplished.

ACKNOWLEDGMENTS

Many people contributed to this book, either directly through their specific feedback and suggestions or indirectly through their inspiration, ideas, and support over many years.

First and foremost, we would like to thank all of our elea entrepreneurs and their leadership teams who bear the torch of making capitalism more inclusive. A particular thanks goes to the founders of our four lead investment examples, Lesley Marincola (Angaza), Zhihan Lee (BagoSphere), Martin Elwert (Coffee Circle), and Gaurav Mehta (Dharma Life), as well as to all other impact entrepreneurs – along with their team members and beneficiaries – who were prepared to share their stories with us for inclusion in this book.

Furthermore, we are immensely grateful to our colleagues from IMD, who embraced the idea of creating an elea Center for Social Innovation and gave this theme substantial space within IMD's fabric of thought leadership. A special sign of gratitude goes to Professor Jean-François Manzoni, the President of IMD, for his support and sponsorship, as well as to Professors Anand Narasimhan and Knut Haanaes for their contributions in the context of the Center's Advisory Board. Further, we much appreciated the help of Delia Fischer and Sally Peck with communication and marketing.

A heartfelt thanks goes to elea's co-founder Susanne Wuffli and to Harold Grüninger, who have helped to guide, monitor, and support elea since its inception as members of its Board of Trustees. In addition, elea is profoundly grateful to the members of its Philanthropic Investors' Circle and its Comité de Patronage for their inspiration and guidance, as well as for their financial and non-financial support. Particular gratitude is due to elea's leadership team, Andreas Kirchschläger (CEO), Stefan Kappeler (COO), and Adrian Ackeret (CFO), for their drive and energy and their hard work in building, directing, and running elea over the years, as well as for their many direct and indirect contributions to this book. Furthermore, we would like to thank all elea colleagues who have been a part of our journey to date for their professional contribution, their passion, and their commitment.

Moreover, we would like to acknowledge all thought leaders, practitioners, scholars, and experts who created, pioneered, and shaped this emerging industry of impact entrepreneurship and impact investing. They continue to inspire us as role models with their ideas, experience, and examples.

Many friends of elea made the effort to read initial drafts of this book and provide valuable comments, insights, challenges, and specific suggestions on how to improve it. Beyond those already mentioned, these include (in alphabetical order): Stéphanie Abels, Urs Baumann, Martin Buess, Ignazio Cassis, Melody Chua, Veit de Maddalena, Bill Drayton, Alnoor Ebrahim, Marietta Füllemann, Paul Geissbühler, Candice Hitzeroth, Jeremy Hockenstein, Lisa Jean-Mairet, Su Kahumbu, Paul Kukuk, Andrew Kuper, Maximilian Martin, Peter Maurer, Thomas D. Meyer, Katherine Milligan, David Li, Damien O'Brien, Paul Polman, Patrick Reichert, Phil Rosenzweig, Tina Ruchti, Adrian Sameli, Juerg Schaeppi, Jutta Schläpfer, Daniel Siegfried, Marcin Stryczek, Elfid Torres, Amanda Turner Ege, Divya Vasant, Camilla Weder, Gerald Weigl, and Urs Wietlisbach.

A further word of thanks goes to our publishers, Rebecca Marsh, Sophie Peoples, Kristie Rees, and Imran Mirza (including his production team) from Routledge, for their passionate interest in the topic, their confidence as well as their care and professionalism in getting the book published. And we are – once more – immensely grateful to our "Power Team," Valérie Keller-Birrer (Valérie Keller Research Services) and Lisa Levasseur Berlinger (Chameleon Language Services GmbH), who assisted us with research and editing, respectively, and whose valuable contributions included challenging feedback, discipline, perfectionism, and humor.

Finally, we would like to thank our families, without whom such a project would be immensely more challenging. Vanina Farber is grateful to her mother Tamara Fuks for showing that one person can make the world a better place and have a multiplier effect on others. She would also like to thank her husband Florencio Gudiño and their twin daughters Ella and Zoe Gudiño-Farber for their valuable support. Besides being grateful to his spouse Susanne, Peter Wuffli would also like to thank his three children and their respective partners Beat Wuffli & Anita Gierbl, Arianne Wuffli & Andreas Egger, and Daniel Wuffli for all their love, care, and support.

ABOUT THE BOOK AND THE AUTHORS

Social entrepreneurship and impact investing are two powerful movements that contribute to a more inclusive capitalism and bring innovative solutions to global societal challenges, such as the fight against poverty and the protection of planet earth. This book provides practical advice and guidance on how to best integrate entrepreneurship and capital for sustained impact and innovation. It draws on elea's innovative philanthropic impact investing approach to derive lessons which can inform and inspire the impact sector in its further development. elea Foundation for Ethics in Globalization was created in 2006 by Peter and Susanne Wuffli. Its purpose is to fight absolute poverty with entrepreneurial means.

Written by two leading experts from both practice and academia, the book summarizes insights from elea's 15-year pioneering journey, from designing and running an investment organization, choosing purposeful themes, sourcing and evaluating opportunities, to partnering with entrepreneurs for impact creation. It includes suggestions on how to build and lead impact enterprises in such areas as creating strategies, plans, and models; building effective teams and organizations; managing resources; and handling crisis situations.

One important insight is that such an evolutionary path is non-linear and calls for continuous reflection on successes and failures, on lessons learned, and on adjustments needed going forward. However, there should be no compromises on ethics. Ethical roots, virtues and guiding principles, such as integrity, humbleness, professionalism, or additionality, should be made transparent and serve as signposts along the way. Another key lesson is how much value can be gained from close and sustained personal collaboration between investors and entrepreneurs in a spirit of partnership. This is particularly true when such collaboration is underpinned by mutual respect, professionalism, skills, and deep expertise gained from sharing experiences.

Using real-life examples of impact enterprises to arrive at practical suggestions, this book is valuable reading for current and future entrepreneurs and investors, corporate executives, philanthropists, policymakers, and anyone who is curious about entrepreneurship and inclusive capitalism.

Authors

Professor Vanina Farber, PhD, born in Argentina in 1969, is an economist and political scientist who specializes in social innovation, sustainable finance, entrepreneurship, and sustainability and has almost twenty years of teaching, researching, and consultancy experience, having worked with academic institutions, multinational corporations, and multilateral international organizations. She holds a PhD in Business Administration (Economics) and an M.A. in Economics from the University of Memphis, as well as a "Licenciatura" in Political Science from the University of Buenos Aires in Argentina. She is currently the holder of the elea Chair for Social Innovation at IMD. Prior to joining IMD, Vanina was an Associate Professor and Chair of Sustainable Entrepreneurship and Social Inclusion at the Universidad del Pacífico in Peru, where she was also the Dean of the Graduate School of Business from 2014 to 2016. Vanina Farber is married to Florencio Gudiño, and they have twin daughters.

Peter Wuffli, PhD, born in Switzerland in 1957, is a senior leader and entrepreneurial philanthropist. He is also the Founder and Chairman of elea Foundation for Ethics in Globalization. In addition, Peter is the Honorary Chairman of IMD (a global top-ranked business school in Lausanne, Switzerland) and serves on the boards of Sygnum, a digital asset bank in Zurich and Singapore, and of Partners Group Impact Foundation. He is also the Vice Chairman of the Zurich Opera House. Previously, Peter was a partner at McKinsey & Company, the CEO of UBS Group, and the Chairman of Partners Group (a global leader for private-markets investments) and IMD, respectively. In 1984, Peter Wuffli obtained a PhD in economics from the University of St. Gallen (Switzerland), with a dissertation on Swiss direct investments in Mexico. He regularly publishes on topics related to globalization, ethics, leadership, philanthropy, and impact investing. In 2015, his most recent book, *Inclusive Leadership – A Framework for the Global Era*, was published by Springer. Peter Wuffli is married to Susanne Wuffli, and they have three adult children.

Institutions

IMD is a top-ranked business school and executive education expert based in Lausanne, Switzerland. Its purpose is: *Challenging what is and inspiring what could be, we develop leaders who transform organizations and contribute to society.* IMD was founded by business executives for business executives as an independent academic institution with Swiss roots and a global reach. Peter Wuffli has been engaged for IMD at the board level since 1995, and he served as the chairman of its Foundation and Supervisory Board from 2010 to 2019. In 2019, IMD had a revenue of CHF 135 million and a faculty and staff of approximately 300 people.

The **elea Foundation for Ethics in Globalization** was created by Peter and Susanne Wuffli in 2006. Its purpose is to fight absolute poverty (i.e., daily incomes below USD 3.00) with entrepreneurial means, and it aspires to be a role model organization with global charisma in the field of entrepreneurial philanthropy. elea is a philanthropic impact investor with a focus on early stage impact enterprises in fields such as global agricultural value chains, informal retail and last-mile distribution, employable skills building, and digital solutions. It employs a professional staff of approximately twenty colleagues. Since inception up to the second quarter of 2020, elea has made forty impact investments.

The **elea Center for Social Innovation at IMD** was established in 2017 with the mission to inspire and encourage leaders in business, government, and civil society to create social innovation in their respective areas of responsibility. The center's distinctiveness builds on IMD's access to the corporate world and business leaders and on elea's expertise as well as its network with impact entrepreneurs and impact investors. It creates and disseminates knowledge through articles and case studies, contributes to IMD's open and customized executive education programs, and forges connections between corporations, social innovation practitioners, and academic experts.

INDEX

Note: Page numbers in *italics* indicate figures and "n" indicate endnote.